S0-ACJ-646

MUSIC MASTER
OF THE MIDDLE WEST

Da Capo Press Music Reprint Series

GENERAL EDITOR

FREDERICK FREEDMAN

VASSAR COLLEGE

Music Master
of the
Middle West

The Story of F. Melius Christiansen
and the St. Olaf Choir

BY

LEOLA NELSON BERGMANN

With a New Foreword by Frederick Freedman
Vassar College

DA CAPO PRESS • NEW YORK • 1968

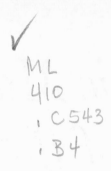

ML
410
, C543
, B4

A Da Capo Press Reprint Edition

This Da Capo Press edition of *Music Master
of the Middle West* is an unabridged repub-
lication of the first edition published in 1944.
It is reprinted by special arrangement with
the University of Minnesota Press.

Library of Congress Catalog Card
Number 68-16222

Copyright 1944 by the University of
Minnesota

Copyright © 1968 by Da Capo Press
A Division of Plenum Publishing Corporation
227 West 17th Street
New York, N. Y. 10011
All rights reserved

Printed in the United States of America

Foreword

MRS. Bergmann's *Music Master of the Middle West*, an unusual double study of the St. Olaf Choir and its founder-director, F. Melius Christiansen, first appeared in 1944. Originally written as a dissertation, it presents a good picture of pre-1900 Minnesota musical life, of the choral traditions prevalent among the American people at that time (with a special emphasis on religious groups and societies), and of the impact and influence of one man, and, indeed, of one family, on several generations of musicians. In the process, curious and exciting aspects of Christiansen's own work and personal life are explored and fully developed.

It would be no exaggeration to say that the St. Olaf Choir has been one of Minnesota's most important cultural ambassadors during the past half century. With innumerable world and national tours to its credit, it has left a strong impact on audiences everywhere. As guiding genius of the Choir, Christiansen received full recognition of his achievements throughout his lifetime. Perhaps his greatest public honor was the official state-wide observance of his eightieth birthday on April 1, 1951, an occasion followed by many concerts in which his compositions and choral arrangements were performed.

The choral tradition which Christiansen developed, though somewhat outmoded today, had a strong impact on choral practices throughout the country. His teachings at St. Olaf, the various summer camps, workshops, and clinics he ran (particularly for public school teachers and church choir directors), his various guest appointments at midwestern universities and colleges — all of these were instrumental in providing choral directors with the sort of training that allowed them to raise the standards of choral singing and repertory throughout the country, and particularly in the Midwest and Far West. Long before his death on June 1, 1955, Christiansen must have seen the happy legacy of his teaching and practice.

As one learns from Mrs. Bergmann's monograph, in 1942, Christiansen's son, Olaf, was called from Oberlin College to assist him with the Choir, and Olaf succeeded his father as director upon the latter's official retirement in 1944. The elder Christiansen's shoes were ably filled as Olaf perpetuated his father's *a cappella* tradition and stylistic choral concepts (fine pitch, highly polished tone quality, sameness of color). But he also implemented significant changes of his own, and programs of the past quarter century indicate that his father's compositions and arrangements gradually assumed a smaller part in the repertory, while performances of contemporary works by leading twentieth-century composers increased in number.

And now after twenty-seven years of successfully perpetuating the Christiansen name and tradition, the retirement of Olaf Christiansen has been announced, effective June, 1968. One cannot but speculate on the course the Choir will now take: will the highly stylized St. Olaf tradition prevail? or will there by a change to modern and more widely accepted choral techniques? There are so many sources of good choral training today, stemming, ironically, from groundbreaking work in the elder Christiansen's day, that the St. Olaf influence is no longer felt as it once was, and the choice confronting the Choir is very real. Regardless of the course ultimately chosen, however, *Music Master of the Middle West* remains an interesting and significant study recreating an important chapter of America's musical heritage.

FREDERICK FREEDMAN

Poughkeepsie, New York
April 1968

MUSIC MASTER
OF THE MIDDLE WEST

F. Melius Christiansen

MUSIC MASTER
of the MIDDLE WEST

*The Story of F. Melius Christiansen
and the St. Olaf Choir*

BY

LEOLA NELSON BERGMANN

THE UNIVERSITY OF MINNESOTA PRESS
Minneapolis

Copyright 1944 by the

UNIVERSITY OF MINNESOTA

All rights reserved. No part of this book may
be reproduced in any form without the written
permission of the publisher. Permission is hereby
granted to reviewers to quote brief passages in a
review to be printed in a magazine or newspaper.

PRINTED AT THE COLWELL PRESS, INC., MINNEAPOLIS

Preface

THE life story of Fredrik Melius Christiansen, in many ways common to hundreds of thousands of immigrants who came to America to realize the dream they felt could not be quickened in the land of their birth, is part of a great American epic. In the broad central Valley of America, Dutchmen planted their tulip beds and their corn; Germans, Swedes, and Norwegians, their wheat. Catholic, Mennonite, Lutheran, Methodist, Seventh Day Adventist, each with his own beliefs, observances, and ritual, worked side by side to clear the wilderness. Common to all was their faith in the land. Where the tents of the Sioux and the Osage had been pitched, first sod and log houses, then frame houses arose. Courage, energy, and forthrightness marked the pioneers as they plowed the virgin wastes and planted their grains.

After the farmers had settled, merchants, millers, mechanics, stove-, lamp-, and furniture-makers came to serve and to supply them. These, too, had need of courage, energy, and forthrightness as they built their cities and laid iron rails on the prairie. And when the land had begun to yield and the factories to turn out their goods, the time had come for pioneers of learning and of the arts, for the Valley was not only fertile for corn and for wheat, but benign to the unfolding of the mind and to the refinement of the heart. And these pioneers, too, had need of courage, energy, and forthrightness when they erected a single building and called it a college or a university.

Within the span of a generation these same institutions were to become centers of scientific research and cultural achievement that would draw the eyes of the whole nation to the Valley. When great symphonies are now performed at a midwest university by students who still remember their grandmothers' tales of canvas schooners, Indian attacks, and the coming of the railroad to the Valley, it is more than a story of epic proportions; it is one of the hopes of mankind. The symbol of this hope lies not so much in the successful emulation of the old, as in the fact that the level of the old has been reached so quickly by a civilization still young and not overshadowed by the dusk of decadence.

With a full sense of the grandeur of this pageant of man, I have here sought to tell a threefold, not a single, tale: the story of St. Olaf College as a center of Norwegian Lutheranism in America; the life story of F. Melius Christiansen as it unfolded in that setting; the story of his work in music and how it grew from regional to national significance.

Christiansen came to the Mississippi Valley in 1890. Had he remained on the eastern seaboard, this story of his life might never have been written. But he went on to the Middle West, and the people, life, needs, and opportunities he found there shaped him for the signal contribution he was to make to America's culture. To that extent this book tells what might be called a regional story, but it is written by one who, though sympathetic to the fighting spirit of the various ethnic groups, is not sympathetic to any kind of separatism—religious, ethnic, geographic, or any other. I am wholeheartedly an advocate of a nationwide, unhyphenated Americanism.

This biography could never have been written had it not been for the invaluable help I received from Dr. F. Melius Christiansen himself. I began it unwittingly while I was a student at St. Olaf College and a member of Dr. Christiansen's choir. When I consciously took up the task,

Dr. Christiansen gave me liberally of his time, and in doing so gave me more than that. Whatever of his personality has been caught in these pages comes from the inspiration of those hours. To him go my first thanks.

Professor Austin Warren of the department of English of the State University of Iowa was generous enough to sponsor my work as a doctor's thesis in American civilization. Professors Louis Pelzer and Harrison John Thornton of the history department taught me in their seminars to see those broader aspects of the American scene that are so essential to an understanding of Christiansen's work and life. References to the numerous institutions and persons who assisted me in various other ways are to be found in the section on "Sources."

Helen Clapesattle, editor of the University of Minnesota Press, kindly and wisely guided my stumbling efforts to bridge the gulf which, alas, separates an academic manuscript from a publishable book. Finally, I wish to acknowledge how very much I owe to my husband, who with untiring enthusiasm and ever helpful criticism has watched over this story of an immigrant boy who became a good and great American.

LEOLA NELSON BERGMANN

April 1, 1944
Iowa City, Iowa

Table of Contents

ILLUSTRATIONS

Prologue

AS THE last note of the bell echoed away into the church tower, the somber tones of the prelude saluted the Sabbath hush of the church. Sunlight poured in through the unstained windows, set deep in thick-timbered walls; a gallery flanked the sides and rear of the church where the choir had assembled in its customary place near the organ. A faint mustiness hovered in the air and seemed to muffle the sound of heavy shoes and the rustle of skirts as the worshipers entered their pews in the Lutheran church at Larvik, Norway.

Up in the gallery a small, light-haired boy sat alone near the organ, entranced as he watched the fingers of the organist move deftly over the manuals. To the nine-year-old lad it was a miracle that such effortless movement could produce the magnificent richness that swelled from the organ pipes. Sunday after Sunday the little boy could be seen in the half-light of the gallery watching and listening. His father had told him that soon he was to be allowed to take piano lessons from this organist.

When the choir rose to sing he bent forward in anticipation, and until the last chord of a familiar chorus from *The Messiah* was clipped of its sound he sat motionless, unconscious of everything but the music. The stentorian tones of the pastor's opening prayer recalled him with a start, and for a short while he listened. Then the voice gradually receded until in the imagination of the child it seemed to come from the flutes of the stiff white ruff that circled the pastor's neck.

When the long sermon was ended, the boy waited for

I

the benediction. Customarily the choir's responses were accompanied by the organ, but today the organist left his bench and raised his hand to the choir; the response came forth in measured tones of solid vocal sound. Slowly the thick chords reached into the vault of the church, ascending and descending in reverent tread.

After the last *Amen* had died away, the congregation rose and murmured its way up the aisle and out into the spring sunshine. But not the lad in the gallery. Never before had singing gripped him like this. Scarcely able to contain himself he stumbled up to the organ console, waiting impatiently for the end of the postlude. When the organist had released the last note, he turned kindly toward the lad, but before he could speak the boy burst out impetuously, "Please let me sing in your choir."

The boy was Fredrik Melius Christiansen.

Half a century later in another city of Norway, historic Trondheim, another and much larger audience gathered to celebrate the four hundredth anniversary of the Augsburg Confession. King Haakon, the Queen, and the Crown Prince were present. High on the list of special attractions was the appearance of an American choir that had been winning critical acclaim throughout Norway. It was a small college choir, and its members were ordinary American young people, drawn largely from the farms and small towns of the sprawling Middle West. Its concert numbers were the traditional hymns and folk tunes of Europe. But with that music these young singers from the western prairies had won the loyal love of thousands of American concertgoers and the highest praise of music critics the country over. Now they were repeating their triumphs in the Old World.

The singers were the St. Olaf Lutheran Choir, and its director, in many ways the real author of its being, was F. Melius Christiansen.

Through the home and church life of his Norwegian boyhood, Christiansen had absorbed the musical culture of his native land. Music was the thread on which his family, every member of it, beaded their days, and Norway's folk songs, her lullabies, her dance tunes, and the sturdy chorales of her Lutheran church were alive in him. Then at St. Olaf College, lying far to the north in the great Valley that is the heart of America, he found a need and an opportunity that demanded all he had to give, the utmost in power and resourcefulness. In a land so new it was without tradition he had to learn how to train untried singers; he had to write songs for them to sing; he had at every step to draw on his originality, to try new methods, to make his way alone.

The sons and daughters of the Norwegian pioneers came to this church college, and Christiansen taught them to sing Bach and Brahms, as well as the chorales and the folk melodies of their ancestors. Then trained in their art by his master hand, they went out to sing in the cities of America, and from their songs a movement was started and a standard set for a cappella singing that has vitally enriched the musical life of the nation.

The story of Christiansen's contribution to American music, his recognized influence on choral singing from coast to coast, is the story of an Old World heritage shaped and enlarged by the free, wide ways and the deep soul-hunger of the New. "Norway gave me much," says Christiansen, "but America has taught me how to use it."

CHAPTER I

Boyhood in Norway

IF ON a summer's evening in 1865 one had chanced to be passing Nordbraaten, the farm belonging to Jon Braaten in the district of Eidsvold, Norway, one might have heard music floating through the open windows of the salon on the second floor. The singing strains of a violin, the soft thump of a bass viol, and the sprightliness of clarinet tones mingled in music that hinted of Norway's foaming water-falls, the wistful lilt of the herd girl's song, and the gay tunes of dancing peasants in their bright-colored skirts and bodices. The Braatens were spending another pleas-ant evening. Tradition has it that there is gypsy blood in the family. Perhaps in the days of wandering minstrels such a one found his way to Norway's southern coast, stayed, and became the ancestor of the sons and daughters of Nordbraaten. However that may be, music was deep in their souls.

Not many kilometers from Nordbraaten in the region of Hurdal's Lake was Smedhaugen (*smed*—smith; *haugen* —hill), a home built generations before by a stalwart smith on the curve of a gentle hill. Here lived the four Christiansen boys, husky and tall like their anvil-pounding ancestor. Soon Anders, one of the four, crossed the meadowlands to Nordbraaten to see one of the Braaten girls, slim, dark-haired Oleana. Oleana's father, a violinist of some ability, had an inflexible rule in regard to the young men who came to court his daughters: they must be able to play some musical instrument. From the father and sons in the Braaten household Anders willingly

4

learned to play several instruments, and in time he came to be a skillful cornetist and bass viol player.

Anders and Oleana were married, and for the first few years they lived at the old Christiansen home on Smedhaugen. Trained to be a mechanic, Anders was employed at the Eidsvold glassworks as a glass blower. A son Karl was born to them in June 1869, and two years later, on April 1, 1871, Fredrik Melius was born.

To the Norwegians Eidsvold is hallowed ground, for in that district on the Carsten Anker estate Prince Christian Frederick and his cabinet, merchants, farmers, and military leaders gathered in 1814 to frame the constitution that declared Norway's independence from Denmark. In this same parish, too, Wergeland, the fiery young poet of liberty, lived and worked during the thirties to carry on the ideal of liberalism that had dominated the group at Eidsvold in 1814. In the church that Wergeland's father had served as pastor, the infant Fredrik Melius was baptized.

Naturally in this family of amateur musicians the musical education of the children was an early concern. When he was three years old Melius was given a three-key clarinet, and with instruction from his Uncle Kristian his training began. Then, of course, on the frequent visits to Nordbraaten his grandfather played his violin for the child, let him hold it, and showed him how to draw the bow over the strings.

Some five years after the birth of Melius the family moved south from Eidsvold to Sarpsborg, where Anders was engaged to work on a large bridge under construction in that city. Shortly afterward they moved again, this time to Agnes, a small settlement built around a match factory, and here Anders Christiansen was asked to be the director of the factory band. Melius, pleading with the ardor of a six-year-old, was finally allowed to play in the band, and with his stubby clarinet he proudly marched, or more truthfully almost ran, beside the men in the parade on the Seventeenth of May, Norway's Independence Day.

Of lasting value in this early period of the boy's life were the evening hours at home around the fire, when the family band made up of the father with his trombone, Karl with his cornet, and Melius with his clarinet played light marches arranged especially for them by Anders or by Uncle Kristian. Oleana would sit in the flickering light of the fire with the new baby, little Kristian, in a cradle beside her, listening above the whir of her spinning wheel and offering encouragement to Melius when he grew impatient at the clumsiness of his childish fingers. His mother loved music deeply and was the driving power behind the musical activities of the family. She herself had a lovely voice, and, although she had had no formal training, her singing had the beauty and warmth of one who is gifted by nature.

The most meaningful of these early years, however, came after Anders had settled his growing family in the city of Larvik. To the south of their home now lay the shining waters of the blue fjord; to the west far across the city rose the smokestacks of the glassworks, the paper mills, and the flour mills. Down by the wharves freighters from England steamed into the harbor with their cargoes of coal and salt; then reloaded with timber and wood pulp they would return slowly down the fjord past Faeder lighthouse, out into the Skagerrak, and across the sea to their English ports. Melius and his brother Karl liked to run down to the piers and watch the sailors with their leather-tan faces shouting to one another in strange tongues as they unloaded barrels of salt. But it was not often that the boys could do this, for they were busy lads with schoolwork and regular hours of practice on violin, piano, and cornet, which their father insisted on rigidly. Anders Christiansen was a man of discipline, of sure-footed and measured habitude. He taught his sons the value, even the necessity, of industrious and prudent living, in matters of both time and money. The spirit that dominated the family was that of the sober, conservative burgher class to which Anders as a skilled worker belonged. In every aspect of his life he exhibited the sturdy traits of the middle class. Politically he aligned himself with the Høiere (Conservative) party, which believed in the status quo, favoring a strong monarchy and the continuance of union with Sweden. In Anders Christiansen's opinion the old order was preferable to the disorder that accompanied liberalism.

Few luxuries were permitted in the Christiansen household beyond the simple necessities for living. Entrusted once with fifty *kroner* (about fourteen American dollars) which he was told to deposit at the bank, Melius unfortunately lost the money. Although his parents did not reprimand him, he knew that to them the loss of fifty *kroner* was almost a catastrophe, for they had worked hard to save the money.

Socially the family was polite, correct, and cautious. In matters of conduct the parents were strict, especially Anders, who reared his children to respect the authority of their superiors in the family, the church, and the state. Familiar friends were accorded the deepest courtesy and were received with the starched manners that prevailed in Norway's urban society. When a guest came to call, Anders Christiansen would offer him a glass of brandy or aqua vitae; soberly they would raise their glasses to each other, nod politely, and drain the glasses. No words disturbed the dignity of the occasion. When Melius returned to Norway for a visit after several years' residence in America, his father had the customary tall silk hat and cane in readiness for his son to use. In the eyes of the elder Christiansen these were essential as an index of their middle class rank.

The religious practices of the family followed the same pattern of sedate and refined taste. They were members of the state church of Norway because their forebears had been, and quietly they walked in the old traditions, untouched by the fervor of pietism that had awakened the hearts of thousands of Norwegian people. A powerful religious revival had been set'in motion throughout Norway early in the nineteenth century by Hans Nielsen Hauge, a lay preacher of remarkable ability. Fighting the lifeless formalism in the state church with the "living word" of Scripture, he sought to revive and purify the religious faith of the people. Hauge gained his strongest support from the long-repressed rural class, which was eager to listen to a gospel that taught the equality of all men. However, the town of Larvik was not without its Haugeaner elements; a Methodist group had organized a strongly pietistic church in the community, and to this group were drawn many who felt that the formalism of the Lutheran church destroyed the regenerative power of religion.

The Lutheran church for its part held fast to its traditions and looked askance at the evils of a changing order. In May of his fifteenth year Melius was confirmed in this church with a group of boys and girls who had completed the specified instruction in the doctrines of Lutheranism. In their social pattern confirmation marked the end of youth and the beginning of adulthood, a turning point that called for solemn and sound advice. On that memorable confirmation day the venerable pastor of the Larvik church turned to his group of confirmands and said very gravely, "As you young people go out into the world,

8

there are two things I want to warn you against—Methodism and Socialism."

On the language question, too, one of the cultural and political issues that was engaging the energies of Norway's leaders at the time, the Christiansens were aligned with the cautious, correct conservatives. They used *riksmaal,* the combination of Danish and Norwegian tongues that during four centuries of Danish domination had become standard usage in official, intellectual, and urban circles. For the newer and more truly Norwegian *landsmaal,* formed from the various folk dialects spoken in the rural districts, the Christiansens had nothing but scorn. Living in the eastern part of Norway, where *landsmaal* had not as yet gained a foothold, they had little contact with it actually, and they were not acutely conscious of the broader social aspects of the movement. Even when *landsmaal* had taken on respectability and its exponents had become powerful enough in 1924 to change the name of the nation's capital from *Christiania,* with its Danish associations, to the medieval *Oslo,* Melius Christiansen, far away in America, disapproved. "To this day I despise *landsmaal,*" he said, "because I was not brought up in it as a child."

The public school that Melius attended from his eighth to his fifteenth year had the usual curriculum of the Norwegian schools, and because each subject had its particular teacher, the instruction was very thorough. The report card young Melius received at the end of his eighth year of school listed the subjects he had studied: Catechism and Explanation, Bible History, Church History, Reading, Norse Literature, History, Geography, Science, Arithmetic, and Writing. Scholastically he ranked well, and for industry and aptitude he was given the ratings *meget godt* (very good) and *saerdeles godt* (excellent) respectively.

Larvik had been awakened musically some years before the arrival of the Christiansens by the coming of an energetic musician, Oscar Hansen. With exceptional talent and unlimited enthusiasm he had organized a community orchestra, a band at the glassworks, another at the flour mill, a summer band, and three singing societies. The somewhat portly figure of Oscar Hansen, walking through the streets of Larvik with a sheaf of music under his arm, was familiar and loved by all the people of the city. When he was not rehearsing with one or another of his bands, he was giving private lessons, arranging a concert for the Soiré Orchestra, or executing his duties as organist at the Lutheran church. His light burned through the late hours of the night and into the morning as he studied a newly arrived symphony score or composed music for his bands and orchestra, or for the cello, on which he was an accomplished artist.

Because of their interest and talents the Christiansen family was soon swept into the musical activities of the little industrial city. Melius' first meeting with Hansen occurred shortly after the family moved to Larvik. As director of the glassworks' band, Hansen called for try-outs, and when the Christiansens appeared, the father and two sons, he was not a little pleased at Melius' performance on the E-flat clarinet. With Melius in the clarinet section, Karl playing trumpet, and Anders the horn, the Christiansens were firmly established in the twenty-seven piece band of the Larvik glassworks.

Feeling that Melius had true talent for music, Anders and Oleana soon arranged for him to take piano lessons with Hansen. The handsome, rotund teacher completely captivated the heart of his young pupil and it was not long before Melius' mother noticed with amusement that her son was imitating his teacher in slight mannerisms of speech and even walked with Hansen's characteristic limp. Practicing was no hardship for this lad, who, besides his love for music, wanted above all to do well for the man he ardently admired. To Oscar Hansen must go the credit for initiating Christiansen into the classical tradition of music. Trained in the spirit of the German classics in Leipzig and Christiania, Hansen through his teaching and directing inculcated very early in Christiansen a feeling for the musical style of the great masters.

From childhood the violin had been the instrument of his choice, and when a wealthy citizen of Larvik offered to pay for his violin lessons, the offer was happily accepted and Melius began studying with the able and very popular teacher, Professor Olsen.

Among his varied musical activities, Melius' membership in Hansen's Soiré Orchestra furnished him with some of the best training of his early youth. This orchestra of some thirty members drew its players from the most talented families of Larvik. Colin Archer, later to become famous as the designer of the steamer *Fram,* in which Nansen explored the wilds of the frozen Arctic regions, played the cello, while in the violin section next to Melius sat his own teacher, Olsen. Working diligently under its exacting director, this group of amateur musicians played some of the easier symphonies of Beethoven, Mozart, and Haydn in the six or seven concerts given each season.

One evening Hansen stopped young Melius after rehearsal, handed him the score of a polacca by Adolph Hansen, a Bergen composer, and told him to prepare it for a solo performance. Happy in the honor, he spent many hours each day practicing over and over the difficult measures of the Polish dance. Finally the eventful evening arrived. The doors of the municipal auditorium were closing; latecomers were hurrying to their places; the orchestra was assembling. Melius felt a tremor of excitement at the sight of the endless rows of upturned faces that fused into a mass before him. Then out of the blur he suddenly saw his mother. Her sensitive face, so softly shadowed by illness, tonight was alive with warm happiness; shy pride gleamed in her dark eyes as she looked at her twelve-year-old son, and the sight of her was enough to melt his first chill of fear.

Midway in the concert came the polacca. The fright that had once more begun to climb into the boy's throat was cut short by the quick nod from Hansen, who sat down at the piano and began the familiar strains of the accompaniment. Melius lifted his bow and with ease and surety swept into the lively strains of the dance, forgetting his fear, desiring only that his instrument sing out what he felt.

Resounding applause told him he had pleased the audience. He had made his debut as a violinist. A sparkling-eyed boy, carrying a violin case, walked home that night through the foggy March sleet of Larvik.

Unlike most countries, Norway did not enjoy the privileges of the international copyright; consequently, composers ran the risk of having their works pirated if they appeared in print. Rather than take that risk, a composer would leave his manuscript with a wholesale music dealer, from whom other musicians could rent the score to copy out the separate parts for their orchestras.

In addition to schoolwork and his practicing young Christiansen assisted Hansen by copying the parts from the symphony and band scores the director rented from Copenhagen. Through this work as a copyist Christiansen gained much valuable training in arranging and scoring music for bands and orchestra, a training that served him well in later years. Knowing that the family means were limited, the boy became quite troubled about the cost of his piano and organ lessons. One day he questioned Anders, "Father, it is very expensive to take as many lessons a week as I do. Would it not be better if I took only organ?"

Anders answered him quietly, "No, Melius. Don't worry about the money. You yourself have paid for your lessons many times." Copying was slow, exacting work for a boy who, although he loved music, was normal boy enough to enjoy also the fun of skating and sliding in the winter and swimming in the summer.

It was only natural that a boy so musically and emotionally alive should try his hand at composition, but the occasional waltz and mazurka he wrote in an old copy-book at the age of twelve were only stereotyped arrangements common for small bands. These early efforts were no musical lispings of a genius, but they were important as an indication of the creative instincts within him.

In the days of Christiansen's youth pipe organs had to be pumped laboriously by hand. Needing someone to pump the church organ on which he practiced and knowing that his younger brother Kristian was passionately fond of liver sausage, Melius would buy a few pennies worth of sausage and offer it to his brother in return for his services. Often the two boys could be seen walking toward the church after school, one carrying music, the other running along beside him munching on a chunk of sausage.

They spent many an hour in the chilly dimness of the church, and more than once as the daylight faded Melius heard frightened little Kristian sobbing wildly but pumping courageously as if to ward off the ghosts that leered from the gloomy depths of the empty church. The fright was contagious, and Melius would snatch up his music, take Kristian's hand in his, and flee from the church, their footsteps echoing behind them. Breathlessly they ran through the graveyard that surrounded the church, and not until they were well away from the shadow-casting gravestones did they slow to a panting walk. The hours of practice were not spent in vain, however, for in Christiansen's fourteenth year he was asked to fill Hansen's place as organist during the latter's absence for a year's study in Leipzig.

Tragedy and sorrow intermittently shadowed the Christiansen household during Melius' childhood and youth. Oleana, never very strong, had contracted tuberculosis, and although she fought to maintain her health, she was not able to regain her strength after the births of the six children who followed her first two sons in close succession. As her health declined, each new infant's hold on life became more tenuous. Three of the girls died, the last when only a baby of a few months. By 1884 Oleana was almost entirely confined to her bed. Frail though she was, she tried to control her family with the discipline that she felt was necessary and that Anders demanded. But gentleness and love were stronger in her than duty.

One day Karl had been into mischief of some boyish kind that called for more than a reprimand. Too weak to get out of bed, Oleana said to him, "Karl, go outside and cut a switch." Not daring to disobey his mother, Karl left the house and in a few minutes returned with a willow switch.

"Take down your trousers and lie across my bed," she ordered. The youngster complied, and, lying with his face buried in the bedclothes, he waited for the first fiery sting. None came. He waited longer, then cautiously raised his head to look at his mother. The switch lay limp in her fragile hand and tears rolled crookedly down her cheeks onto the pillow. Weakly she brushed them away and said brokenly, "Get up, Karl, and after this be a good boy." She knew she would not be with them much longer.

Oleana Christiansen died in 1885. The death of the

mother who had bound her family together with her stanch, bright spirit seemed to have a disintegrating effect on the little circle. Restlessness, dissatisfaction, and a sense of loss gnawed within Karl until he was driven to quit his home and join the stream of Norwegian emigrants moving toward America. Melius, too, was troubled about the future.

Although Anders had constantly urged his son to study music, he felt that for the boy to follow it as a profession was another matter. To depend solely on it for a livelihood was too uncertain; so he advised Melius to become a schoolteacher. Since his graduation from public school, Melius had been taking classes in mathematics at evening school, but he knew that for him happiness lay only in working with scores and scales and intricate harmonies. Planning for a life of music, therefore, he continued with his lessons, his copying, and a little teaching as well. But knowing that Oscar Hansen's sons would soon succeed their father in his work, and realizing that Larvik offered scant support for more than one or two professional musicians, young Christiansen decided that he must go elsewhere.

CHAPTER 2

Immigrant with a Fiddle

ON A spring day shortly after his seventeenth birthday Melius walked north along the winding streets, past close-set houses, toward the edge of the city, which lay horse-shoe-shaped on the inner side of a hill. Above him was Larvik's famous Beachforest, where he had played so often with the band on warm summer nights. Memories of gay music, couples strolling under the trees, wide night of stars leaning over still water, and the distant horn-call of an unseen steamer far out in the fjord filled his mind as he walked the familiar streets. He knew this was his last spring in Larvik, for he had decided that in the autumn he must leave.

From the top of the hill he looked across the housetops with the wood smoke curling from their chimney pots, across the fjord where sea gulls swooped in gray-winged circles; blue stretched on into blue as far as he could see, and beyond that again lay his new home. For his destination was to be America. He could hardly have chosen otherwise; there was so much talk all around him of this rich, fair land to which Norway for decades past had been losing thousands of her people.

There was ample reason for the exodus that so alarmed the church and state officials, but beneath it all lay the economic situation. Bare, rocky mountains and dense forest made three fourths of the land untillable; the remaining quarter alone had to support more than a million inhabitants. Long winters and the grubbing toil it took to coax grain to grow in the few weeks of summer were disheartening even for the Norwegian peasant, who by nature endured hardship patiently. At best he could make only a bare living from the land; crop failures meant debt and often the loss of his farm. Prizing his independence and hating debts, he found the mounting economic burden intolerable and was easily susceptible to vivid tales of the wide, open reaches of rich, black soil in America.

Although Norway suffered no such severe political upheavals as were contributing to the emigration from other countries of Europe, the discontent of the peasants had begun to voice itself in political opposition to the domination of the upper classes. Religious unrest, too, played a part, giving rise to rebellion against the barren formality and dominant hierarchy of the state church. The emigrant who returned from America to visit his homeland and dared to stand in the presence of the pastor without removing his hat might be looked at askance by his kinsfolk, but he was secretly envied for his democratic bravado. The clergy did their best to discourage their parishioners from deserting the home of their fathers, but the most eloquent of pulpit efforts could not compete effectively with the letters from across the ocean.

These "America letters" from friends and relatives already settled in the cities or the wilderness of the West were the most potent factor in swelling the tide of emigration. In Norway anxious parents waited for the first letter from their emigrant son, and when it arrived the neighbors were called in to share the precious news about Lars or Halvor. Soon the whole district had heard of the letter, and singly or in groups they came, some of them from many miles distant, to read it and return home with their imaginations fired. On winter evenings young and old gathered around the fire to talk over again the America tidbits, which were always relished however often they had been passed around the circle.

It was of little matter that these letters often departed

17

from the truth. In most instances the first few years of fighting against odds to clear the land, build homes, and get enough to eat meant back-breaking labor the like of which the Norwegian settlers had never known in their homeland. Splitting rails at a wage of twenty-five cents a day, with a family of five or six to provide for, was not uncommon in the pioneer days of the Middle West, where most of the Norwegian immigrants settled. But stern pride prevented them from giving too candid an account of their plight in the letters they sent back to Norway. Instead they garnished reality with exaggerated descriptions of the beauties that surrounded them and of the wealth and freedom America offered to all who came.

So in Norway the poverty-ridden, the unhappy, and the ambitious succumbed to dreams of America's rich meadowlands, her waving fields of grain, or the shining yellow gold in the hills of California. Every community, almost every farm, had its virulent attack of the "America fever" that Wergeland had called "the most dangerous disease of our time," and family after family bade farewell to the fjords and fjelds with exciting hopes of a better future across the sea.

In this atmosphere the children of Anders Christiansen had grown up. All through childhood America had been for Melius the distant place from which came the letters of Abraham and Kathrine, relatives of his mother who had left Norway before he was born. Then two of his father's brothers went to America and their letters were added to the others. He had undoubtedly picked up more news of the country from the two Mormon missionaries who had lingered on in Larvik after the last great Mormon drive in Norway in 1872, and to whom he had given violin lessons in exchange for instruction in English.

And now Karl was in America, apparently happy and doing well. He had gone directly to Wisconsin, where he was settled in the north woods town of Washburn, working as a mechanic in a sawmill with his Uncle Fredrik. Already he had become the director of the Washburn band of thirty members. Melius, however, wanting to become a professional musician, thought the opportunities would be greater in a larger city and accordingly planned to go across the continent to the coastal city of Oakland, California. Hans Petter Christiansen, another of his father's brothers, also a mechanic and something of an inventor, lived there with his family.

Anders Christiansen did not at any time oppose his sons' desire to go to America. His approaching marriage to Thrine Gullickson, the widow of a sea captain, kept him from urging them to remain in Norway. He was very fond of his two boys, but he realized that children from a first marriage sometimes create problems in a second. Consequently he did not protest but willingly provided money for the journey for Karl in 1887 and for Melius in 1888.

As August days crept into September, a queer mixture of emotions confused and delighted Melius. He lived in the unknown excitement of the future, but tugging within him was the love for his home, for his little sister Ragna Josephine, who was ill, for Larvik with its familiar streets and houses, the market where he had bought liver sausage for Kristian, and Lund's bookshop where he had bought violin strings and copy paper. On the thirteenth of September six-year-old Ragna succumbed to tuberculosis, and of the once large and happy circle of children only thirteen-year-old Kristian and eleven-year-old Anna remained. It was hard to think of leaving them.

But Melius had made his decision, and he went about arranging his affairs in a methodical manner. He secured his exemption from military service and permission from the authorities to leave Norway. On October 4 the resi-

dent assistant to the parish priest wrote out his permit
to leave Larvik, which also certified his vaccination, gave
his birth, baptism, and confirmation dates, his standing
in the church records, and concluded with an official wish
for God's blessing upon his "prospective journey to California in North America."

The time for departure came. Farewells to his music
teachers and his friends had been made, and now his
father, Kristian, and Anna were at the pier where he was
to board a small steamer bound for Antwerp. They stood
silently in the evening dusk watching the sailors heave
trunks, bundles, and crates up the gangplank and onto
the steamer. The whistle sounded. Melius shook hands
with each of them, tried to smile, then hurried up the
gangplank to the deck, where he stood by the rail waving
to them, the lump in his throat swelling tighter and tighter
as the boat nosed its way out into the fjord. When the
three figures were but dim specks and the buildings were
blurred against the side of the hill, he turned away, went
into his cabin, and threw himself on the bunk in a burst
of weeping. He was alone and afraid.

The small steamer docked two days later at Antwerp,
where Christiansen, unaccustomed to traveling, was somewhat dismayed to learn that his boat for New York would
not sail for another week. Fortunately he found a hotel near
the harbor, and there was much to be seen in the picturesque city of ancient guild halls, cathedrals, and parks.

Roaming the crooked stone-paved streets one day, he
found himself in front of the ancient Cathedral of Notre
Dame. A ticket from the concierge gave him permission
to enter the church, famous for its Rubens paintings.
Renowned paintings held no interest for the young fiddler,
but he was greatly impressed by the organ music, which
seemed to float among the many arches and columns high

into the vaulted ceiling. Sitting in a dim recess, he lost himself in the shadowy medieval setting that surrounded him, momentarily forgetting the disturbing world of tickets, boats, and strangers. When he rose to leave, he was confused by the maze of aisles and the many exits and could not find the door through which he had entered. He knew, however, that his hotel lay down by the harbor on a lower level of the city; so he reasoned that by walking only on streets that led downhill he would eventually reach the waterfront and from there could find his hotel. He did.

The week passed and once more he was on board ship, his third-class ticket providing him with a bunk in the men's quarters on the lowest deck. A few days off land the boat encountered stormy October seas; the ocean boiled and heaved, and Christiansen, miserably sick, could only struggle from bunk to rail and back, bitterly reproaching himself for the folly that had prompted him to leave Larvik. But violence must sometime be spent, and the last days of the three-week crossing were more pleasant.

The first glimpse of New York and its busy harbor was a novel experience to an immigrant even in 1888, before skyscraper architecture had made its jagged appearance. Not for another four years were the twenty stories of the Flatiron Building to rise imposingly above the modest five- and six-story buildings that made New York's skyline at that time. The one feature that then lent distinction to the entrance was the Statue of Liberty, towering in coppery glory from its pedestal in the harbor. Melius was at the rail to see this statue about which he had heard so much, but the stories had not prepared him for the thrill he felt as the boat crept nearer and nearer and the outline of the tremendous figure became more distinct.

This first wonder of the new land made a deep impression on him, as it had upon thousands before him.

Christiansen reached America during the uproar of the presidential election in which the protectionist Republicans downed the Cleveland Democrats and settled the mediocre Benjamin Harrison in the White House for a term. It was the era when Morgan, Hill, Carnegie, Vanderbilt, and Rockefeller were beginning to wield their corporate power over millions of American people and dollars. It was the age of feminists, of the beginning of sailor hats, mannish coats, and bicycle suits, of temperance lectures, brownstone fronts, and mid-Victorian morality. William Dean Howells, the most realistic novelist of the day, carefully refrained from offending the refined taste of feminine readers in Back Bay drawing rooms. Musical New York was listening to Theodore Thomas' Philharmonic Orchestra, which sometimes had as its guest artist a comparatively unknown cellist, Victor Herbert. At the Metropolitan, Leopold Damrosch was introducing Wagner to America, but the populace preferred to listen to the rollicking melodies from *The Mikado,* the latest by Gilbert and Sullivan. The gay nineties, Diamond Lil, and "After the Ball Is Over" were just around the corner. America was entering upon an energetic phase of her national life.

Of most of this the young Norwegian was quite unaware. He was in New York only long enough to go through the tedious examination at the Castle Garden immigrant station and to find his way through the streets crowded with carriages, horse-drawn trolleys, and vegetable stands to the depot. After the noise and confusion of the immigrant station, his stumbling attempts to answer the innumerable questions, and the uncertainty of finding his way through the babel of strange tongues on the streets of New York, Christiansen was glad to board the train for California and settle down in relative safety.

A somewhat awkward routing took him first to Montreal, then across the Canadian provinces to Vancouver, and finally south down the coast to Oakland. In Winnipeg he had an experience that almost paralyzed him with terror. Scores of Indians in full tribal dress, painted faces, feathered headgear, and beaded belts trooped onto the train. All the tales he had heard of the tomahawking American savages flashed through his mind, and he thought his doom was upon him. Should he try to escape? A quick glance showed him that the passengers around him were either engrossed in their newspapers or watching the entrance of the Indians with only faint curiosity. He sat in rigid anxiety, and not until the train had lurched forward again and the redskins had settled down pacifically was he able slowly to relax from his fright.

The snowy reaches of land, flat, treeless, and townless, at first excited his interest, then bored him. Until the train approached the Rockies! In Norway he had been accustomed to low, wooded mountains nestling shoulder to shoulder in friendly proximity. The bold, impersonal grandeur of these rocky masses with their white peaks piercing the sky startled him into wonder.

From this journey across America a profusion of new impressions, significant and insignificant, pinned themselves to his memory: the patter of English, of which only isolated words were meaningful to him; the smell of orange and banana peelings and apple cores mixed with the fetid odor of the airless coaches and the leaking gas from sputtering lamps; glimpses of herds of cattle corralled for the winter, of towns with board walks and swinging saloon signs; in the evening the crimson bulge of sun at the western edge of the snow-crusted prairie; grinding halts and the wheeze of steam as they came into towns, and the nervous jerk as they left; the melancholy, long-drawn whistle of the train as it rushed into the dark funnel of the night.

When the train cut through the low, overlapping hills into Oakland, Christiansen noted eagerly that several church spires rose above the other buildings. Naïvely he concluded that with so many churches in one city it would be a simple matter to get a position as an organist. People were right when they said America was the land of opportunity. In five years he would be able to save enough money to go back to Norway to live. Relief cloaked the anxious curiosity he had felt before he saw the spires.

Uncle Petter and his family welcomed the boy happily, and for Melius there was once again the warm safety of the Norwegian language around him, good food, and friendly gossip about the family in Norway. After adjusting himself to life in his uncle's home, he began to think about finding a job. He read newspapers and books in an effort to learn English as quickly as possible, and watching others, he tried to act as much like an American as he could. Behind this behavior lay the sense of inferiority so frequent in immigrants. Handicapped by ignorance of the language, they often felt inadequate and not so clever as the Yankees.

Melius thought that if he could *look* American it would increase his chances for employment. He could see that his upright shock of curly hair marked him apart from the slick-haired Americans he met on the street; so on one of his first mornings in Oakland he went to a barber shop and asked for an American-style haircut. With deft scissors, a dose of highly scented oil, and a fine-toothed comb the barber brought the boy's mop of unruly blond hair into a neat swirl far down on his forehead.

Fascinated by his new image in the barber's mirror,

Christiansen was scarcely aware that the man was asking him questions. Not understanding the chattering American anyway, the boy merely nodded in answer. The result was a shave, a massage, and a bill for two dollars. Melius, so frugally reared, blinked in astonishment, and with a sinking heart realized that his splurge of vanity had taken disastrous toll of his few remaining dollars. Now a job was imperative. His spirits rose, however, when he remembered the church steeples, and, stealing pleased glances at his reflection in the store windows, he jaunted down the street. He was a good-looking young man with a well-proportioned figure of medium height, straight shoulders, and a shapely head, the tilt of which bespoke an unconscious youthful pride.

His naïve self-assurance waned in the next few days; musicians were not needed. Every church had its organist, and no one wanted to take lessons from a young unknown violinist who could scarcely speak English. Discouraged, he began to look for any kind of work, and finally with the aid of his uncle he found a job in a shoe factory, operating a machine that polished the soles. He had difficulty adjusting the machine correctly and struggled clumsily with it. Too frequently instead of polishing the soles it ripped them off. Again and again this embarrassing accident occurred, and at the end of three days the foreman decided the new Norwegian was a hopeless dud; too many shoes were being sent back for resewing. Christiansen was hardly sorry when they told him his services were no longer required.

What next? He was somewhat perplexed but not seriously troubled when he set out once more in search of work, reading the "help wanted" columns of the newspapers and walking the streets. Melius liked the foggy air of Oakland and its sister city, San Francisco, their narrow streets with the sharp inclines and different levels; he liked the small, boxlike, buff-colored houses built up on the sides of the hills with steep stairways leading up to them, bright red geraniums in the windows and palms growing in the tiny dooryards. Everywhere he went the buildings and houses had one thing in common: bay windows, myriads of them. When the last rays of the sun slanted across the bay in the late November afternoons the windows caught the glow and from below it seemed that the whole hillside was aflame.

The two cities were pulsing with life, gay and picturesque. Elegantly groomed women in bustled taffeta gowns, tortoise-shell combs, and gold earrings walked through the dirt streets to the open markets, where Chinese, Russians, Spaniards, Japanese, and moon-faced Mexicans hawked their wares, some squatting in the dust, others shouting at each other as they jostled along with baskets of fish or vegetables on shoulder poles or on their heads. Sailors in neat blue suits, caps, and knotted neckerchiefs sauntered in and out of trinket shops, enjoying port for the first time in months. Down Montgomery Street in San Francisco hack drivers rode with a flourish, swept through the grilled gates of the carriage entrance, and deposited their whiskered and bowlered gentlemen at the steps of the Palace Hotel. Parks, handsome mansions, and wrought-iron hitching posts graced the heights above the bay, while down toward the shore the lanes were crowded and dingy, roofs sagged forlornly over houses that almost tumbled into the water, and children and dogs played in the garbage-cluttered streets.

All these new sights and sounds made job-hunting something of an adventure for the Norwegian newcomer in spite of disappointments. After several days he found a place where his Norwegian tongue and lack of experience were not counted against him. The *Pacific Scandinav,* a Danish newspaper in San Francisco, needed someone to

set type and address papers, and Christiansen was hired
for the job. For about three months he worked at it, glad
to have it, but not satisfied; every impulse within him
yearned for music. Writing addresses and working with
type faces and ink-smeared copy kept his body from
starving, but inwardly he felt lean and unfed.

Hearing of a Norwegian who played in a symphony
orchestra in San Francisco, Christiansen looked him up
and found him to be a congenial companion. Occasionally
they spent evenings together, playing, talking music,
reminiscing of their homes in Norway. Christiansen enjoyed these evenings. A few times, too, he was asked to
play violin solos at functions held in the home of the
Norwegian consul. But for one who had determined to
enter the ranks of the professionals, this was discourag-
ingly little.

Ferrying back to Oakland after an evening with his
friend, Christiansen stood on the deck in the cold damp-
ness of a February wind, watching the angry churning of
the water. He thought of what he had left in Norway,
how confident he had been when he came to America,
and how little he had to show for his stay here. He, who
had come to America to make his way as a musician, was
working in a newspaper office doing things that anyone
with two hands could do, while Karl, who had come with
no particular intent to carry on his music, was directing
a band. Had he made a mistake in coming to a city instead
of to a small town? Melius did not like to admit that he
was lonely and discouraged, but as he walked home from
the ferry he found himself trying to think of ways to get
enough money to go to Washburn.

Karl had evidently sensed his brother's dissatisfaction
in his letters. As if he knew what Melius wanted, he sent
him sixty dollars for a ticket to Washburn, and Melius
at once made plans to leave Oakland. Sixty dollars, he

learned, would take him as far as Ashland, Wisconsin, a town some nine or ten miles from Washburn. That was close enough. Once more he packed his trunk, said good-by to his relatives, and left the city he had entered so hopefully a few months earlier.

His journey east took him back over the same route by which he had come to California. Upon arriving at Winnipeg early in the evening, he found that his train for Minneapolis did not leave until four in the morning; so he arranged his baggage and settled himself on one of the benches for the tedious wait. Glancing around, he noticed that he was alone except for several tramps, sly-eyed, unkempt creatures, with bearded faces and surly voices. Christiansen watched them furtively, and his agitation increased as they cast glances in his direction and muttered to each other in a guttural lingo that was entirely meaningless to him. Then an idea came to him—his violin! He took it out of the case, tucked it under his chin, and began to play a lively dance tune. The men looked at him in surprise, then began to tap their feet and nod at each other in approval. The boy knew how to play. Soon they were dancing and shouting in merriment.

On and on he fiddled; on and on they danced, calling for more, clapping and stamping to the rhythm of the Norwegian dance tunes he played. When his train was finally called, Christiansen gladly escaped from the riotous tramps and the close, stuffy station. He was weary but he had kept them busy, and that was all that mattered. First Indians, now tramps! Christiansen never forgot Winnipeg.

Late afternoon shadows were lengthening the spindle-trunked pines when he arrived in Ashland, a lumber town on Chequamegon Bay at the southwestern end of Lake Superior. Eager to reach Washburn that night, he walked up the street, saw a saloon with the sign "Norway House" above the door, and went in to inquire the direction. A man stepped outside with him and pointed across the snow-covered bay to a cleft in the dark woods on the opposite shore. "There, that's Washburn," he said. "By cutting across on the bay it's only about five miles. Nearly ten by land."

Christiansen thanked him and started through the snow for the V-shaped slice of sky that cut into the belt of forest across the bay. After living in a train for many days, he was relieved to be out in the open, breathing cold, fresh air.

The distant woods were soon muffled in the darkness of approaching night, so Christiansen could only keep walking in what he thought was the right direction. Suddenly he was aware of foot tracks in the snow. Stopping to look more closely, he saw they were his own. He stood still. It was out of the question to continue now, for he had lost all sense of direction and was only going in circles. But neither could he spend a shelterless night on the ice and snow of Lake Superior. Then came the thought that lights would soon be turned on in Washburn and they would guide him. There was nothing to do but wait.

He shivered as he sat down on the snow, partly from the sting of the wind, partly from nervous fear that animals might be prowling around. Munching a crust of dry bread left over from some his aunt had given him when he left Oakland, he sat waiting. It was not long; soon in the distance he saw a twinkle, then another and another. On the opposite side of the bay two lights, fainter than the others, appeared. The first group of seven, he decided, were the lights of Ashland, the fainter ones the lights of Washburn. Toward the latter he walked as fast as his cold feet would permit.

One hour, two hours passed. When trees and a few buildings began to take shape out of the darkness, he knew he had at last reached Washburn. He climbed up the snowy bank and, numb with fatigue and cold, walked down the town's one street, wondering how to find Karl. The houses he passed were all dark—all but one. A lamp shining through its window threw a square of light across the snow. He walked past the house slowly. Then a door squeaked on its hinges, someone came running out, a hand grasped his shoulder and turned him around.

"Melius!"

"Karl!"

By chance Karl had stayed up later than usual to chat with a shoemaker who played piccolo in his band. As they sat talking, Karl had glanced out just as a figure who walked like his father Anders passed by the window.

Karl took his brother up to his room, and for the second time since leaving Larvik Melius threw himself on the bed and burst into tears.

CHAPTER 3

Wisconsin Bandmaster

IN THE weeks that followed, Melius settled down with Karl, who felt a father's responsibility for his younger brother and was glad to give him what he needed in clothing, food, and incidental living expenses. Karl was earning good wages for his work at the sawmill and managed his money carefully.

Melius soon felt more at home than he had at any time since leaving Norway. The people in Washburn were friendly folk, and many of them were of his own kind, for in Washburn was one of the many early Norwegian settlements that dotted the central plains of America. From the first Norwegian colony in Orleans County, New York, groups of pioneers had pushed westward in the thirties to settle on the northern prairies of Illinois. Many went to the already busy trading center of Chicago, and others moved north to the swampy flats of Milwaukee, farther north into the pine forests, and west onto the rolling meadowlands of Wisconsin. Into Missouri, Iowa, and Minnesota they spread, gradually working toward the flat stretches of the Dakotas, where ceaseless wind whispering through the tall prairie grass was the sod-hut dwellers' sole companion for weeks on end. But they stayed, fought blizzards and prairie fires and drought, watched black clouds of grasshoppers ravage their fields, and lived to build schools and churches for the nurture of their minds and souls.

Other Scandinavians and some Frenchmen had drifted into the flourishing lumber town of Washburn, which ten years earlier had not even existed, but which now had three large sawmills and over three thousand inhabitants. Since Norwegian, Swedish, and Danish immigrants comprised the band that Karl directed, he had given it an appropriate name, the Scandinavian Band. Melius played the baritone and his Uncle Fredrik played cornet in this group, which met weekly for rehearsal.

Melius, however, was not content to remain in circles where only Scandinavian was spoken. He wanted to learn English, which he still spoke only hesitantly. Karl soon introduced him to a group of young people with whom he often went bobsledding on brisk, starlit nights. He enjoyed the gaiety of the parties, and from the banter of the young Americans he was able to pick up the idioms of the language he was trying to master. They in turn gladly accepted the young immigrant, who was full of life and prankish jokes.

When the public school opened the next fall, Melius made arrangements to enter. Since his training in Norway had been more than equivalent to the courses offered in the Washburn high school, he took only English. Under the tutelage of his French-Canadian teacher he rapidly learned to read and write the new language, but at the end of the year he still did not feel wholly at ease in speaking it.

Parties, Karl's band, and high school kept him occupied and happy. He enjoyed life in Washburn, particularly since he could be near the water. The atmosphere of fishing boats and nets, waves beating into spray against the rocks or licking insatiably at the sandy shore, leaving a deposit of weeds, clam shells, and corky splinters of wood, brought a clean content to this sea-loving Norwegian boy. He particularly liked to walk along the shore early in the morning when the sunlight was filtering through the drifting mist. He watched long-billed bitterns and sandpipers tracking the wet sand as they stalked about probing for buried grubs, and he was delighted by the call of the snipe—three short notes followed by a long one a third below. Imitating it with a whistle, he would try to coax the bird from its nest, half-hidden among the fallen leaves in some shadowy retreat.

Pleasant as his life was Melius knew that it was his duty to find a job. When a circus came to town the next summer the director offered him a place in the band. The novelty of the circus with its fanfare and spangles appealed to the happy-go-lucky Melius, but not to Karl. When Melius informed him of the offer, Karl advised him to ask such a high price for his services that the band could not afford to hire him. He remained in Washburn.

To all appearances Christiansen was not greatly perturbed about the future; yet there was a restlessness, a question of where to turn, what to do. Undoubtedly it was this feeling of uncertainty and insecurity that prompted him, when he was in Duluth one time, to seek out a fortuneteller famous the country round for his ability to reveal the past and peer into the future. The black-bearded oracle announced that three opportunities were soon coming to him, that among them he was to choose a place situated on a river, that in this place he would meet his future wife.

His first move toward securing a position was to advertise himself in the *Skandinaven,* a Norwegian-American newspaper published in Chicago. This newspaper had been established in 1866, and like so many of its kind, played an important role in the life of the immigrant. It brought news and gossip from Norway, preserved the culture of the homeland in the hearts and minds of the Norwegian Americans, and was the organ through which the immigrants became acquainted with American institutions and

33

governments. Advertising in a paper that was read every day in over ten thousand Norwegian-American homes was almost certain to bring results.

Christiansen had offers from three places: The Third Regiment of Wisconsin at Eau Claire offered him the directorship of its band; the city band of La Crosse wanted a conductor; so did the Scandinavian Band at Marinette. Studying the map, Melius made his choice. Marinette seemed to offer the most opportunity, for across the river from it lay the city of Menominee. If he was unsuccessful in Marinette, he reasoned shrewdly, he could always cross the bridge and ply his trade in the neighboring city.

In the late autumn of 1890, when he had been in America for two years, Christiansen was on his way to his first real position—nineteen years of age, a little taller and broader, again bushy of hair, and still more Norwegian than American.

Located at the mouth of the Menominee River on Green Bay, Marinette was active with the commotion of eighteen sawmills. In the spring the river was clogged with logs that had been floated downstream from the lumber camps. Mill whistles and the shrill whining of saws were familiar sounds to the people of Marinette. Here, too, the mills had attracted many Scandinavians.

It was cold the afternoon Christiansen arrived in Marinette; snow flurries appeared and disappeared fitfully in the bleak air as he walked down the street. The town was like any town that has grown up in the haste of a boom. Ten years earlier its population had numbered less than three thousand, and its streets had boasted a few frame buildings and scattered houses. Now the town had almost quadrupled in size; the buildings were crowded on both sides of the streets; stores were busy with a steady flow of customers; horse-drawn trolleys stopped at the corners; and many teams of horses and sleds were tied to the iron hitching rails near the livery stable.

Continuing down the street, Christiansen noticed a clock suspended over the entrance of a store with "M. Nelson, Jeweler" lettered below the face. Attracted by the Scandinavian name, he went into the shop, but his entrance was scarcely observed by the proprietor, busy with his customers. As Christiansen stood by the coal stove warming his hands, he heard a man speak to the proprietor in Norwegian. Christiansen knew then that "M. Nelson" was one of his own countrymen. He stepped up to the counter and spoke to the man. "This is a nice store you have."

"Thank you. Is there something I could do for you?"

"My name is Christiansen. I have just come to Marinette to direct the Scandinavian Band."

The look of surprise on the jeweler's face was unmistakable. "Well, so you are the new director. I hadn't expected you to be so young," was the frank greeting. "But welcome to Marinette. What have you been doing before this?"

Glad to have an opportunity to convince the man that he was no greenhorn, Christiansen told him of his training in violin and organ, of his band experience both in Norway and in America. He learned that the jeweler was a violinist as well as the director of a male chorus and quartet.

Then remembering his manners, Nelson said, "You must be tired. I'll get my coat and take you over to the Tremont Hotel. Tomorrow we'll go to see the president of the band. He will tell you what you need to know and help you get some place to live."

Good as his word, Nelson came to the hotel shortly after breakfast the next morning and hurried Christiansen off to meet the president. Again Christiansen's youth produced surprise. The president was clearly doubtful about the ability of one so young, but he decided the young chap should at least be given a trial at a rehearsal, which he immediately called for that evening.

The members of the band arrived, eyed their new director with curiosity, and looked at each other with skeptical faces. When they were all settled, Christiansen asked them to play one of their numbers, but before they were half through he stopped them, went over to one of the members, picked up his instrument, and demonstrated how it should be played. From one to the other he went, clarinet, trombone, and trumpet players, showing them how to finger and blow. Their skepticism gave way to amazement. From that time on there was no further comment about his youth or question of his ability. With his knowledge of music and his natural energy Christiansen in time raised this band of butcher-, tailor-, and baker-musicians to a fair level of performance.

Christiansen soon moved from the Tremont Hotel into the home of the Prescotts. The Prescotts were considered the most prominent family in the town, well-to-do middle class, Yankee, active members of the Methodist church, cultured and refined. From them Christiansen received his room and board in return for giving piano lessons to the two small girls in the family. He was treated as one of the family, and with the privileges of reading in their library and practicing on their piano, he found life with them enjoyable from the start. The arrangement was a happy one professionally, too, since having the Prescott girls for pupils undoubtedly meant that the new music teacher would be quickly accepted by the rest of the town. Before very long he was giving lessons to several piano, violin, and organ pupils.

Hired to direct only the band when he came to Marinette, Christiansen was asked almost immediately to be the organist and choir director in Our Savior's Lutheran Church. On his first Sunday as organist he demonstrated the independence that became so characteristic of him. In Norway the Lutheran congregations, particularly in the rural districts, had what was known as a *klokker* (precentor), a man whose duty it was to open and close the service with a brief prayer. This official had been transferred by the immigrants into their churches in America, with the additional duty in some congregations of leading in the singing of hymns.

As Christiansen was finishing his prelude, he saw a man walk to the front of the congregation and stand near the organ. He saw no reason for the man to be standing there, so, expecting him to be seated soon, he modulated and lengthened his prelude. But the man remained. Finally Christiansen leaned over and whispered to him, "Sit down." The man remained standing as if he had not heard. Slightly annoyed, Christiansen leaned over again and in a louder whisper repeated, "Sit down." Nothing happened. Exasperated, Christiansen called out in a voice audible to all the startled worshipers, "Sit down!" Chagrined, the *klokker* obeyed, but it took him a long time to forget his embarrassment and forgive the young organist.

Gossip at the dinner tables of the Lutheran families that noon was largely confined to speculations and comments about the daring action of the new organist. However, the *klokker* disappeared from the church in Marinette that Sunday never to reappear, and the custom finally fell into disuse generally as the American-born children assumed positions of control in the churches.

In Christiansen's choir were the usual businessmen, clerks about town, young schoolteachers, and willing spinsters—

37

untrained singers who belonged to the choir out of devotion to the church or for social reasons. Among the members were Jake Lindem, his wife, and his daughter Edith, a girl of fourteen. Lindem, who had been trained as a carpenter and cabinetmaker in Norway, in America worked first for his father selling lumber, then at a foundry, and finally in a sash and door factory of his own. He had become one of the established citizens of Marinette, and in their home Christiansen was always a welcome guest.

The new organist would not admit that anything more than general friendliness and hospitality attracted him to the Lindem household, but Edith, young as she was, sensed that she was partly responsible. One evening he dropped in ostensibly to convince the Lindems that the organ which had served their musical needs adequately for several years should be replaced by a new piano. Whether he was successful or not was of minor concern to him; it offered a plausible excuse for seeing Edith. With her golden-brown hair done in ladylike smartness on the top of her head, her corseted figure, long sweeping skirts, and fashionable leg-o'-mutton sleeves, she appeared several years beyond her early teens.

More and more frequently thereafter Christiansen accompanied the Lindems home from choir practice or stopped for a casual visit after his evening band rehearsal. Edith was not displeased, but for the most part she was so engrossed in her high school activities and in "reading for the minister" in preparation for confirmation that she had little time to be serious in her affection for the good-looking and lively young musician.

Karl continued to act as a steadying influence on Melius by coming from Washburn to visit him occasionally and to watch his progress with almost fatherly concern. But Melius was young and carefree. Life was to be enjoyed; he had a job; he was doing well; the world was full of kind people. Unconsciously he was trying to capture the style and complexion of his new environment, while consciously he was reveling in the freedom of a mildly bohemian existence after the control and order of his life in Norway. As if to compensate for the good times he had missed in his early youth, Christiansen threw himself energetically into the brighter pursuits of living after he had become established in Marinette. The inevitable results were carelessness and neglect of his work, especially his pupils, until one by one he began to lose them. Although this holiday mood lasted but a short time, the consequences were serious enough to make Christiansen realize even at that immature age that "it never pays to neglect your work," as he often said in later years.

Whether he liked it or not, circumstances forced him to mend his ways. Handicapped by a dearth of choral music, Christiansen had to draw upon his own talents, and during the two years he spent in Marinette he composed a few sacred songs, among them "Et Raab, Et Bud" (A Cry, A Message) and "Kom Barn, Kom Brud" (Come Child, Come Bride). Christiansen apparently enjoyed a modicum of success with his small church choir, for the group sang his "Et Raab, Et Bud" at a *sangerfest* (song festival) of Lutheran singers held in Duluth.

Christiansen sometimes appeared as a violin soloist, and on one occasion he gave an organ recital with little Sadie Prescott as the vocal soloist. To her he dedicated his first published work, "Bonny Castle Waltzes," a composition for piano. Its title grew out of frequent conversations about Bonny Castle, a home the Prescotts were building on Lake Superior. This light, nondescript composition, published in Chicago in 1892, did not bring the youthful composer a single penny in royalties.

In the summer of 1892 a male quartet from Augsburg Seminary, a Lutheran institution located in Minneapolis, came to Marinette to sing in the local Lutheran church. With a program of popular Scandinavian melodies both secular and sacred, the quartet made a hit in the communities it visited. One of the purposes of the tour was to interest young people in the liberal arts course that Augsburg offered in conjunction with the seminary work. A member of the quartet, Theodore Reimestad, talked to Christiansen about the need for continuing his education if he intended to go further with his music, and finally convinced him of the advisability of going to Augsburg.

On a September evening when the wind hinted of forest fires far to the north and the moon rose late over the dark river and the twinkling town, the members of the Scandinavian Band gathered for their final meeting with the young conductor. This time it was not a rehearsal or a concert, but a party in honor of the director whose leadership they had enjoyed during the past two years. Speeches were made and glasses were raised in wishes of good fortune for him in his new venture. This young lad with his gay and impulsive ways had won their hearts, while his honest, blunt tongue and undeniable musical ability had earned their respect.

Around him were the friendly faces of the men who had looked askance at him two years before when he had been introduced as their new director. He joined in the banter of jokes among the Scandinavian members concerning the respective demerits of the other fellow's nationality. His hearty laughter scarcely indicated the uneasiness he felt. The uncertainty of his finances troubled him; he had earned enough to take care of himself well in Marinette, but he had not anticipated becoming a college student. Reimestad had assured him that with his musical ability and experience he would be able to earn enough to cover at least a portion of his expenses, but he wondered.

CHAPTER 4

The Ole Bull of Augsburg

"RELIGION is a private affair," Christiansen briefly retorted when one evening in Washburn a member of the
Salvation Army approached him and asked him if he was
saved. He was not accustomed to assaults on his inner
life; he had not lived with people who knew God so inti-
mately that they could speak of Him in the conversational
tone of the household and the street.

Now he was at Augsburg College, and it was a world
very different from Washburn or any other place he had
lived. Without realizing it, he had come into a miniature
religious revival, part of the larger movement that swept
through the nineteenth century like successive prairie
fires, breaking out now in one place, now in another, but
always moving westward with the frontier. Christiansen
found himself in an atmosphere that throbbed with religious emotion, and there was no brushing it aside with a
brief retort.

Originally established in 1869 in Marshall, Wisconsin,
Augsburg Seminary had been moved in 1872 to a plot of
ground on the edge of Minneapolis, still a comparatively
young city of some twenty thousand inhabitants. Through
the years a four-year college department and a four-year
academy were added to the seminary, and when Christiansen entered in October of 1892, the student body numbered one hundred and sixty-seven. A few small buildings
on a city block in South Minneapolis constituted the
campus. There was nothing imposing about the college,
but it was a center of cultural activity in this predomi-
nantly Scandinavian section of the city. The professors,

students, and friends of Augsburg formed a racial and social unit by themselves, taking very little part in the larger life of the city. They clustered in small homes near the college and were diligent members of Trinity Lutheran Church. Their social functions, usually sponsored by church organizations, were held in the church basement, in nearby Dania Hall, or on the third floor of the Norwegian YMCA building.

The majority of the students, particularly those in the seminary, had been born in Norway and had come to America in their youth. Most of the professors, too, were Norwegian born and educated. They preferred to preach and to listen to Norwegian sermons, to sing Norwegian music, to mingle exclusively with people who spoke their own tongue. One of the theological students was regarded as a "queer one" by his associates because he went to the opera, to symphony concerts, and to the recitals of visiting eastern or European artists in the downtown auditoriums. "Why do you go to those 'Yankee concerts'?" they asked him suspiciously. So long as they could hear the Augsburg Quartet sing their favorite Norwegian hymns they were content. In the church the social and intellectual life of the school moved and had its being.

Naturally, then, Augsburg shared actively in the confused and stormy life of the Norwegian Lutheran church in America. The groups and conflicts that had been tangling religious life in Norway were transplanted with the immigrants to America, and intensified by the heady spirit of independence in the new land, they led to a long succession of divisions, mergers, and renewed secessions among church bodies. The various conferences and synods were more or less in agreement on fundamental doctrines, but they were sharply divided by temperamental differences on matters of ritual and governing policy.

The merging of three major synods in 1890 carried

Augsburg into the United Norwegian Church, which inclined definitely toward the high road in ritual and toward authoritarian control of the congregations. For twenty years, however, Augsburg had been a center for the faction that favored low church ritual and free congregational action, and its leaders could not be convinced that the spirit of the stiff white ruff was right. After three uneasy years in the new body, they, together with a few loyal congregations, withdrew from the synod. In the lean years that followed, the Friends of Augsburg, as they called themselves, had little but their faith in God to support them. Their prayer meetings and Sunday services took on added fervor, and united by their adversities, the little group experienced a deep spiritual revival that was later referred to as "the awakening of the Nineties."

It was in the midst of all this politico-religious turmoil that Christiansen entered Augsburg in the fall of 1892. The fact was important, not because he cared very much about the specific points at issue, but because high-pitched and emotional as he was, accustomed to thinking and living conventionally in regard to spiritual matters, he now for the first time came in contact with strong personalities given to positive and unwavering convictions. They not only guided his moral life, but they molded his aesthetic taste and forced him to stiffen his intellectual fiber.

Important among these new friends was a student in the theological department, Hans Andreas Urseth. A few years Christiansen's senior, Urseth had a more mature outlook and was an intelligent and refined person with a bent toward the poetic. As a devout Christian, he exerted a quiet influence on all his associates, with whom he was very popular.

Another influential friend was the energetic young professor, Sven Oftedal. Educated at the University of

Christiania in Norway but refusing to be ordained in the state church, Oftedal had joined the faculty of Augsburg Seminary and was a militant leader in its religious recalcitrance. He was captivatingly handsome in a burly way, with bushy, overhanging eyebrows and a drooping black mustache, and his brilliant wit and infectious laughter assured the success of any social gathering he attended. His keen mind stimulated Christiansen, to whom his "lyric nature" strongly appealed. Intensely interested in music and poetry, he quickly recognized the new student's musical talent and encouraged him to develop it.

Christiansen in later years came to look back on this Augsburg period as a turning point in his life. A few days after his arrival in Minneapolis, he went to the courthouse, applied for citizenship, and received his first papers. As a student in a small college and a prospective citizen of his new country, he acquired a measure of security, felt that he was not quite so much a member of the outgroup as he had been for the past four years.

During the first few days of college Christiansen was so occupied with learning what to do and where to go that he had very little opportunity to get acquainted with his fellow students. He had found two rooms near the campus in which to do his studying and practicing when he was not in classes. One afternoon as he was leaving the building where classes were held, a fellow student came up to him, introduced himself as John Hendrickson, and invited Christiansen to walk downtown with him. Christiansen's ready acceptance seemed to indicate a need for companionship.

In the course of their walk to and from town, Christiansen learned from Hendrickson something of the topography of the city, the streets, trolley lines, the river and its bridges. Reluctant to leave his new acquaintance at the end of their walk, Christiansen asked him to come up to his rooms. They were sparsely furnished, but conspicuous against one wall was a reed organ. Upon it lay a violin. "Do you play the fiddle?" asked Hendrickson curiously.

"Sure," answered Christiansen, flinging his cap on a chair and picking up his instrument. He plucked the strings to see if they were in tune, then dashed off a few phrases. For the next hour Hendrickson listened delightedly to the stream of music that flowed from the bow of the young fiddler, and that evening he announced to his student friends that he had discovered a superb musician in their midst. A few days later Christiansen made his first public appearance as a violinist before the members of the Debating Society, the leading organization on the campus. His reputation as the Ole Bull of Augsburg had begun.

But in expanding this role, so entirely satisfying to him, Christiansen encountered a real obstacle in the gulf that separated the Augsburg circle from the "worldly set" among their Norwegian countrymen. Minneapolis was growing rapidly at this time, and it was characterized by all the talkative, energetic gregariousness of adolescence. The Norwegian immigrants had caught the spirit of the city, and with the added incentive of a desire to preserve their old cultural ties, they organized singing clubs, literary clubs, rifle clubs, and debating societies; they called themselves the Sons of Norway, the Leif Erikson Lodge, the Odin Club, the Grieg Club; they erected halls, furnished clubrooms, hung club emblems and the Norwegian and American flags on the walls, and sang club songs; they gave balls and theatricals and entertained such distinguished Norwegian visitors as Björnstjerne Björnson and Knut Hamsun. Because many Norwegians had been accustomed to wines and liquor in their European homes, they continued the practice in America, particularly at their clubs, where foaming beer or a whisky toddy added congeniality to an evening's rehearsal or entertainment.

Christiansen was soon in some demand as a violinist at these Norwegian clubs, and he might easily have achieved real popularity and profit among them, but the disapproving frowns of his Augsburg friends kept him from accepting as many of the engagements as, given his own fun-loving temperament, he would have liked. The Augsburg circle looked with hearty disfavor on the jolly Norwegian societies with their free and easy ways and convivial drinking, and they thought it much more fitting that Christiansen's talents as a musician be used to promote the cause of temperance, with which the college was actively allied.

The temperance movement was sweeping the country in waves of song and speech that called the drunkard to repentance. Pamphlets were distributed picturing the tortured inebriate and his unhappy family, while righteous, nondrinking people flocked to the tents and auditoriums to listen in horrified enjoyment as impassioned speakers sought, with gesture and graphic detail, to arouse them against the satanic foe that was inflaming society. When the meeting was over, refreshments were served and a short musicale was given by local artists.

In his role as a musician Christiansen became a familiar figure at the temperance meetings. He enjoyed the work, but it made no bulges in his thin purse. He was told by the temperance enthusiasts that he was doing it for Christ and the cause of Christian living, and furthermore, they rationalized, he was gaining a fine reputation that would ultimately reward him with pupils. As a matter of fact, he acquired only a few violin pupils during the year and two others to whom he gave reed organ lessons.

His busy life with almost nightly appearances as a soloist soon reduced him to a state of pale fatigue. Fear of the disease that had taken the lives of several members of his family made him naturally apprehensive about his health. The prescription of the doctor he consulted was, "Quit school for six weeks and drink beer."

This was no simple advice to follow. He knew that even beer for medicinal purposes was not legitimate for the Augsburg student. What if he should be seen entering the dens of iniquity where beer was to be obtained? And even if he slipped in on his way to or from some engagement, it would be hazardous to arrive either at a temperance meeting or at the dormitory with a telltale breath. Disturbing as the prospect was, his health was of greater concern to him, so for a few weeks, he has confessed, he managed "to sneak into beer taverns without the faculty's knowing about it." When he appeared at the doctor's office six weeks later, he was "fat and rosy," and apparently no one was the wiser.

From the start most of Christiansen's attention and time were occupied by music; in the academic life of the school he did not cut much of a figure. That he took his classes lightly is evident from the fact that records of his work, aside from his initial enrollment, do not exist in the office of the registrar. No examinations were given until the close of the school year, and these Christiansen apparently failed to take, for no grades have been recorded for him.

But the classes were not a bore to him; there were a great many things to occupy one's attention that did not come under the name of scholarship. In that generation college students were not too sophisticated to enjoy perpetrating jokes on unsuspecting professors, and experienced teachers had learned to look carefully before they leaned too heavily on their lecture tables. The front legs had been known to be too close to the edge of the lecture platform to brook pressure without disaster. Christiansen is reported to have been familiar with this little method of destroying a professor's dignity, and he willingly entered into plots to create classroom diversions.

One morning Christiansen's geometry class was busily droning out the correct answers to the day's problems. Unfortunately for those who had not prepared well, the lesson was proceeding smoothly. Their only hope of salvation lay in the chance that someone would arouse the disapproval of their professor, Wilhelm Pettersen, who if he became irritated would spend the rest of the hour scolding the offender. The unprepared squirmed in their seats until Professor Pettersen called on Christiansen to solve a problem. In masterful style the young man went through the steps of the solution, triumphantly concluding with the correct answer. But all was not right. The professor's expression was dour. "Young man, I can only conclude that you have not prepared your lesson. You have used a method for solving your problem that has never been taught in this class."

"No," answered Christiansen, "I was taught to do it that way in Norway."

The professor's irritation mounted. "In Norway that might be acceptable, but not in America where we do things in an American way."

Not downed that easily, Christiansen retorted, "But I don't see what difference it makes anyway. What has a way of solving a geometry problem to do with a way of life?"

This was too much for a mathematical pedagogue without philosophical inclinations. "Sit down, young man, and let me give you some advice." For the rest of the hour he lectured the blond Norwegian on the necessity of adapting himself to the culture of the New World. With a sigh of relief the uneasy ones in the class settled back to scribble messages and play "cat and rat" with their neighbors.

The episode was not forgotten. Across the campus in Murphy Square a ram was tethered to a tree. In the classroom there was a closet. In the half-light of dawn the following morning three boys, one very blond and with a roguish smile, tugged at a rope, patted and cajoled a four-legged creature, opened and shut creaking doors.

When Professor Pettersen began to call roll in the geometry class that morning, another sound suddenly merged with the names. Ba-a-a-a, ba-a-a-a-a. All eyes turned toward the closet in the front of the room. A student walked to the door and opened it. Out shot the ram. Opposite the closet stood the good professor, and for a ram as well as a geometrician the shortest distance between two points is a straight line. Before he knew what had happened, Professor Pettersen had been butted to the floor by two curved horns on a lowered head. Several students rushed to rescue him from his humiliating predicament, while others harnessed the ram and escorted it back to its plot of grass. The professor had no strength left for castigation that day.

The Augsburg curriculum was centered on the Greek language, undoubtedly because of its value for the study of the New Testament. Students in the college course were classified not as Freshmen, Sophomores, Juniors, or Seniors, but as members of the First, Second, Third, or Fourth Greek Class. Latin, though not ignored, was treated with more reserve, perhaps because some elements of the Lutheran church at that time tended to regard it as slightly heretical because of what they believed to be its "humanistic" implications. History was stressed, but it was church history (from Norwegian texts) and Norwegian history. Norwegian literature, too, was given a prominent place in the course of study. McGuffey's *Readers* furnished the students with the meager English they were taught. Lectures were delivered and class discussions were carried on for the most part in Norwegian.

Classes were held in "Old Main," by 1892 a twenty-year-old building primitive in equipment and worn in appearance. Three times a day the welcome smells of frying bacon, roast beef, or gingerbread filtered into the classrooms from the kitchen below. Restlessly the boys waited for the gong that would end their Greek lessons and give them the signal to rush down the stairs to the dining room. Board was good and inexpensive, costing each student not more than a dollar and a half a week. Each year the boys elected a student manager whose duty it was to provide them with the best food possible for the least possible cost. The students also took turns serving and carrying out the duties in the dining room. Because of its democratic organization, the boarding club served as the major social center for the students.

Although some of the students lived off campus, the majority of them were housed in a dormitory on the grounds. No luxuries graced their living quarters. Halls were dark and drafty. Rooms were small and plain, each with an iron bed, a bureau, a desk and chair.

Christiansen was among the group of boys who frequently gathered in Urseth's dormitory room. Smoking their pipes and lolling on the bed, they discussed "God and the world." Since athletics were frowned upon as unbecomingly boisterous for a Christian college, there were no home-run heroes, no basketball stars to discuss. Instead the conversation centered on philosophical and theological matters, particularly the relation of art and music to the church and to religion. Always a lover of argument, Christiansen invariably took the other side from the rest and so acquired something of a reputation as a radical. He has said that during this time he received most of his education through discussions with intelligent people.

The few free hours his schedule afforded were spent with his friend Urseth. Facile with his pen, Urseth was the poet among his student friends, writing satires, humorous verse, and in more serious moods, religious verse of a sensitively lyrical quality, a type that appealed strongly to Christiansen's taste. The two formed a happy combination, Christiansen setting to music the poetry from Urseth's pen. Fortunately the two young artists were able to make their efforts public in *Ungdommens Ven* (Young People's Friend), a small Norwegian magazine designed for the young people of the Lutheran church. Every issue contained a page or two of music, and to these Christiansen and Urseth became frequent contributors.

The editor, K. C. Holter, and his wife were loyal friends of Augsburg College and Seminary, and at their home the students were always welcome. Mrs. Holter took a keen interest in music and literature and contributed stories and articles to her husband's publication, besides assisting in editing it. She wrote a few verses that Christiansen set to music, but in all probability they were known only to the coterie of writers and music lovers who gathered at the Holters'.

Quite within the pattern of its culture, Augsburg encouraged the musical interests of its students as a means of expressing their Christian faith and of keeping alive their Norwegian heritage. The Augsburg Quartet sang frequently at church functions and social gatherings in Norwegian circles, while a student chorus rehearsed regularly under Christiansen's direction, singing the familiar male chorus numbers of the Norwegian composers Kjerulf and Grieg.

During this year of rehearsals, solo appearances, and incidental composition, Christiansen's desire to become a concert violinist remained unchanged. He practiced conscientiously and undoubtedly dreamed of the day when he would earn his living playing before large audiences. His friends realized that he had talent, and when it was evident that he had but slight interest in translating Greek sentences and working trigonometry problems, they encouraged him to study music. Undecided himself what course to follow, Christiansen sought advice from Sven Oftedal. Unhesitatingly the professor told him to continue his music rather than try for an academic career. "You are a musician by the grace of God," he said.

Finances would be the problem. Christiansen could continue to direct the student chorus at Augsburg and to teach a class in singing and theory. Besides the meager pittance the school would pay him for this he would have only the income from a few violin pupils and whatever odd playing engagements he could pick up, but by frugal living he would be able to study music once more, the thing he had been yearning to do ever since he came to America. So instead of returning to Augsburg as a student in the fall of 1893, he enrolled at Northwestern Conservatory of Music in Minneapolis.

Begun quietly in the middle eighties, Northwestern Conservatory was now exerting a decided influence on the musical life of Minneapolis. On its staff were several musicians who did much to give the city a preeminent place in the musical annals of the Upper Mississippi Valley. Among them was Fritz Schlacter, teacher of violin and the city's leading cellist. Another was the head of the orchestra department, the violinist Heinrich Hoevel, who had been well trained at the Cologne Conservatory. During Christiansen's year at the conservatory this excellent musician organized the Hoevel String Quartet, whose weekly concerts became an institution in the cultural life of the city for the next twenty years. More than anyone else Hoevel was responsible for the development of chamber music in Minneapolis.

The outstanding attraction in the piano department was Carl Lachmund. He had studied at the Cologne Conservatory, had worked with the brothers Scharwenka in Berlin, and had been one of Liszt's last pupils. J. Warren Andrews, who had given distinguished service as an organist in several prominent New England churches, was the director of the department of church music. His Sunday afternoon organ recitals in the fashionable Plymouth Congregational Church on Nicollet Avenue drew large audiences of wealthy and influential citizens.

With these and other teachers Christiansen spent the year 1893–94 studying violin, piano, harmony, and counterpoint. Students of all nationalities and from all occupations were at the conservatory: a Swedish cabinetmaker, a young German girl whose father worked at a flour mill, and an Italian grocer from Washington Avenue, as well as the sons and daughters of the leading pioneer families.

For a young city just beyond the pioneer stage, Minneapolis had developed a remarkably active musical populace. Choral societies, instrumental groups, and sundry musical clubs had literally mushroomed into life. The active participation of the citizenry is charmingly exemplified by one of the city's recognized musicians, A. M. Shuey. On Sundays he officiated at the organ of one of the largest churches in the city, St. Mark's Episcopal Church, while during the week he worked as a ticket agent at the station of the Milwaukee Road.

Music had been a part of the city's life since its beginnings. In the fifties Ole Bull pleased the town with the extraordinary voice of his thirteen-year-old protégée, Adelina Patti, and his own amazing fiddle, while the Hutchinson Family Quartet brought whistles of approval from large audiences with their songs of abolition, temperance, and women's rights.

During the sixties and seventies oratorio seems to have been the favorite musical fare, and lavish performances by the Musical Society or the later Minneapolis Choral Society attracted sleighloads of listeners from St. Paul and other places as distant as Faribault. For one such effort of the Musical Society five hundred dollars was spent on the costuming alone. The performance starred a Mrs. Whitney, who, according to one honest critic, "showed great control of voice for one who has been out of practice so long."

Exceedingly popular during the seventies were the Saturday night "Dime Concerts" held in the Market Building on Hennepin Avenue and First Street. Socialites as well as the rank and file of the city came to hear Emil Weinberg's orchestra, the Union Brass Band, and other local instrumental groups, which were often assisted by soloists from Red Wing, St. Paul, and even Chicago. Informality was the keynote, with the audience promenading the hall during the concert.

With at least five performances of *Pinafore* in 1879 an operatic tone was set for the eighties. *The Mikado, Patience,* and *Mascotte* were heard again and again. Henry Clay Barnabee and his Boston Ideal Opera Company offered English light opera. The Hess Opera Company brought grand opera, and Emma Abbott and her troupe always drew large audiences, particularly the year the "silver-voiced tenor" Brignoli sang with her company.

Music festivals were numerous and popular. In April of 1883 a huge Theodore Thomas festival was held, with the Amherst and Oberlin glee clubs, the Chicago Church Choir Opera Company, and such renowned soloists as Minnie Hauk and Marie Litta taking part. After another festival a few weeks later, in which Theodore Thomas' orchestra again took the spotlight, a special train to Owatonna returned concertgoers to their homes. A year later a third Thomas festival was held in the new University Coliseum. That year also brought to the city a trio of German singers, Frau Materna, Herr Winkelmann, and Herr Scaria, said by Wagner to be the first dramatic singers in the world.

The nineties ushered in an era of concert, with opera receding into the background, although Barnabee's Bostonians continued to sing to packed houses, particularly when they gave De Koven's *Robin Hood*. And in 1896 when the Damrosch Opera Company brought a Wagner series to Minneapolis, audiences were highly enthusiastic, especially with the performance of *Tristan*. But on the whole orchestras and single artists commanded the attention of concertgoers in the nineties.

Great bands and orchestras visited the city: Sousa's with all its novelties; Victor Herbert guest-conducting a local band; Anton Seidl and the Metropolitan Orchestra in an all-Wagner program. The greatest musical event of 1890 was the evening in May when Arthur Nikisch, director of the Gewandhaus Orchestra in Leipzig, conducted the Boston Symphony in an unforgettable concert at the University Coliseum. To accommodate the crowds, trains coming into the city stopped at the university station; all horse and streetcar facilities were increased. In spite of the annoying hiss of the electric lights throughout the concert and the unsatisfactory acoustics of the build-

55

ing the event was considered a triumph for musical art.

One season during the nineties Krehbiel was heard in a series of lectures. The Minneapolis Institute of Arts sponsored recitals by the French organist, Alexandre Guilmant, and the promising boy pianist, Josef Hofmann. Eccentric Madame Schön-René came to Minneapolis to visit her sister and stayed to give direction to the first efforts of more than one fledgling musician. She organized the University Choral Association; she instituted a series of concerts that brought the most notable figures of the musical world to the city. Many a student of that day will recall the evenings spent in Schön-René's home when she entertained Calvé or Melba and invited promising students to sing for the great artists.

Minneapolis was a singing city. For the purpose of cultivating a taste for good music, almost a hundred singers, including the foremost musicians of the city, organized themselves into the Minneapolis Choral Association early in 1890. Immediately active, the group took charge of the opening of Century Hall, an auditorium on the second floor of the Century Piano Company. The occasion was remembered as one of the most elaborate social and musical affairs of the year. Dr. F. A. Dunsmoor, president of the club and one of the state's foremost surgeons, acted as head usher; Paul A. Schmitt, owner of a large music store, was one of the doorkeepers; while two of the city's favorite singing stars, Olive Fremstad and Maude Ulmer, managed the flower booths. The leading artists of the city were on the program. A five-hundred dollar profit from the venture was a propitious beginning for the new organization. After performances of *Elijah* and *The Messiah* the Choral Association was acclaimed a shining success.

Musical life was also in full swing among the smaller social and cultural units within the city. Each racial

56

group had its singing societies. The German Harmonia Society, started in 1861, for many years held the reputation of being the most accomplished singing society in the state. Particularly active were the Scandinavians, who had swept like a migratory horde into Minneapolis after the Civil War. The Scandinavian Society of the late sixties was followed by a succession of choral groups, men's quartets, and the like in the next three decades, and the performances they gave and the soloists they sponsored became a marked feature of the community's music.

The Norwegian newspapers carried frequent notices of the meetings and festivals of the various *sangforeninger* (song societies) to be held in Minneapolis, with similar Norwegian societies from Chicago, Fargo, Sioux Falls, and Duluth coming to participate. Exchange visits were well attended by the music-loving Norwegian Americans, who kept the spirit of their mother country warm in their hearts by frequent singing of "Ja vi elsker dette landet" (Yes, We Love This Land), Norway's national anthem.

It was to be expected that the Norwegian societies in Minneapolis would unite in their efforts to honor the memory of their beloved countryman, Ole Bull. The Ole Bull Monument Association spent two years raising funds and making elaborate plans for a huge celebration at the unveiling of the statue of Bull, wrought by the sculptor Jacob Fjelde. When the statue was unveiled, an international singers' tournament was held, with nine Norwegian, Swedish, and German singing societies competing for the prize. Over six thousand people jammed the auditorium, the largest crowd ever assembled in the Northwest under one roof, reported the newspapers. The climax of the celebration came when a violinist, hidden from view, began to play the strains of "Saeter Jentens Søndag" (Chalet Girl's Sunday) while the curtain was slowly withdrawn. There stood the plaster cast of the statue of Ole

Bull with his familiar smile and tilted head seemingly playing the melody the audience was listening to. When the bronze statue was unveiled at Loring Park the next year, nearly every local musician of note took part in the program. Bull's widow Sarah and his son Alexander, also a violinist, were present.

All this musical activity made the year at the conservatory a very enjoyable one for Christiansen. He had no money, but free concerts were plentiful, and occasionally students were given special rates for the big recitals. Of all the visiting artists, the eccentric Reményi remained the city's favorite. Traces of the age of the virtuosi still clung to the performances of this extraordinary fiddler, and his mannerisms grew more pronounced with each visit, until even Schubert's "Serenade" was scarcely recognizable under his bow. Christiansen heard him and marveled. Then there was Lillian Nordica, who gave a brilliant concert that winter, and Olive Fremstad, the "Norwegian nightingale" of Minneapolis, who was gathering laurels for herself in the East and abroad. With the many recitals by local artists, held in the several downtown churches that had large auditoriums, Christiansen could have spent every night of the week at a concert if time had permitted.

In May he graduated from the conservatory with a degree in music. He had done well, but he was not satisfied. More study was necessary but there was no money for it, and the only way he could secure it was to get as many pupils as he could, continue his odd jobs of directing and teaching at Augsburg, and appear as a recitalist when opportunity presented itself.

At Augsburg, meanwhile, where he was still part and parcel of the college scene, arrangements were being completed for a meeting of the Norwegian Lutheran Singers' Union. The interest in music on the part of the Augsburg student body, and particularly the inspiration of Theodore Reimestad, had provided the stimulus for organizing this body of singers to include the Norwegian Lutheran churches in the outlying districts. The first festival had been held in the spring of 1893 at Eau Claire, Wisconsin, and under Reimestad's vigorous directorship had proved so successful that plans had been made to meet the following year in Minneapolis.

On the seventh of May, two hundred and thirty Norwegian Lutheran singers, together with pastors and officials of the United Norwegian Lutheran Church who were meeting for their annual convention, assembled at the Swedish Mission Tabernacle, whose main auditorium was the largest in the city. At the opening concert a large chorus of the combined Lutheran church choirs of Minneapolis sang the "Velkomstsang" (Song of Welcome) which Christiansen and Urseth had written for the occasion.

The festival was so successful that it was repeated in March of 1895, again at the Swedish Tabernacle in Minneapolis. Where there had been twelve choirs in 1894, there were now fifty-two, besides three men's quartets, an octet, and two men's choruses, making a grand total of more than a thousand singers. This large chorus was assisted by an orchestra recruited for the occasion. The choir that Christiansen had directed in Marinette very proudly appeared in two solo numbers, both by their former director.

In the spring of 1894 the Augsburg Quartet began to make plans for its annual summer tour. The group had recently lost one of its singers, so the remaining three, Theodore Reimestad, Johannes Nydal, and Bernt Sundal, invited Christiansen to fill the vacancy. When the school year was over, the quartet left Minneapolis to tour the hundred and one small Norwegian communities scattered throughout Minnesota, Iowa, and South Dakota. Theirs was a serious purpose. They were stumping for prohibition. To old Scandinavian melodies they wrote appropriate temperance texts, emotional and exhortatory, and sang them with high relish to the listeners who crowded the churches. Christiansen's contribution as the first bass was not outstanding, but his general musicianship was valuable to the group and his violin solos lent variety to their concerts. The young men had a successful and congenial summer together, and in the congregations they visited, people vied with one another to entertain them.

Once, however, this was not true. In one Iowa village Christiansen and Sundal were told to go to the home of a certain Danish family for supper. The boys found the house and introduced themselves to the lady who answered their knock, but they were admitted somewhat reluctantly and were left standing in the hallway. They waited several minutes for some sign of hospitality. "I don't believe they want us very badly," said Sundal. "Don't you think we'd better leave?"

As he spoke a young girl passed through the hall on her way to the living room, where she seated herself on the piano stool and began rustling through some sheets of music. Apparently she had been taking music lessons and was eager to display her talents before the two young men. With much aplomb she thumped out the opening bars of the popular song, "After the Ball Is Over." Christiansen's eyes began to twinkle; without saying a word he opened his violin case, took out his fiddle, and joined in the melody, lending it the much needed grace. The father and mother immediately appeared in the doorway and with pleased smiles invited the boys to come into the sitting room. The fiddle had saved the day! It brought them an abundant and pleasant meal.

Christiansen was good company; he had a ready tongue for a joke and an inclination toward prankishness. One day he and Sundal stayed at the home of a farmer in southern Minnesota. While wandering about inspecting the premises, they noticed a pasture where a litter of baby pigs were enclosed. As they stood by the fence watching them, the animals crowded up expecting to be fed. Turning to Sundal, Christiansen asked, "How do you suppose they'd react if I played my violin for them?"

"I don't know, but it's worth trying," answered his friend.

Christiansen hurried back to the house for his violin, returned, sneaked carefully up to the fence, and pulling the bow across the strings, made a terrific squeal, worse than any pig could ever produce. The frightened animals rushed to the other side of the pasture, falling all over one another in their haste; but they soon returned, only to hear the dreadful noise again and to repeat their mad tumbling across the pasture. As the boys stood laughing at the result of their experiment, the farmer, who had observed it, walked by and remarked, "Denne karen maa vaere en fael spissbur." (This fellow must be a real scamp.)

But there was another side of Christiansen's nature. He could be blunt and outspoken in his speech and stubborn in his ways. His temper would flare in a spurt of anger, then quickly subside. Because of this strain of irascibility in his temperament and his occasional streaks of obduracy, it was not always easy for fellow students to get along with him, but most of them willingly overlooked those qualities in his make-up, feeling that his honesty toward all people, his sincerity, and his gaiety compensated for his lack of control over his less agreeable emotions.

At the end of the summer the musicians returned to

Minneapolis well fed and rested; moreover, they had made twelve hundred dollars, which they divided equally among themselves.

In the years that followed, Christiansen carried on his work in many quarters of Minneapolis, playing, teaching, and directing. On Sundays he officiated at the organ and directed the choir at Trinity Lutheran Church, where the eloquent Falk Gjertsen served as pastor. In Lutheran church circles Christiansen was gaining a reputation as a capable young musician, and frequent notices in the Minneapolis *Tidende* (Tidings) show that his chorus and choir were in constant demand. On March 1, 1895, the *Tidende*, in announcing that the Augsburg student chorus would sing at the Trinity Society for the Needy, made the following comment about its director: "Det er bekjent, hvilken sukces koret gjorde forrige aar under ledelse af sin fortraeffelige instruktør Melius Christiansen . . ." (It is well known that the chorus was successful in former years under the leadership of its excellent director, Melius Christiansen . . .)

On January 31, 1896, the *Tidende* informed its readers that a mixed chorus, to be called "Nordlyset" (Northlight), had been organized in the Trinity Lutheran congregation with Professor F. M. Christiansen as director. The story behind this is that Christiansen wanted a chorus over which he could have sole jurisdiction; church choirs were of necessity at the beck and call of the pastor or any organization in the church. Although Nordlyset was made up of members from Trinity congregation, it was independent of the regular choir. As it happened, however, the group did frequently sing in the churches, particularly Trinity.

One day when Pastor Gjertsen asked Christiansen if the chorus could sing at some special meeting, for unexplained reasons Christiansen refused. Without notifying the director, and certainly without taking heed for the morrow, Gjertsen called each member of the chorus and informed him that the group was to sing at the function in question. When the news reached Christiansen the next day, he went immediately to Gjertsen and in irate fashion flatly refused to let the chorus sing, exclaiming in his hotheaded way, "You are not the only one who has bone in his nose!"

Unlike the vast majority of older American churches, where a well-paid quartet furnished the musical climax for each service, the Norwegian-American churches all maintained some sort of choir, poor though it might be. Musical training in the majority of the Norwegian-American families was pitifully meager, and untrained singers constituted the membership of the struggling church choirs. The director usually had had a brief exposure to a course in music; if he had come from Norway, it had probably been obtained at a two-year normal school whose purpose was to give the rural youths a chance to acquire a smattering of culture after high school. Consequently, the quality of church music was still on a fairly low level, despite the awakening interest betokened by the annual singing festivals.

The anthems written by Dudley Buck, then the great figure in American church music, were not readily adaptable to the Norwegian Lutheran service. Because of the dearth of choir music, his songs were used, but the people preferred the melodies and texts to which they had been accustomed in Norway. Although English had penetrated into the business and social life of the immigrants. Norwegian to a large extent still remained the language of worship. The immigrant had been taught the way of salvation from his Norwegian Bible and the Norwegian translations of Luther's Catechism and Pontoppidan's "Explanation"; so for him all the emotions, sensations, and associations of his faith were attached to the Norwegian words. It was well-nigh impossible for him to transfer the significance of these words of his inmost beliefs to their English equivalents. Among some of the uneducated and more pietistic immigrants there still lingered inarticulately the belief that the words of the Scripture were sacred only in the Norwegian tongue.

Lanstad's hymnbook, a standard hymnal in the churches of Norway since the 1870's, had been carefully packed in every immigrant trunk and was faithfully used in the pioneer homes and churches. The more progressive, however, felt the deplorable lack of a new Norwegian-American church music, and slowly it was being created. Up to the turn of the century the leader in this process was John Dahle, who wrote for male and mixed choruses and edited and arranged the only two songbooks that were widely used by church choirs. Although Dahle's musical training at Hamar Seminary in Norway had not been extensive, he had a good sense of form and harmony. While Lutheran church music was in its infancy he served it well, but it remained for a sounder and more creative musician to become the real leader in this realm.

The attention given to music at Augsburg stimulated Christiansen and Urseth to try their hands at a collection of songs for mixed chorus. This book, entitled *12 Korsange* (Choir Songs), appeared in 1894 and was used by church choirs in Minneapolis and by some elsewhere in communities served by the Augsburg professors and graduates. Two years later, even though Urseth had by then accepted a pastorate in Rochester, Minnesota, the two enterprising friends began to publish a monthly bulletin, *Sangserie* (Song Series), devoted entirely to music. In addition to original compositions, it included excerpts from oratorios and arrangements of familiar Scandinavian hymns. This attempt to provide music for church choirs lasted

64

until 1898, when the bulletin was changed to a religious literary monthly and given the new name of *Idun.* The music was not discontinued, however, but was issued in supplementary sheets with each publication. A few years later, in 1901, Christiansen and Urseth again joined their talents in the publication of *Korsangeren* (The Choir Singer), which contained English as well as Norwegian texts. This book immediately became popular among the church choirs of the synod and remained so for several years.

Meanwhile it had been decided that the music which had been appearing through the years in the young people's magazine, *Ungdommens Ven,* should be collected and reprinted in book form. The result was the issuance of four such volumes over a period of years, bearing the title *Frydetoner* (Joyful Tunes). The volumes contained music by Scandinavian, German, English, American, and Scandinavian-American composers and were rather widely used by the choirs in the Lutheran churches.

All this music that was coming from the pens of Norwegian-American composers was simple, rhythmically melodious, appealingly sentimental, and thus easily learned by the great body of amateur singers who comprised the choirs for which it was intended. Composed in the shadow of the tent-meeting, the songs called the sinner to repentance, urged him to hear the Lord knocking on the door of his heart, and pleaded with him to make his decision quickly before the gates of hell closed in upon him. The majestic dignity that had characterized the church music of Norway was entirely lacking. Some watched dubiously this trend toward the revivalistic type of gospel hymn brought to the fore by Moody and Sankey. Others nodded approval, believing that religious music must be made accessible to all and therefore must be "easy to sing."

65

For Christiansen composition was at this stage most certainly subordinate to his interest in the violin, and these early efforts merely reflected the spirit of his environment. As a matter of fact, his compositions at this period were an unfortunate combination of a text full of emotional clichés and a stereotyped harmonic pattern. But one of them in particular, "Kun et Skridt," became a favorite at Lutheran prayer meetings. It was then known as "But a Step" but is now used in Lutheran circles almost entirely in a translation made by Oscar Overby entitled "One Resolve."

It must be borne in mind that Christiansen was literally educating himself in composition during his early twenties. He took composition as a matter of course, creating because necessity forced it upon him. His childhood had been spent among amateur composers—his father, his uncles, and both his teachers. When the family band needed a new number, Anders Christiansen wrote one in the copybook. When Melius needed new exercises for his violin practice, Professor Olsen jotted down a few in his exercise book. This training was of value in that it taught Christiansen not to be helpless in the face of exigencies.

More successful than his composing was his teaching; gradually as his reputation spread through the Norwegian circles in the city, the number of his pupils increased. During 1895 he was living in a modest room on Seventh Street and Twenty-first Avenue, juggling his many scattered duties as adroitly as he could to give himself a few free hours a day for his violin. Deeply absorbed one afternoon in practicing a new concerto, he was interrupted by a knock on his door. Opening it, violin still in hand, he saw a plainly dressed woman and a little boy with a clumsy, boxlike affair under his arm, standing in the darkened hallway.

"Are you Professor Christiansen, the violin teacher?" the woman asked.

"Yes, come in. What can I do for you?"

"I am Mrs. Olsen, and this is my son Adolph," she explained. "We have heard that you are a music teacher, and we would like to have Adolph take lessons—that is, if it isn't too expensive."

Christiansen nodded. He liked the woman's quiet manner. Obviously music lessons in this household would mean a sacrifice on the part of the parents. He turned to the boy, smiling at the eager expression on his face. "Have you ever had any lessons, Adolph?"

The boy shook his head. By this time he had brought into view the instrument he had been carrying under his arm. It was a crude attempt at a violin, made from a cigar box with a few strings stretched across a wooden bridge.

"Will you play something for me?" Christiansen asked, wondering how it was possible to produce a recognizable sound with such a makeshift.

The lad produced a clumsy bow and on one string played in halting fashion the simple melody of "Home Sweet Home." Christiansen saw immediately that he was playing by ear and that he knew nothing about fingering. While the boy struggled manfully through the piece, Christiansen stood with his hands folded behind his back, smiling broadly. When the child had finished, Christiansen walked over to him, patted him on the head, and said, "There is one thing about you, young man; you have a good ear."

The Olsens were very poor and so was the violin teacher, but he wanted to teach the youngster. A simple exchange of favors was finally arranged: Christiansen was given a room at the Olsens'; Adolph received violin lessons—and, Christiansen being generous with his time, piano and theory lessons as well. He was an exacting and thorough teacher, but so enthusiastic that he inspired his pupil to apply himself assiduously. Christiansen took a fatherly interest in the lad, and the relationship he had had in his youth with Hansen was now reversed. The boy went to the church where Christiansen was the organist to watch him play and learn from him; he began to dress, act, and speak like his teacher; frequently he went to choir rehearsals with Christiansen.

One winter evening teacher and pupil arrived at the church a few minutes before the appointed hour to find that only one or two singers had arrived. When the hour struck and only eight members had appeared, Christiansen lost his patience, turned to the boy and said brusquely, "Come, Adolph, if they can't get here on time, they can practice alone." He was a decisive and stern disciplinarian; punctual in his own habits, he demanded that those with whom he worked be the same. After one such episode no one dared again to keep him waiting.

The struggle for existence was maturing Christiansen; he had learned that only hard and constant application would keep him alive and bring him the thing he wanted most in life: the opportunity to become a great artist. He had no time to waste waiting for people. There was too much to be done.

CHAPTER 5

Widening Horizons

TWO themes recurred constantly in the pattern of Christiansen's thoughts as he occupied himself with the struggle to make a living. Fixed in his mind since childhood had been the idea that all musicians at some time in their lives study in Leipzig. He realized more keenly all the time that he must continue his study, and a year in Leipzig became his goal.

The other thought was Edith Lindem. He had not forgotten the girl with the attractive smile and the friendly manner who had sung in his Marinette choir. They had exchanged letters regularly, and whenever he could scrape together a few dollars he had gone to see her—on her confirmation day, during Christmas vacations, and particularly in the summer when his work was lighter.

One warm summer evening after her graduation from high school, Edith and Melius sat on the porch steps of the Lindem home. The tiny orange bulbs of darting fireflies glowed on and off in the darkness about them; a sharp smell of pine scented the air. From upstairs the slap of bare feet on the hall floor, shouts, and the squeak of bouncing bedsprings informed them that they would have peace from the teasing remarks of Edith's young brothers. Edith broke their comfortable silence. "Papa told me I could go to school next fall if I want to."

"Oh, is that so? Are you going to?"

"I don't know. What do you think I should do?"

"Would you like to go?"

"Well—yes. I've been thinking about the normal school in Oshkosh."

Melius puffed on his pipe. "Oshkosh. That's pretty far from Minneapolis."

"Yes, but I would come home for vacations."

"What's the matter with Minneapolis?" questioned Melius. "There are plenty of good schools there. And then I could see you once in a while. Your father and mother think you're too young to be serious about a fellow, but if we had a chance to be together more often and learn to know each other better, then we could tell if we'll keep on liking each other as well as we do now." He spoke slowly, not looking at her.

Her heart was thumping as she answered him sedately, "Yes, I think that would be very sensible."

Melius continued almost as if he had not heard her, "Edith, will you talk to your father again and ask him if you can go to school in Minneapolis? That is, if you want to be in Minneapolis."

"Of course I want to be there. All right, I'll talk to him." She looked at Melius, handsome and well dressed, his white shirt front making a patch of light in the surrounding darkness. She liked to tease him about his formal manner of dressing—a Prince Albert coat, high stiff collar, and boiled shirt front. When she once asked him why he dressed so formally for everyday occasions, he answered seriously and with a hint of reproof, "I am an organist." He was the son of Anders Christiansen!

Edith went to Minneapolis in the fall of 1895. She was eighteen, lively and energetic, and naturally very happy to be near Melius. Enrolled at Normal College, a little-known school on Franklin Avenue, she took ladylike lessons in elocution, voice, and piano, with some literature and algebra of sorts. She acted in a few plays and took part in musicales, but never could she persuade Christiansen to attend these performances. He was too busy playing for his bread and butter. But if he did not take her dramatics seriously, at least he was serious in his feelings toward her, and on the evenings when his chorus, Nordlyset, rehearsed in Normal College Hall he usually had a good reason for whistling gaily as he walked up Franklin Avenue.

Her mother's illness took Edith back to Marinette in the spring of the following year, but Christiansen wrote to her and went to visit as before. With her he discussed his artistic and religious beliefs and the kind of professional life he hoped to live. In religion he and Edith did not always agree, Edith having followed her parents into the prophetical path of the Russellites, but Christiansen, demanding independence of thought and action for himself, believed in it for others as well. Religious differences were no stumblingblock for his growing love.

Edith and Melius were married on the afternoon of July 14, 1897. The Lindem home was festive with summer flowers and fragrant with the smell of cooking coffee and freshly baked cakes. In the recess of a bay window the bride and bridegroom received the felicitations of their friends and relatives. Bridal happiness had brought a radiance to Edith's otherwise plain, honest face, and she looked charming in her high-necked gown with its puffed lace-trimmed shoulders and long tight sleeves, its satin ribbon sash and ruffle-edged overskirt of sheer white. Beside her Melius was as dignified as a curly-haired young man of twenty-six can look in a wing collar, a white bow tie, and a long-tailed black coat with a white rose on its lapel.

It was a simple wedding without music, a point upon which Melius had been unyielding. However, above the chatter of wedding pleasantries the sound of male voices was heard in the strains of a popular Norwegian song. A quartet of friends had come to serenade the couple; they would not permit an old comrade to be married without some token of recognition.

Christiansen was achieving his other desire too. With a little money he had saved and with assistance from relatives, he and Edith were going to Leipzig. Karl, who had come from Washburn for the wedding, was to accompany them, also to study music in the famous German city. They had already decided to spend a few weeks in Norway on the way, so they left Marinette in happy anticipation of good times ahead.

When Melius had come to America, he had fully intended to return to Norway in five years. Though nine had passed, the idea of carrying on his profession in Norway had been kept alive by his emotional attachment to his homeland. The heavy trunks and bulging boxes were evidence that Edith and Melius were leaving America with the intention of establishing themselves in the country of their fathers.

Melius' younger brother Kristian, who was in the Norwegian naval service, had arranged for a short furlough and was to meet them in New York. When they reached the city, they found, not Kristian, but a message from an official in a South American port informing them of their brother's death. Tuberculosis had found another victim in the Christiansen family. With heavy hearts they sailed, knowing their homecoming would be saddened by the tidings they were bringing to their father.

The few weeks in Norway were crowded with visits to all the Christiansen friends and relatives, who welcomed Melius' bride and the two brothers with joy and curiosity. At every turn they were met with the same questions. Was America as great as most people said it was? What were the houses and shops like? What did the people eat and wear? Their friends enjoyed hearing the visitors speak

The Christiansens at Sister Bay, Wisconsin, 1938
Left to right: Jacobi, Olaf, Mrs. Christiansen, Elsa, Dr. Christiansen, Paul

English, but they were pleased that Melius and Karl still preferred to talk in Norwegian, and they approved of Edith because she, too, spoke their language.

In the homes of their many friends the tables were heaped in their honor, and it was with delight that Melius and Karl once more sat down to good Norwegian food: creamy fish soups, smoked and pickled herring, fish balls, boiled codfish *(lutefisk)* dripping with melted butter; tasty meat balls *(kjøtboller)* in rich brown gravy; cheese made from goat's milk *(gjetost)*; brown-speckled potato bread *(lefse)* as crepelike and flat as elephant's ears; the endless variety of buttery Norwegian cakes and pastries, fluted *sandbakkels,* wreath-shaped *Berlinerkranser* decorated with chopped almonds, crinkly *fattigmand*; and succulent fruit puddings spiced with cloves and cinnamon.

It was only natural that the Christiansen boys, who had taken such an active part in the musical life of their home town, should be asked to give a public performance, and to their joint cornet and violin recital Larvik's citizens and newspapers responded with manifest pleasure. But when the summer drew to a close, the three Christiansens packed their trunks once more, bade good-by to their old friends, and sailed for Germany, going first to the old Hansa city of Stettin, and from there by rail to Berlin and finally to Leipzig.

They rented two pleasant and inexpensive rooms on the second floor in the *Hintergebäude* of No. 26 Alexanderstrasse, a crooked street near Johannespark and the conservatory. A small room for Karl; for the young couple a larger one with two big windows, a piano, a bed, and across the room in the corner a shiny, bluish tile stove. They were to spend two happy years at No. 26, close to the park and to the "concert quarter" where the conservatory, the Gewandhaus, and some of the university buildings were huddled in convenient proximity. Near by, too, was St. Thomaskirche, which had played such an important part in the musical life and musical education of Leipzig.

Christiansen was often among the two or three thousand who thronged to the huge church for the Saturday motet sung each week by the boys' choir of Thomasschule. For generations this had been customary and there were many Leipzigers who had not missed a performance in several years. With ease, precision, and marvelous accuracy of intonation the boys sang the most difficult motets of the great masters, the early Netherland and Italian composers, their own Bach, and the modern polyphonic writers. Although Christiansen was absorbed in developing his skill as a violinist during this period, without a doubt the hours he spent listening to the impressive singing of this choir unconsciously enriched him for the work he was later to do.

The conservatory required its students to attend all Gewandhaus concerts. During the years the Christiansens were at the conservatory, the director was the incomparable Arthur Nikisch. Not since the days of Mendelssohn had the Gewandhaus known such a brilliant conductor. All Leipzig was at his feet. The regular weekly concerts were given on Thursday evenings, and to them Leipzig society went in full dress. On Wednesday evening or Thursday morning it was customary to have a *Hauptprobe* which was open to the students and the public for a small charge, and this, a duplicate of the formal concert, came to be almost as popular as the Thursday night performance.

There was scarcely a night that the two Christiansen brothers did not leave No. 26 Alexanderstrasse, light their pipes, and walk toward the concert quarter for an evening of chamber music by some string quartet, the Joachim or the Gewandhaus Quartet perhaps, or the popular Bohemian Quartet; or it might be to hear Herr Schelper and Frau Bauman in Weber's *Oberon*, or a recital by one of their fellow students.

Christiansen's days were spent at the conservatory in classes and violin practice. In view of his later concentration on choral work, it may seem strange that he should have manifested such slight interest in it at this point, but the atmosphere of the conservatory was not conducive to it. Attention was centered almost entirely on instrumental training; choral study was quite openly snubbed. One of the compulsory classes at the conservatory was chorus drill, but apparently no efforts were made to enforce the requirement. Christiansen confesses that not once during his two-year period did he report for the class, yet nothing was ever said about his absence. Singing ranked low in the conservatory's musical scale, so it was natural that Christiansen should adopt a similar attitude of indifference.

He took classes from the quiet and scholarly Gustav Schreck, cantor of the Thomasschule and teacher of composition and counterpoint at the conservatory. At the first meeting of the class in October some twenty to thirty students sat at the long table in Schreck's classroom; before the year was over all but ten had dropped out, unable to keep the pace their teacher set for them. Aside from class exercises for Schreck, Christiansen did no composing during his two years at the conservatory. There was no time, for he was spending six hours a day practicing on his violin, besides an hour or two at the piano.

He studied violin with Hans Sitt, a grumpy and unsociable man but an excellent teacher. During a lesson he would sit with his violin on his knee, a cigar in his mouth, ashes dropping carelessly on his vest. While absorbed in a concerto, the student would suddenly be surprised to hear an accompaniment, and turning, would see Sitt, violin still resting on his knee, playing an incredible harmony part with three fingers, plucking with his little finger. Sitt was never lavish with his praise, but that he considered Christiansen an able violinist is known from his incidental comments made to others.

Carl Mellby, a senior at Augsburg Seminary during Christiansen's year in the college, was now a theological student at the University of Leipzig. He had formed a tennis acquaintanceship with Hans Sitt, and during one of their rests between matches, Mellby spoke of his home in Minnesota; whereupon Sitt, amiably conversational, remarked that he had a very talented young pupil who was also from Minnesota, Minneapolis in fact. On several subsequent occasions Mellby heard him speak of Christiansen as his "gifted pupil from America."

Oddly enough, among the Christiansen brothers' conservatory acquaintances were three other young people from Minneapolis: Grace and Verna Golden and Carlyle Scott. All of them were to become prominent in the Flour City's musical life, and all good friends of the mature Christiansen. Verna Golden became Mrs. Carlyle Scott and for many years served as the manager of the Minneapolis Symphony and of the University of Minnesota Artists Course. Mr. Scott accepted a position in the department of music at the University of Minnesota on his return from Germany and in time became its head. Grace Golden, upon the death of her husband, James Davies, succeeded him as music critic for the Minneapolis *Tribune*.

Late one afternoon Karl and Melius were in the crowd that poured out of the Gewandhaus in a gay holiday mood. Carriages and horses filled the street, and friends were greeting each other with smiles and a merry, "Viel Glück zum neuen Jahre!" as they elbowed toward the sidewalk. Joachim, in his late sixties now but still a great master of the violin, had made his annual New Year's Day appearance at the Gewandhaus.

Melius began to talk excitedly as they left the crowd and walked through the gathering dusk toward Alexander-strasse. "It certainly was a surprise to hear him play that simple little Viotti, especially when we all expected the Beethoven concerto. They say he's played the Beethoven for the last four years at this concert, but he fooled us all today."

Karl agreed, but judiciously added, "He did the wise thing. He showed us that simple things are beautiful if they are played with perfect technique and with dignity. Too many of us think we have to play something difficult in order to make an impression, but a great artist like Joachim knows that simple things can sometimes be the most effective." They walked in silence for a few minutes, then just as they approached No. 26 Melius said soberly, "Yes, it's probably one of the best lessons I've ever had."

In the spring of 1899 Christiansen received his diploma from the Royal Conservatory at Leipzig. The two years had been spent in diligent work, but Christiansen looks back on those student days in Leipzig as among the happiest in his life. During the stay in Germany the Christiansens' plans had again undergone a change, and now it seemed more expedient to return to America than to settle in Norway. With the infant Elmer, born in the spring of 1898, the Christiansens sailed for their American home in the summer of 1899.

Knowing full well how precarious an existence musical free-lancing provided, Christiansen felt the times ahead might be too lean for his little family; so Edith and the baby went to Marinette to live with the Lindems until he could re-establish himself in Minneapolis after his two-year absence.

He was soon offered a position as organist at Bethany Lutheran Church, which, though not very promising, at least brought him a few dollars. More encouraging for his future was the invitation to join the violin department of Northwestern Conservatory. Through the contacts he would make at the conservatory he might expect to be drawn into the very center of musical life in Minneapolis. And in this there had been no let-down. Concerts, recitals, song festivals, all were as many and as good as before. Minneapolis now had three conservatories of music, a creditable symphony orchestra, and three outstanding choral clubs—the Philharmonic, the Apollo, and the Thursday Musicale—to say nothing of a host of lesser groups, including the active singing societies of the various nationality groups.

A few public appearances revealed the remarkable progress Christiansen had made during his absence, and, free now from the restraining influence of the Augsburg circle, he was soon making frequent appearances as violin soloist at the concerts of one or another of the Scandinavian singing societies. As director of the Kjerulf Club too, he quickly advanced to a front-rank position in Norwegian-American musical circles.

The Kjerulf Club was a men's singing society. For it, as for others of its kind, the caliber of the voice was not important; the only requirement for membership was that the person be a "good fellow." A few such jolly souls organized it, and after getting enough members to provide amiability and an ample treasury, they looked for the best director in the city. Christiansen was glad to accept their offer of four dollars a rehearsal and began immediately the difficult task of making a singing chorus out of a group heavily weighted with poor voices. At first they rehearsed in a room over the Lee Brothers' Photograph Gallery on Nicollet Avenue and Third Street. Later they moved into a larger studio at Northwestern Conservatory, which was then located above the Metropolitan Music Store on Sixth Street between Nicollet and Hennepin Avenues.

As a social venture the Kjerulf Club was a success. It was a loose-jointed affair with only one prohibition: no English could be spoken at the rehearsals. It was a Norwegian club, and the members were seriously patriotic about the land of their fathers. When rehearsals were over, they crossed the street to a smoke-filled tavern to exchange business gossip over their beer and tobacco.

Christiansen rarely participated in the social activities of the club. When he came into rehearsal, loose chatter ceased and business began. His sharp tongue was quick to lash out at anyone whose attention wandered from the work at hand. Sometimes taciturn and moody, he could at other times be high-spirited and humorous. The members of the club genuinely liked him; they enjoyed singing for him, and they appreciated the effort he expended to make singers of them. He even wrote a few male chorus numbers for them to sing. In fact, one of the most charming numbers Christiansen ever wrote for men's chorus is one composed for the Kjerulf Club. It is a choral setting for "Ungbirken" (Young Birch), a sensitive lyric by the Norwegian poet, Jorgen Moe.

One evening while singing at a meeting in a North Minneapolis church, the Kjerulf choristers lost their bearings in the middle of the selection and became hopelessly mired in a false chord. They knew it was impossible to go on. Christiansen, never slow of decision in moments of stress, or at any other time for that matter, calmly turned on his heel and walked off the platform, leaving the vowel-mouthed chorus to face the audience on a suspended chord until they could swallow it and follow him, helplessly embarrassed.

Christiansen by no means confined his activities to Scandinavian circles. One of his pupils at the conservatory was Sister Marie Josephine, a violin teacher at St. Agatha's Academy of Music and Arts in St. Paul. In addition to giving her lessons, he went once a week to observe and supervise her teaching. Occasionally he would appear as soloist on the literary and musical programs held in the school auditorium for the students and friends of the academy.

Most notable, perhaps, in the broader sphere into which his conservatory position took him was his membership in the violin section of the Philharmonics orchestra, the germ of what is today the outstanding musical organization of the Central Northwest.

Early in the 1880's a group of local musicians, both amateur and professional, had formed an orchestra under the leadership of Frank Danz. A few years later Frank Danz, Jr., concertmaster in Theodore Thomas' Chicago orchestra, succeeded his father as director and developed a symphonic organization of considerable merit. Public favor was won when Danz inaugurated a series of summer concerts at Lake Harriet which attracted a bevy of gay couples and an impressive array of carriages. This popularity carried over to the Sunday afternoon concerts of the following winter season, and in 1894–95 a Friday evening series was begun, mainly as dress rehearsals for the Sunday performances but also to accommodate the puritanical souls who thought it sinful to indulge in any tickling of the senses on the Sabbath, particularly when it took place in a theater. By the last years of the century the audiences had become so large that the concerts were moved from the Metropolitan Theater to the more commodious Lyceum Theater.

In addition to its regular weekly performances, the Danz Symphony appeared in special concerts with the city's numerous choral clubs. A typical program is one given with the Normanna and Svea singing societies on April 10, 1898, at the Metropolitan Theater. The choruses sang the usual Norwegian and Swedish numbers of the popular composers Kjerulf and Wennerberg. The orchestra played Grieg's *Peer Gynt Suite,* Liszt's "Rhapsodie No. 3," and selections by Raff and Nicolai. For a brilliant climax the joint chorus and orchestra presented Grieg's "Landkjenning" (Landsighting). Such concerts were festive occasions. Socialites drove back to their fashionable Park Avenue mansions in shiny carriages, proud of their city's talent, while the families of Scandinavian carpenters, bakers, and machinists returned by trolley to their small homes in South and North Minneapolis, rejoicing that the culture they knew and loved was finding its place in a new land.

Early in the nineties the Segelbaum brothers, local musicians, were responsible for the organization of a club known as the "Filharmonix." It consisted of a small orchestra and a men's quartet. Later the club was increased to include women's voices and was renamed the "Philharmonic Club." In 1901 a young German musician, Emil Ober-Hoffer, who had been the conductor of the Apollo Club in St. Paul, slipped quietly into the musical life of Minneapolis as a piano teacher at Northwestern Conservatory. Among other activities he directed the choral section of the Philharmonic Club.

Because salaries for symphony members were scarcely enough to live on, the director of an orchestra, in order to maintain his group, had to secure private concert or accompanying jobs for his members. Danz was becoming neglectful in these duties to his men, and when the young German director of the Philharmonics chorus began to find outside positions for the members of the orchestra, Danz found that his men were leaving him to work with

81

Ober-Hoffer. Before long Ober-Hoffer was directing an orchestra of his own and, aggressive, able leader that he was, he lost no time in recruiting Christiansen for its violin section.

The first important engagement of the new orchestra was accompanying the Philharmonic Club in *The Messiah* during the holiday season of 1899. Christiansen long remembered that gala performance, in which the orchestra scored a triumph that boded well for its future. Four years later, in 1903, the group was formally organized into a corporation under the name of the Minneapolis Symphony Orchestra. Ober-Hoffer, later dropping the hyphen from his name and restoring its original German form of Oberhoffer, continued as its director.

Naturally these varied activities brought Christiansen an increasing number of private pupils, and old programs show that he presented them frequently in recitals. His most promising student still, however, was the lad who had come to him five years before with a homemade violin under his arm. Now newspaper reviews were praising the talent of "Master Adolph Olsen." On March 26, 1901, Master Adolph appeared with two well-known Minneapolis artists in a benefit concert at which Christiansen conducted the Northwestern Conservatory orchestra.

Every hour in the day now was filled with lessons and rehearsals; the evenings with concerts and recitals of one kind or another. During a free hour Christiansen would work at his desk writing out a melody that had been humming in his mind. He was composing for his violin as well as for choruses and choirs. Audiences often heard his lilting lullaby, "Kjølstavisa," and a longer, more serious work, "Romance." His motive books were full of themes that he wanted to work into compositions; there was not time enough for all that he wanted to do.

As the new century began, Christiansen felt that a new

era had begun for him, too. His had been no spectacular success, but in a year's time he had lifted himself from the obscurity of a nameless musician on the second floor of a house on some forgotten street to the rank of an artist who fulfilled engagements in all quarters of a growing metropolis.

Wealth was pouring into the city from the golden prairies of the West; immigrants continued to find their way to the city above the yellow-rocked banks of the Mississippi, to lend their sturdy, honest efforts in the building of its culture. A mixture of provinciality and growing sophistication marked the taste and mentality of the city. In its urban swirl Christiansen played a minor role, and yet he was part of its spirit; he was growing with it; he was learning from it. It had disciplined him, but still he was tempestuous; it had polished him, but still he was crude; it had matured him, but still he was young.

With signs pointing to a more substantial income for the future, Christiansen made arrangements to bring his family to the city. In April 1900 Edith and Elmer and a second son, Jacobi, born in Marinette two months before, moved into the furnished house that Christiansen had rented for them in Minneapolis. For the first time in all the years Christiansen had lived in America he had a sense of real security. With Edith and his family about him his confidence rose.

Shortly after the Christiansens had settled in their new home, Melius' brother Karl came to make his home with them for three years while he studied engineering. In August of 1901 a third son, Olaf, was born, but a year later the family was shocked by the sudden death of four-year-old Elmer, who was stricken with spinal meningitis. It was difficult for the sad father to accept the loss and to justify in his mind the ways of God to man. In the spring of 1903 the family prepared for the arrival from Norway of Christiansen's brother-in-law and his two small children, who had been left motherless by the death of Christiansen's younger sister. In June of that year the Christiansens' first daughter was born. Although she was named after her mother, the child was affectionately called "Tulla." Edith had a large household to manage now, but she was strong, capable, and devoted to them all. Christiansen, on the other hand, had little time for his children, for he had to give all his energy to his profession in order to supply the needs of his growing family.

On August 21, 1903, friends of the Christiansens were surprised to learn from the Minneapolis *Tidende* that violinist F. Melius Christiansen had been called to head the music department at St. Olaf College in Northfield, Minnesota. Christiansen, the announcement stated, would direct the band and the chorus and teach violin and music theory. Christiansen's family would remain in Minneapolis and the violinist would devote two days a week to his pupils in the city. His friends had heard nothing of such a plan. How had it come about, they wondered.

CHAPTER 6

College on the Hill

A FEW weeks before, while the Christiansens were living in a cottage on Lake Amelia (now Lake Nokomis), a few miles out of the city in the wild woods near Minnehaha Falls, Christiansen had received a postcard from John Nathan Kildahl, the president of St. Olaf College, asking the violinist to meet him for an interview about a position. Christiansen had never heard of St. Olaf, but he went into the city to meet the president. Apparently impressed by the young man during their conversation, Kildahl asked him if he would like to go to Northfield to see the college. Christiansen agreed.

They took the train southward through forty miles of rolling farmland. Rows of shocked grain dotted the stubbled fields; here and there threshing machines were already spouting streams of golden straw; waist-high corn rustled in the July wind; neat red barns and white farmhouses indicated thrifty owners. The landscape seemed to breathe simplicity, peace, and security.

The scene hardly changed when the train rumbled into the village of Northfield—a few more trees and houses, carriages on the streets, people passing each other leisurely with nods of greeting. Leaving the station, the two men took a street leading west to the edge of the town. On a distant hill Christiansen saw the pointed tower of a light-colored brick building. "Up there's the college," said President Kildahl, "and the building you see is the Main Building, as we call it." A dirt street curved up the hill; scattered frame houses with lawns in front, pasture land and woods at the back, marked their progress up to the college.

The campus was green and pleasant. Tall trees shaded the walks between the buildings. Except for a few workmen, who were spading and hauling dirt near one of the buildings, the place seemed deserted. "The new building over by the Main," Kildahl explained, pointing in the direction of the workmen, "is our library, given to us by Consul Steensland of Madison, Wisconsin. It has just been finished." The bricks were shiny and barelooking, the pillars gleaming white in the bright sunshine. "The red brick building you see through the trees is our men's dormitory, just three years old. It houses two hundred men. In that plot across from the library we shall soon begin building a chapel, which some day, we hope, will have a fine pipe organ."

The men paused in the shade to talk, for the trudge up the hill had made them hot. As they rested, Kildahl told Christiansen the story of the college.

St. Olaf College, then beginning its thirtieth year of existence, had been founded by the Reverend Bernt Julius Muus, a pioneer pastor in southern Minnesota. In 1859, a year after the state had been admitted to the Union, the young pastor, fresh from the University of Christiania, arrived in Minnesota and established himself in Goodhue County. Rich soil made this southern section of the state a mecca for the land-hungry Norwegian immigrants. Coming from older settlements in Illinois and Iowa and directly from Norway, the settlers converged upon these valleys. The Norwegian names they gave to their settlements still add to the Old Country illusion that might befall even a contemporary traveler as he drives through the dense woods and down a steep hill into the Sogn or the Vang Valley. Settled in some sections exclusively by Norwegians, Goodhue County played an important role in the life of Norwegian-American institutions in Minnesota and furnished many able leaders for church and school.

Among the early settlers in the community, and one of the few with a substantial education, Muus became a pioneer leader and missionary. As he traveled on foot or horseback from farm to farm, baptizing, preaching, teaching, he became concerned about the education of his people. There was at this early date no Norwegian Lutheran school that admitted both men and women. At Luther Academy and College in Decorah, Iowa, the course was designed to prepare men for the study of theology and accordingly followed the model of the Latin schools in Norway with their emphasis on the classics. Augsburg College in Minneapolis, similarly planned to attract would-be clergymen, also kept its doors shut to women.

Muus anticipated the need that was bound to arise. As the children of the Norwegian settlers grew up, many of them would leave the farms to seek employment in towns and cities. They would need an education to fit them for service in the many fields of activity that America offered. They could not remain isolated from American thought and manner of living. He saw the necessity for a coeducational institution which would be democratic in structure, but which at the same time would not be alien to their culture and religious background.

Muus tried to interest neighboring pastors, leaders of the synod, and other men of influence in his project to establish a school in some strategically located city or town, but for the most part the response from these gentlemen was lukewarm. Harold Thorson, a wealthy merchant of Northfield, was a striking exception. Refused support by those from whom they could legitimately have expected it, Muus and Thorson turned to the citizens of Northfield.

The town had been built in the pleasant valley of the Cannon River. What little business was carried on there was centralized in two or three blocks parallel to the river. Around the town square, which was in reality more triangular than square, were clustered the banks, grocery stores, clothing stores, and harness shops. Most of the people had built their homes on the east side of the river, and in their midst was Carleton College, a co-educational school founded in 1866 by men of New England heritage.

The town was peopled with quiet, scholarly professors and their families; with some retired farmers who had made their money from the rich soil of southern Minnesota; and with owners of small business establishments who were content to spend their three score years and ten making change from the sale of a spool of thread or a pound of nails in a small village where one could own one's own home and rear and educate one's children without too much trouble. The idea of another college was welcome to these people.

A group of public-spirited men, most of them of New England background, began a campaign for funds, and, after two town meetings, it was announced that almost six thousand dollars had been pledged for the support of the school. A corporation of five members—Muus, Thorson, and three farmers from Goodhue County—was formed, and on November 6, 1874, the articles of incorporation were signed. The general purpose of the institution was stated in this characteristic fashion: ". . . to give a higher education to pupils fifteen years of age or over and to preserve them in the true Christian faith as taught by the Evangelical Lutheran Church, nothing to

88

be taught in contravention with the Apostolic, Nicene, and Athanasian creeds, with the Unaltered Augsburg Confession, and with Luther's Small Catechism."

St. Olaf's School, as it was named, was in this first stage just another "academy," not unlike the average of its kind that marks a period in the history of American education. For the first three years it was located in temporary quarters. The students, about fifty in number, boarded and roomed with townspeople; most of the faculty members lived in rooms above the stores on Division Street, the principal business thoroughfare. To the majority of the students, who had lived only on farms, this new environment, simple and unpretentious as it was, undoubtedly afforded many a thrill. A plot of ground in the south end of the town was used by the boys as a baseball field; a bend in the river served as a swimming hole.

A young St. Paul pastor, Thorbjörn Mohn, became the first principal of the school at a salary of six hundred and fifty dollars a year. Coming to America from Norway, Mohn had taught a country school before entering Luther College in Decorah, Iowa, and after his graduation from that institution, he had studied theology at Concordia Seminary in St. Louis. Pastorates in Chicago and St. Paul had shown him to be a wise and farsighted leader of men.

By 1877 four teachers were giving courses in religion, Latin, German, Norwegian, algebra, and music in addition to the common school subjects, and a permanent site had been chosen. Sloping upward from the Cannon Valley west of town, the ground gradually rises a hundred and thirty feet to a plateau called Manitou Heights, which overlooks the village, the curving river valley, and the distant wooded hills. On the brow of the hill above the grainfields of the villagers, some of whom still farmed on a small scale, the first structure, the Main Building, was erected in 1877–78. It was a hazardous venture for an institution with no assured backing, but on that wooded hilltop the builders of St. Olaf took their stand.

Though the church refused to promise support for the school, the academy was from the start guided and staffed by clergymen. The close connection with the church and church politics shows clearly in the events that led to the establishment of a college department.

In the late 1870's and during the 1880's the age-old Calvinistic idea of predestination reappeared to plague the Lutheran theologians of the Norwegian Synod.* The faction accused of having Calvinistic sentiments were called "Missourians," because of their doctrinal affinity to the German Lutheran Missouri Synod, and their opponents were known as "Anti-Missourians." When it became apparent once again that no ecclesiastical body could peacefully harbor both wings, the Anti-Missourian Brotherhood seceded from the Norwegian Synod.

The new group was immediately faced with the problem of finding schools to educate its young and train men for the ministry. Muus, Anti-Missourian in sympathy, seized the opportunity for his school and early in 1886 invited the secessionist leaders to meet at St. Olaf. At this folkmoot, or *folkemöde* as they called it, Anti-Missourian clergymen and laymen from far and near voted an annual appropriation to St. Olaf, which in turn undertook to establish a college department and a divinity school.† The necessary arrangements were soon completed, and in September 1886 the first freshman class entered St. Olaf College.

*This was one of the major synods among the Norwegian Lutherans at that time; others were the Hauge Synod, the Norwegian-Augustana Synod, and the Norwegian-Danish Conference.

†After several changes the seminary was finally established in St. Paul, Minnesota, and has since been the official divinity school for the Norwegian Lutheran church.

Although the purpose in founding the school had been to provide a more elastic course of study, the majority of the early teachers had had a strictly classical training and were reluctant to admit the value of other subjects, particularly those of a scientific nature. But as the college began to draw men who were ambitious to enter professions other than the ministry and women who wanted to be trained for teaching, the Greek, Hebrew, and Latin of the early days were gradually supplemented by courses in science, literature, and the social sciences.

For six years preceding 1899, when he became president, Kildahl told Christiansen, the college had been left to support itself, but now it had been named the official college of the United Lutheran Church of America, and continuing support from that body was assured. It seemed the moment to undertake a program of experiment and expansion, to the end that the college might better serve the needs of its students.

Since its founding it had been a school for the children of middle class homes, and it attracted almost exclusively men and women of Norwegian, or at least Scandinavian, descent. Most of the students came from homes in which Norwegian was the language of everyday conversation, or at best homes that were bilingual. They had thus retained their feeling for Norwegian culture, and their concentration in relatively closed farming communities, together with the control exercised by the orthodox, tended to preserve their group character and made them somewhat refractory to the broader currents of American thought. The need Muus had foreseen was here, and the college was facing the problem of how best to meet it. It had been suggested that music was one road for development.

On the faculty were two men whom Christiansen knew: Carl A. Mellby, the Augsburg student he had met in Leipzig, and Paul G. Schmidt, whom he had known in Minneapolis. Both nonprofessional musicians of creditable ability, these two had already aroused a lively interest in oratorio on the campus. Under their leadership the students had acquired enough proficiency to sing cantatas and the easier oratorios with pleasure, and the preceding May the Choral Union, as the student-faculty chorus was called, under Mellby's direction and with the assistance of Twin City soloists, had given Gaul's cantata, *The Ten Virgins*.

Neither Mellby nor Schmidt, however, could give the time necessary for such extracurricular activities without damage to his regular classwork. Consequently they had suggested to President Kildahl that a full-time director be secured and they had recommended Christiansen for the post. Kildahl had approved the suggestion and was acting on the recommendation. The job was clear-cut: to build a music department. It was a large order with small pay—six hundred dollars a year. Christiansen could have the position if he wanted it.

He asked for time to think it over. He was attracted by the place and he liked Kildahl, but he hesitated over the risk of moving his family for such a small salary to a place he knew little about. In the end he worked out an arrangement with Kildahl for a trial year, leaving his family in Minneapolis and maintaining some professional contacts there, but agreeing to spend the greater part of his time at the college.

Regarding his new position as an experiment, Christiansen during that first year kept aloof from the general life of the faculty and students, but living in the men's dormitory when he was on the campus, he could not be unaware that he had entered what was quite definitely the atmosphere of a midwestern denominational school with all its doctrinal intensity and intellectual limitations, but also with its great integrity of purpose. Student recreation was circumscribed both by means and by the faculty's disposition toward gravity. Under these conditions music and literary societies naturally became the most acceptable activities for those who desired a measure of excitement which they did not find in the classroom and the religious exercises.

Though the records of college activities reveal that a school band, class glee clubs, and choruses within the literary societies, as well as the Choral Union, were in existence before Christiansen came, a heightening of interest in music was noticeable after his arrival. The November issue of the college paper, the *Manitou Messenger,* reported the change:

At last music is about to receive the attention it deserves at our institution. . . . Prof. Christiansen came highly recommended, and his work here during the past two months has convinced everyone that he is the man for the place. As a result of the new order of things interest for the art melodious has taken an upward shoot, and our various musical organizations are in a flourishing condition. A class in Harmony has been organized; the Choral Union is larger than ever, and its members are filled with enthusiasm; embryo violinists are sprouting and coming to the front, and the band is on the highway to achievements unexcelled. The only organization not yet revived is the orchestra, but that undoubtedly will be reorganized in the near future. The latest development is a College Glee Club of sixteen charter members.

There is little doubt that the new head of the music department made an impression on the students. Certainly for the members of the band he was an experience. Local success had made them complacent, and now for the first time they were confronted with a musician who was exacting and harsh. They had been taught to play a piece from its beginning to its end without interruption, to repeat it so again and again until the number was battered into some sort of recognizable shape. But Christiansen had no admiration for the homemade style; he drilled the entire band, as well as each section, on one short phrase after another, sometimes spending the hour's rehearsal on only a small part of the selection. At first this unheard-of practice seemed wearisome to the boys, whose musical training had been acquired in a hit-or-miss fashion, and their reaction after the first rehearsal was not enthusiastic. There is even a touch of juvenile arrogance in the letter one of the young men wrote home to his family: "We are going to miss Onstad—this man isn't much good. He is a violin player."

But the boys soon realized that the "violin player" knew his business. They were surprised and mildly impressed when he paused in rehearsal to demonstrate the correct way of playing the melophone, and their appreciation grew as he found it necessary to teach a clarinetist how to finger and a cornetist how to avoid a sputtery tone. Gradually they came to realize that Christiansen's technique of practicing difficult passages in isolation until they were mastered was producing a marked improvement in their performances. By the middle of the year they had attained a level never before reached. They had become a good band.

Christiansen accomplished this by the relentless will and the intense energy that already characterized the man and his work. He did not spare himself, nor did he spare the boys. He roared at them, lost his temper, and sometimes, if a member was so absorbed in the execution of his own score that he forgot to watch the conductor's baton, the little wand itself came crashing down beside the sinner, a near hit. No wonder the boys lived in awe of their stormy director. From one note to the next they did not know when this unpredictable man would stop them with a bark and let his wrath explode at one or all of them. With his sharp, darting eyes, flushed face, and vigorous movements he was the most electric personality they had ever seen. He demanded their best, drove them fiercely. But, though somewhat terrorized by him, the boys came to admire him unrestrainedly.

The thing that saved Christiansen from being a tyrant in his profession was his audacious humor. At any place, at any time, the unexpected might happen. An amusing incident occurred during a band concert in a small North Dakota town. It was, one must remember, the era when the tobacco cud was still very common. An Englishman who traveled in America some years earlier observed in his journal that this phenomenon seemed to increase noticeably as he approached the frontier. By Christiansen's time the frontier had disappeared, but the Middle West was still chewing its cud. Anyway, in that little town of North Dakota, while Christiansen was directing in his usual energetic way, his attention was suddenly drawn to a knothole directly in front of him in the floor of the platform. He eyed it for a moment, measuring the distance, then—pht!—a brown cud disappeared neatly into the hole, and Christiansen grinned broadly at the band players, who had watched his performance. How they got through the number the boys never knew; their sides ached with suppressed laughter.

Early in the spring of 1904, toward the end of Christiansen's first year at St. Olaf, the band made its first concert trip away from Northfield, visiting several towns in southern Minnesota. The success of this initial venture encouraged Christiansen to take the band annually on tour and the custom was maintained for many years. President Kildahl gave hearty support to the idea, for the college needed the advertisement that a snappily uniformed band provided. Although the enrollment was increasing yearly, the needs of the college were far greater than its income.

Gradually enlarging its itinerary to include such towns as La Crosse, Eau Claire, Stanley, and Chippewa Falls, Wisconsin, Fargo, North Dakota, and Sioux Falls, South Dakota, as well as many Minnesota towns, the band brought St. Olaf College to the attention of Lutherans of the North Central area. The programs opened and concluded with brisk marches, featured selections from Wagner, Verdi, and Rossini operas, included a waltz or two, and usually one light number with a student soloist. Christiansen himself often appeared as a violin soloist, playing Schubert's "Serenade," or perhaps one or two of his own compositions.

The sudden and startling leap from these local jaunts to a tour of Norway in the summer of 1906 was, as it were, an act of musical reciprocity. In the spring of 1905 the Norwegian Student Singers toured America. At St. Olaf they were entertained by the band, and to mark their appreciation of the fine welcome accorded them, the singers invited Christiansen and the band to make a tour of Norway the following year under their auspices.

While the band was crossing the Atlantic, Christiansen did not allow the members to forget they were on business. Each day he rehearsed them strenuously. One day in the midst of the rehearsal a player had the temerity to suggest that it was mealtime, whereupon Christiansen glared and shouted, "You can't go! You belong to me!" Perhaps this possessiveness was one of the fundamental traits of his artistic personality.

The tour of the St. Olaf Band took place during the spirited period when Norway attained sovereignty by severing her ties with Sweden. National feeling was running high. As the boat, *Oscar II,* moved slowly into

Christiania harbor, the band played first "The Star-Spangled Banner" and then the Norwegian national anthem, "Ja vi elsker dette landet." The Norwegian Singers, waiting at the wharf, answered with a song of welcome. Undoubtedly the patriotic fever mounted another degree as the uniformed band marched up the crowded street toward the capitol buildings. Flags, flowers, and banquets greeted them at every point. They were entertained by Statsminister Michelsen at his villa, played for the King and Queen at Trondheim, and at Larvik were driven in carriages with liveried coachmen to their concert in the Beachforest park, where Christiansen had played many a concert in his youth.

For the boys the tour was one of the most stirring experiences of their lives. And for the Norwegian people there was a glamour about the band from faraway America where so many of them had relatives. To them Christiansen symbolized the success of their own kinsfolk in the New World, and they were proud of it. Nearly every band member was welcomed at some city on the tour by grandparents, uncles, and aunts. Newspapers carried articles about the organization, its director, and the school, and spoke self-consciously about its close ties with the people of Norway. These visitors from America still spoke Norwegian fluently.

Christiansen enjoyed the band, the youth and enthusiasm of the members. Once a year, after Christiansen had established his home in Northfield, he and Mrs. Christiansen entertained the group. At this party the new officers for the following year were elected, after which Christiansen spoke to the members about the work of the band, what it was striving toward, what their spirit should be—in short, gave them the annual "pep talk" that invariably sent the boys home glowing with ambition.

The experience with the band was a stimulus to the young director. Early during his first year at St. Olaf he began the composition of his first band piece, "Norwegian Rhapsody," which was performed by the band on its spring tour the same year. The composition has been popular with generations of St. Olaf College students and became familiar to many audiences both in this country and in Norway. Since its publication in 1932, it has been a required number for state music contests and has also appeared on national contest lists for high school bands.*

Although the band with its tours and numerous local appearances continued to absorb much of Christiansen's time, his attention was increasingly demanded by his growing department, the choir, and composition. Finally in 1919 it became necessary to turn over the directorship of the band to a colleague in the department. Christiansen for brief intervals of a year or so resumed the conductorship of the organization, which he called his "first love," but, in general, enthusiasm for the band waned and the glory it once enjoyed faded with the passing years.

Next to the band in importance when Christiansen began his work at St. Olaf was the Choral Union, a body of some eighty singers, both students and faculty. Three months after the new director took charge this organization gave Schnecker's cantata, *The Fatherhood of God,* after which it promptly began rehearsals for an oratorio to be given in the spring. Christiansen did not approve of wasting time. A little item in the December issue of the *Manitou Messenger* suggests that the students had discovered the serious intentions of their director, for we read, "Members of the Choral Union declare that it is essentially a labor organization."

The musical high light of that first year was the music

*Since the composition of Christiansen's "Second Norwegian Rhapsody" in 1938, this composition has been known as the "First Norwegian Rhapsody."

festival held on May 17 and 18, thus serving, too, as a celebration of the Norwegian Independence Day. In establishing a spring festival, St. Olaf College was merely adopting a practice that had been gaining popularity in the Middle West since Civil War days. In the same month that St. Olaf instituted her festival, the Boston Festival Orchestra under Emil Mollenhauer was making its tenth annual appearance at the Ann Arbor May Festival of the University of Michigan, and the Chicago Symphony, having begun its visits to Cornell College, Iowa, the year before, arrived to participate in its May Music Festival. The St. Olaf Music Festival, though less pretentious, followed the general pattern established by these and other similar celebrations.

A few selections by the male chorus and the band and two addresses by visiting pastors opened the two-day festivities. Less refined than the older music festivals, St. Olaf's featured a baseball game on the afternoon of the first day, a habit that has persisted to the present. The evening, however, was again given over to music, a full band concert at the Ware Auditorium in downtown Northfield. The activities of the second day began with a faculty recital by Christiansen and the piano and voice teachers. Then with the performance of Haydn's *Creation* by the Choral Union, assisted by three soloists and the Danz Symphony from Minneapolis, the festival, the first in a long series to come, was brought to a spirited close. It certainly was the most ambitious artistic undertaking the college had ever attempted.

Ever since 1904 the St. Olaf Music Festival has borne the imprint of Christiansen's personality, though in later years he has been relieved of many of the details. Certainly Christiansen's bias against oratorios was the reason for their early disappearance from the program. After gallant attempts at tackling such works as *The Messiah*

(1905), *Elijah* (1907), and *St. Paul* (1908), the performance of oratorio was abandoned. In 1909–10, moreover,
Christiansen divided the Choral Union into a ladies'
chorus and a male chorus, training each separately. This
was a phase of the experimenting process by which he
learned his art. For the last fifteen or twenty years outside
singing groups, attracted by the growing reputation of
the St. Olaf Choir, have eagerly accepted invitations to
join in impressive mass performances by several hundred
voices. Though Christiansen thinks the artistic value of
these mass performances is negligible, he welcomes the
educational opportunity they offer to the participants.

In view of its later development, another organization
that Christiansen took under his baton upon arrival, the
choir of St. John's Lutheran Church, assumes greater
significance than the rest. The choir was not strictly a St.
Olaf group, but the connections between the college and
the church were close. St. John's was the place of worship
for all the students and faculty, President Kildahl sometimes served as its pastor, and St. Olaf faculty members
were among its trustees. During Christiansen's first few
years the choir, like the Ladies' Aid and other organizations, was a meeting place of town and gown.

Here again, as had often happened in his work, Christiansen found himself face to face with a deplorable lack
of suitable music. The days of substantial music libraries
in the churches and colleges of this region had not yet
arrived; nor were there means to secure them. Providing
music had become part of Christiansen's job. Songs that
he had written for men's voices he now arranged for mixed
voices, and to them he added new songs in increasing
numbers. A booklet, *Sangerfesthefte* (Song Festival
Pamphlet), published in 1905, contains a few Christiansen
compositions, the most interesting of which are two original songs based on the Biblical texts, "It was meet that

we should make merry and be glad," and "Behold what manner of love the Father has bestowed upon us that we should be called the sons of God," both written in the very simplest polyphonic style. Also in this booklet were his arrangements of songs by Kjerulf and Grieg. The latter's "Den store hvide flok" (The Great White Host), was a favorite in every Norwegian community, and Christiansen's arrangement of it became very popular.

Up to the time Christiansen came to St. Olaf there had been no organized department of music; in fact, formal instruction in the subject had been of an extremely haphazard nature. True, there had been a piano teacher at the college since its earliest years, and a smattering of musical theory and singing had found its way into the curriculum. But for the most part the students acquired what little musical knowledge they had largely through their own efforts.

Although Christiansen taught a course in harmony during his first year, he made no attempt to outline a serious course of study until his second year on the campus. In that year a School of Music was officially established, with courses of study including musical theory, harmony, counterpoint, canon and fugue, musical composition, history of music, and advanced courses in piano, voice, and violin. Though he was aided in the department by instructors in piano and voice, Christiansen himself assumed a large share of the teaching load. As the student body increased in number during the next few years, more teachers were added, also such courses as double counterpoint, musical analysis, and advanced harmony. In 1911–12 a course in orchestration and instrumentation was added, and in the following September the department offered for the first time a two-year course in public school music.

The work of planning and directing a department was

a difficult task that demanded new powers from Christiansen. When he began it as a young man of thirty-two, he knew nothing about the administration of a college department. As he later said, if the work in the music department grew it was because he himself grew; his duties and responsibilities taught him what to do.

Christiansen's enthusiasm for his work had indeed put new life into the musical activities of the college. At the end of his first year there was no question in President Kildahl's mind about the success of the new department. Christiansen, too, had enjoyed his work; furthermore, he had observed that the quiet village life of Northfield was an ideal environment in which to rear a family. When the school year closed, he was given the rank of full professor with a salary of one thousand dollars; so in the summer of 1904 he rented a house on St. Olaf Avenue and moved Edith and the three children, Jake, Ole, and Tulla, to Northfield.

In 1908 Tulla, at the age of five, died from peritonitis. The loss of two children within the space of a few years was a traumatic shock for Christiansen. It made him rethink the meaning of life and death, question and reformulate his beliefs. He had always accepted the orthodox Lutheran belief in a divine plan for life. But now doubts arose. Nearer to the facts, he argued with himself, was the view that life is governed by the physical laws of nature. What you eat, what you do, determines whether you live or are deprived of life, he thought. Man may plead for help, for divine interference, he may rage with grief, but he is incapable of changing these laws.

There was in Christiansen no bitter resignation to a fatalistic philosophy of life, but a matter-of-fact recognition of the matter-of-fact basis of existence. Shortly after Tulla's death he was walking down the street one day when he met a little neighbor girl. She was pouting and scowled up at him in her childish way as he came toward her.

"You don't look very happy," he said. "What's the matter?"

"I'm mad," she answered briefly.

"Why?" Christiansen asked her.

"Because Tulla's dead."

"So am I mad because Tulla's dead," he said, repeating the child's phrase, realizing that the reaction of the five-year-old youngster at the loss of her playmate was much the same as his own feeling of angry helplessness at being caught by the laws that determine human experience, laws that man has only begun to control.

The Norwegian temperament is little given to expression of its emotions. Christiansen felt the loss of his children deeply, but to forget he withdrew more and more into his music. Though he was fond of his children and ready to answer their questions and advise them when they came to him, he did not himself take the time to join them in their play or to guide them in their development. Nor did he make any special effort to search out any latent musical talent they might have. Devoted as he was to his profession, he did not force his children into music. He believed that if the talent was there, it would reveal itself spontaneously.

Both Jake and Olaf, however, learned to play the B-flat and E-flat clarinets, and when they practiced in the basement during the summer months, Christiansen went down to count out the time for them and teach them the key system. During band rehearsals the two youngsters appeared on the campus with tin pans and sticks, and stationing themselves outside the windows of the auditorium, they beat noisy but accurate time on their primitive instruments. Christiansen the elder could never conceal a proud smile.

But for the most part he was too engrossed in his own work to give the two youngsters any consistent musical training. And the boys, approaching grammar school age, became more interested in athletics than in music. Christiansen wanted his sons to develop strong, healthy bodies, so he encouraged their interest in baseball, football, and basketball. When in later years he went to St. Paul once a week to teach a class in church music and liturgy at Luther Theological Seminary, he usually came back to Northfield with baseball bats, mitts, skis, or skates for the boys.

It will be remembered that Christiansen had taken an active part in the annual meetings of the Norwegian Lutheran Singers' Union during his affiliation with Augsburg College. The practice of assembling choirs for an annual song fest continued within the United Norwegian Lutheran Church, and Christiansen's position at St. Olaf made it possible and logical that he continue his participation.

Many of the chorales sung by these choir groups were those arranged by the Lindemans, father and son, Norwegian hymnodists of the nineteenth century. In Norway the chorales were generally sung in unison, the four-voice mixed choir being practically nonexistent there at that time. Although the Lindeman chorales were written in parts, the harmonization was obviously for organ accompaniment and not for the voice. The disadvantages of these arrangements became more and more apparent to Christiansen, and he realized that new arrangements must be made for the average church choir if this genre of music was not to fall into disuse. His desire to take a middle course between Bach's too difficult arrangements of the chorales and Lindeman's organ arrangements was the motive for his second period of study in Germany.

Instead of returning to America with the band after

the Norway tour of 1906, Christiansen proceeded to Leipzig for a winter of concentrated work under the guidance of his revered teacher, Gustav Schreck. During his ten months' stay he made a thorough study of folk music and its influence on church music, and reharmonized into contrapuntal style about seventy of the most familiar chorales.

Along with this major purpose, he took the opportunity to increase his knowledge in other musical fields as well. Richard Hofmann, teacher at the Royal Conservatory, had recently completed an exhaustive work on instrumentation and orchestration, and Christiansen was fortunate enough to secure him for private instruction. The regular instrumentation course at the conservatory covered a two-year period, but Christiansen was determined to complete it in half that time. This, of course, meant double work for him and for his teacher as well, and when Christiansen appeared at Hofmann's door with a sheaf of exercises, he was invariably greeted with the growling remark, "Der Amerikanische humbug!" Christiansen had the highest admiration for Hofmann's knowledge and ability, but the man's chronic ill-humor precluded any sort of enjoyable relationship between teacher and student.

While in Leipzig Christiansen composed the first movement of a symphony which he has never completed. Hans Sitt, his former violin teacher, was very pleased with this first movement and would have given it a performance had not the program of the student orchestra already been filled for the year. Too difficult for the St. Olaf College orchestra, the symphony was put aside to be forgotten in Christiansen's music cabinet. His other compositions during the winter months in Leipzig included several songs—experimental exercises for Schreck in writing accompaniments—a few sonatas, and some incidental "stuff," as

Christiansen called it, for the piano. None of this was published.

This intensive work allowed him few idle moments. His only occasional companion was his former violin pupil, Adolph Olsen, whom Christiansen had placed in the St. Olaf Band as a clarinetist as a means of getting him to Europe. Once in Germany Olsen remained for the next five years to study with Sitt. Upon his return to America, Olsen joined the music faculty at St. Olaf College and acquired a reputation as a competent violinist through his appearances as a soloist with the band. Later he returned to Minneapolis to establish himself as a private teacher.

The nature of Christiansen's second period of European study suggests certain observations concerning the direction and scope of his work. Evident is his waning interest in the violin and his waxing interest in composition. Of his compositions of that year none except his chorale arrangements were to reach the public; nevertheless, his creative talents had been stimulated. Significant, too, is the fact that he began to think in terms of symphonic structure. This broader scope in his thinking undoubtedly gave him confidence to attempt the more ambitious works that were to come from his pen in the next decade. Then, too, Schreck had steadied him; he was moving away from his former somewhat loose style toward a more strictly classical form, the form in which he was to make perhaps his richest contribution to church music. Most significant, however, was his study of chorales, for it deepened his knowledge and appreciation of the splendid body of music native to the Lutheran church. He had never before been so aware of the possibilities this accumulated wealth offered for his own work. Moreover, his concentration on chorales had a lasting effect on the music of the Norwegian Lutheran church in that it enabled him to play an important role in the compilation of an official hymnal for that church.

For several years there had been a growing dissatisfaction with the Norwegian hymnals used in the Lutheran churches in America. Both in the United Synod and in the Norwegian Synod committees had been appointed to revise the hymnals to fit the needs of the new generation of English-speaking Norwegian Lutherans. In 1908 it was proposed that a joint committee be formed with four members each from the United Lutheran, Norwegian, and Hauge synods. The purpose of the committee was stated in the preface to *The Lutheran Hymnary,* published in 1913:

The considerations which prompted the creation of the joint committee were, chiefly, the common need of an adequate and satisfactory English hymn book; the fact of a common faith and confession as well as a common inheritance of Lutheran hymnody; the probability of getting a better hymn book through united endeavor than by separate effort; and finally, the desirability of a common hymnary, especially in the event of a union of the Church bodies concerned.

In the succeeding four years this committee of twelve met every summer for several weeks at a time. Mellby and Christiansen from St. Olaf College served on the committee throughout its duration. Among the other members were the Reverend Carl Døving of Chicago, owner of one of the most extensive hymnological libraries in the country at the time, and an authority in the field; the older musician, John Dahle, who served the church well with his numerous chorale books; and Carlo Alberto Sperati, the Italian-Danish director of the Luther College Band. Heated arguments often flared up between Sperati and Christiansen. With his impulsive Italian nature Sperati naturally leaned toward the sentimental, which Christiansen, having reacted against the emotionalism of his earlier compositions, could not tolerate. But Sperati was also the humorist of the committee and perhaps often saved a tense situation when he sat down at the piano and tossed off a clever parody.

To this group Christiansen presented his newly arranged chorales. But the committee, particularly the conservative representatives of the Norwegian Synod, favored Lindeman arrangements, thinking that Christiansen's contrapuntal style, simple though it was, was too difficult for unschooled singers. Christiansen made the counter-claim that Lutheran congregations must be taught to sing more difficult music, and unless presented with it in their hymnal, they would never rise above their present level. The committee eventually accepted all the Christiansen arrangements except those of which the original melody had been written by Lindeman. These the committee preferred to leave as that Norwegian chorale writer had harmonized them himself. Twenty Christiansen arrangements appeared in the collection, which includes over six hundred hymns from American, Scotch, English, German, and Scandinavian sources.

Christiansen often disturbed the committee members with his unorthodox statements about music, church liturgy, and religion. They were uttered largely in a spirit of teasing, for Christiansen was amused by the startled look of dismay they brought to the countenances of sober Lutherans. One such incident occurred in the home of a Lutheran pastor in a southern Minnesota town where the committee was in session. Mellby and Christiansen were staying at the pastor's home during the meetings. One day at dinner Christiansen by way of conversation asked the pastor what had occupied his time that day.

"Well, I had a funeral this afternoon," answered the pastor. "A man was buried."

"Was he a good man?" questioned Christiansen.

"No, I would hardly call him that," the pastor said. "He drank a good deal more than he should, abused his wife and children, and in general was not a very desirable citizen."

"What did you say about him?" asked Christiansen.

The pastor hesitated a moment before answering. "In a case like that it is better not to say anything about the man, but to preach to the assembled congregation."

If the pastor and his guests thought Christiansen would drop the subject at this point, they had never before encountered his Socratic persistence. "But you must have some opinion about the man yourself," he said with an inflection that demanded an answer. "You said he drank too much and abused his wife and children."

"Yes, I don't think he was a man of very good character," said the pastor with finality.

But still Christiansen had not finished. "Do you think he went to hell?"

If he had not been a minister of the gospel and a host, the pastor might have shown his irritation. "Well, that is something I am in no position to judge. That isn't for me to say."

Musing for a moment as if he hadn't heard, Christiansen said, "I wonder if there really is such a place."

The pastor's wife, a busy Martha attending to her guests, had entered the dining room with a platter of food just in time to hear the last few remarks. So shocked was the poor soul that she dropped the platter with a crash. Somehow the general embarrassment was glossed over, but when Mellby and Christiansen returned to their room later in the evening, Mellby admonished his partner, "Don't you know better than to talk like that in an orthodox minister's home?"

"Well, I just wanted to find out what he thought about it," smiled Christiansen with unruffled equanimity.

CHAPTER 7

The Nation Listens

NEW YORK concertgoers moved slowly through the foyer of the Metropolitan Opera House after an evening of music by the St. Olaf Choir. The gay chatter of an after-concert crowd filled the air as people stepped out into the snow of the February night and into their waiting cars. Phrases filtered through the general hum:

"A heavenly tone . . ."

"They did the Bach with such purity . . ."

"How do they get the pitch?"

"I heard them five years ago, but they are even better now . . ."

The next day a critic wrote: "Some two score youths and maidens from Northfield, Minnesota, put on immortality for approximately one hour and thirty minutes last night at the Metropolitan Opera House, for the most exacting listener surely must admit that the choir of St. Olaf's College, during the moments they are intoning, can only have been recruited from the angelic host."

When asked once how the St. Olaf Choir began, Christiansen did not immediately reply, but took from his vest pocket an old-fashioned gold watch. He opened the back of the watch; engraved on the smooth surface was "St. John's Church Choir, May 4, 1911." "This," said Christiansen, "was the beginning of the choir."

The St. Olaf Lutheran Choir did not spring into existence full grown. It was not a direct development from any one source, nor was it brought about by any single purpose. Religious, aesthetic, and even economic motives have crossed and recrossed in its history. Christiansen is, of course, the personality around whom the many factors revolved, but behind him loomed the figure of President Kildahl, who left his imprint on the entire life and work of the college, and, not least, on the work of Christiansen.

The quality most frequently attributed to Kildahl by those who remember him is "saintliness"; a familiar remark is, "Kildahl was the most saintly person I have ever known." The students admired him, but the more extrovert among them did not always understand him, nor he them. His "otherworldliness," as one of them termed it, prevented him from appreciating their desire for occasional practical jokes and harmless mischief. In Kildahl's sedate and ordered world there was no misbehavior; when it cropped up on the campus, he was bewildered by it and was often vexed into impatience with those who erred. This streak of impatience made him exhibit very human qualities.

One day Christiansen was sitting at his desk transposing some music when the door of his room burst open, and Kildahl stormed in. "I thought I could depend on your word, but now I see I can't. You don't seem to realize that plans have to be made far in advance. Just because you have a whim at the last minute someone else must take the consequences and worry about it."

Christiansen had just begun to write another note when the door was flung open, so he had not turned around to greet his angry visitor. Kildahl did not like it. "Nor does it seem to concern you that I am upset about it. You go your way and refuse to be disturbed by things you are responsible for, which is not very commendable on your part. That's all I have to say." The door slammed and he was gone.

Christiansen was puzzled rather than angered by this outburst. He didn't know what the president was talking about. A few days later the explanation came. Again he was working at his desk. Fräulein Mellby, the German teacher, came in. "Professor Christiansen," she said, "I owe you an apology. I told President Kildahl that you said your band would not play at the Foundation Day celebration. I had no right to say it, and I'm very sorry if it has caused you trouble." She looked so miserable that Christiansen thought it kinder not to ask her why she had said such a thing. The president, who later learned that he had been misinformed, never again referred to the matter, but Christiansen felt he should have apologized for his unjustifiable reprimand.

Be that as it may, Kildahl was known and remembered more for his "sweetness and light." Profoundly religious and idealistic, sincere to the core, emotional and evangelistic in his manner of bringing the word of God to the people, he was the force behind the almost annual religious awakenings on the campus. His power lay not in oratory, but in eloquence born of earnest, heartfelt piety. When preaching, he was so overcome by emotion at times that tears would run down his face. Though other men have done much for St. Olaf College in a tangible way, Kildahl was the person who "gave utterance and expression to its soul," as a faculty member wrote of him.

Christiansen was of a different mold. Emotionally responsive to the revivalistic elements in his environment, he had religious upsurgings from time to time, but for the most part he took religion calmly, as an institutional affair. Personal beliefs he thought should be respected, but to doctrinal issues he was stolidly indifferent. He felt that one creed was as worthy as another so long as the individual sincerely believed. In spite of this latitudinarianism and in spite of some strands of inarticulate liberalism and skepticism in his personality, he has always remained loyal to the Lutheran church. There is no denying that Christiansen's strong artistic emotionality has found its means of expression within the mold of Scandinavian Protestantism. It was to the emotional side of his nature, not to "the spirit" in him, that the evangelical Kildahl appealed.

In the sequence of events that produced the St. Olaf Lutheran Choir, these two men frequently appeared side by side. Unique in plan were the Kildahl-Christiansen *sang-gudstjenester* (song services) at St. John's Lutheran Church, in which the talents of the one as a speaker and the other as a musician were brought into effective harmony. The service was made up entirely of chorales and sermonets in alternate succession. By weaving phrases of the hymn through his talk, Kildahl prepared the congregation for the chorale which the choir was to sing. The service was a series of emotional climaxes, which had a marked effect on the listeners and participants. During one such service Christiansen was so moved by Kildahl's preaching that, unable to direct the singing of the chorale himself, he was obliged to hand his baton to one of the choir members.

The first of these services was given and published in 1907, and for each service thereafter a booklet was issued. Although Kildahl contributed to only three of them, seven in all were published between 1907 and 1916, Numbers 4, 5, and 7 in English; the final four appeared with the music alone. In the preface to Number 4, however, Christiansen suggested that the songs be supplemented by "a short sermon on repentance and the love of God."

The forty-four chorales in the seven *sanggudstjenester* were all Christiansen arrangements, and the successive booklets reveal a striking progress from a simple contrapuntal style toward the more complex arrangements of his "developed chorales," eighteen of which appear in this series. Among these are his well-known "Beautiful Savior," "Praise to the Lord," "O Bread of Life," "Built on a Rock," and "Wake, Awake."* In these arrangements Christiansen elaborated upon the chorale theme, writing not only for four voices, but for as many as eight, with the occasional inclusion of a solo part. These "developed chorales" show indeed the rapid strides Christiansen was making toward a bolder style, and his deft manipulation of the voices reveals a firmer knowledge of the polyphonic mode. One feels for the first time that the artist was approaching his maturity.

That Christiansen had entered upon a period of prolific composition is manifest. In 1910 the first booklet of a series of religious lyrics made its appearance. Between 1910 and 1916 eight numbers of *Lette lyrisk-religiøse sange* (Easy lyric-religious songs) were published, with a total of fifty-two songs for mixed choir, all of them original.

Another factor that certainly influenced the emergence of the St. Olaf Choir was the mixed octet organized in 1908. The purpose behind this move, one that was motivating a good deal of Christiansen's work at the time, was described, perhaps somewhat naïvely, by one of the octet members in the October issue of the *Manitou Messenger*:

If there is one man among our people who fully realizes what a treasure we have in our Lutheran Church music, it is Prof. F. Melius Christiansen. . . . He has studied the sources and traced the development of our choral melodies. . . . Observing that our chorals were not being sung as they should be sung, and that many of the young people in the congregations were getting "tired of the dragging and monotonous hymns of the old folks" due to the faulty rendition of the hymns and that in some places even the light and worthless "up-to-date" hymns, with a superabundance of "rhythm and time" were substituted for our dignified and stately church melodies, Prof. F. Melius Christiansen decided to awaken an interest and an appreciation for our choral music.

*The first two of these compositions appeared in Norwegian here; later they were published in English in the *St. Olaf Choir Series*.

During the winter of 1908 this octet prepared a program of Christiansen chorale arrangements and made plans for a summer tour, the proceeds of which were to go toward purchasing an organ for the new college chapel, which had been completed in 1906.* Their tour took them through western Minnesota, eastern South Dakota, and northern Iowa. In Ellsworth, Iowa, they sang with one hundred and fifty other singers under Christiansen's direction at the annual *sangerfest* (song festival) of the Central Iowa Choral Union. Their concerts were ordinarily given in Lutheran churches, but in Ames, Iowa, they were asked to sing both in the morning and in the afternoon at the chautauqua then in session. That they were a success with this more "American" audience is evidenced by the fact that the chautauqua management tried to book them for a three days' engagement the following summer.

At the end of the tour sixty-two concerts had been sung and four hundred dollars accumulated for the organ fund. How much direct influence the octet actually had in reawakening interest in the fine Lutheran music of a bygone age is impossible to ascertain; nevertheless, this tour fixed more firmly in Christiansen's mind the belief that, difficult though the task might be, the people could be educated to appreciate and use the best in Lutheran church music.

These intermingling strands—the St. John's Church Choir, Kildahl and the *sanggudstjenester*, the octet, and Christiansen's own artistic growth toward a more mature expression—made the cloth from which the St. Olaf Choir was cut. Christiansen was developing not only as a composer, but as a director as well. He was forced to raise his church choir to a level where it could sing the more difficult works he was composing, and this he did by giving more time and thought than hitherto to its work. Except

*The Hoyme Memorial Chapel, which burned to the ground in the summer of 1922.

for a few voices, the personnel of the St. John's Church Choir was by 1910–11 a combination of the ladies' chorus and the male chorus at the college. However, the close relation between St. John's Church and the college made the choir still seem as much a part of the one as the other.

In the spring of 1911 this choir of St. Olaf students, still calling themselves the St. John's Church Choir, gave a series of concerts in Northfield and some adjoining communities. And on May 4 the choir members presented Christiansen with the engraved gold watch that has become familiar to several generations of students. The procedure at the end of choir rehearsals has never varied. Christiansen puts down his baton, takes the watch out of his vest pocket to check his own infallible sense for the end of the hour, snaps it shut, and says, "That's all."

Ever since the octet's successful tour of 1908, Kildahl had nourished the hope that the same thing could be done again, perhaps on a more extensive scale. St. Olaf College was still an obscure and struggling institution. The faculty was too small; classroom and laboratory facilities were inadequate; money was needed in many places. Fully aware of the needs of the school, Kildahl and Christiansen both felt that St. Olaf must be brought before the people in a tangible way. The economic motive coalesced with the religious. Kildahl believed, as all St. Olaf's presidents have, that through its religious character and purpose the college could most vitally contribute to the education of the Lutheran people.

The tours of the band and the octet had established a precedent and provided experience as well, so that the idea of a tour for the choir was not considered without knowledge of the difficulties as well as the advantages of such an undertaking. When a Lutheran pastor in Eau Claire, Wisconsin, suggested in January of 1912 that the choir come to that state, the proposal met with immediate approval. Professor Paul G. Schmidt was sent to Wisconsin to discuss the possibilities with various Lutheran pastors and community leaders, and he returned with an extensive itinerary. The choir was to sing not only at Eau Claire and a few surrounding towns, but also at Madison, Milwaukee, and Chicago.

Advertisements of the tour, which was to be taken during the Easter recess, were immediately sent out, and for publicity purposes the name of the choir was changed from "St. John's Church Choir" to "St. Olaf Lutheran Choir." This, then, marks the official beginning of the choir that has played so stellar a role in the otherwise ordinary story of a small midwestern college.

Christiansen began a rigorous schedule of rehearsals, announcing that the concert had to be sung entirely by memory—and of course a cappella; Christiansen's choirs and choruses had always sung without accompaniment. "It seemed a tremendous task, but the end to be gained was a worthy one and the choir set itself resolutely to work," wrote a reporter of the tour in the *Manitou Messenger*. With a few exceptions the program, consisting largely of Christiansen's arrangements of chorales and Norwegian folk melodies, was to be sung in Norwegian.*

Two days before leaving, the choir gave a concert at the Congregational church in Northfield, and the next day Christiansen rehearsed the weak places that had appeared. When the choir left Northfield in a special train on March 27, it was not the polished and somewhat professional group it later became, but the students had a fresh, unsophisticated spirit, and they were very conscious of the importance of their mission for the college.

A capacity crowd heard the choir in its opening concert at the First Baptist Church in Minneapolis. The next day took them to Eau Claire, and the next to Madison. For

*See Appendix C for the program.

the concert at Our Savior's Lutheran Church in Milwaukee on April 1, standing room was at a premium. After the concert, at the surprise party celebrating his birthday Christiansen was presented with a handsome loving cup from the members of the choir. The next evening's concert at Wicker Park Hall in Chicago was gratifying to those who had planned the tour, for the choir proved its ability to draw a sizable crowd in a city full of other attractions. After a performance in Ottawa, Illinois, the choir turned toward home, giving its last performance on April 4 in Albert Lea, Minnesota.

The tour was both work and pleasure for all concerned. The constant travel, one and sometimes two concerts a day, and the numerous entertainments that awaited the group at every stop were fatiguing. The students beguiled the tedium of the train rides by playing Somerset and Rook, two popular card games of the day, while the faculty members in the party, Christiansen, Kildahl, Schmidt, and Paul M. Glasoe, spent the hours in conversation. The pros and cons of numerous issues, political and theological, kept the conversation lively. Christiansen could always be counted on to argue against the rest of them. Aside from his knowledge of music, Christiansen's range of information was somewhat limited, but undeterred by lack of facts, he unhesitatingly expressed his opinion with great certainty.

Singing the same program, the choir took a second tour through Minnesota and North Dakota directly after Commencement that same year. At the conclusion of these two successful tours, Kildahl, Christiansen, and Schmidt decided that unless unexpected circumstances interfered, the choir tour should be made an annual event.

As early as 1912 the possibility of a trip to Norway for the choir seems to have been a common topic of conversation. Perhaps since the successful band tour in 1906, the idea had never wholly left the minds of those who wanted to perpetuate the ties between the people of Norway and the Norwegian Americans. On its tour in June 1912 the choir sang at the annual meeting of the United Lutheran Church in Fargo, North Dakota, and while they were there Professor Schmidt discussed the prospects of a tour with two of the Norwegian delegates, Bishop Bøckman and the Reverend Hans Nielsen Hauge. Encouraged by their opinion that Norway would welcome such a visit, Schmidt opened negotiations with Norwegian groups and individuals. Sufficient financial support was guaranteed by eleven interested Norwegian Americans, and late in 1912 the tour was publicly announced for the coming summer.

Activity and excitement stirred the campus. The fortunate choir members were envied, but everyone was happy that St. Olaf College was again to be represented in Norway by so able a group of musicians. J. Jørgen Thompson of the St. Olaf College faculty went to Norway in March as an advance agent to arrange the details of transportation there. Before embarking at New York on the *S. S. Kristianiafjord* on June 24, 1913, the choir gave concerts in several Wisconsin towns, Chicago, and Brooklyn, all of which gave them confidence to sing before the audiences awaiting them in Norway.

From the moment they docked at Bergen their tour was an outstanding success. Choruses, state officials, church dignitaries, and personal friends greeted them wherever they went. Banquets, sight-seeing trips to Stiklestad, where St. Olaf fought his last battle in 1030, to the tomb of Harald Haarfager near Haugesund, and to many other places significant in Norway's history, kept them occupied between concerts. Everywhere they were treated with the utmost kindness and cordiality. The Norwegian people enjoyed the visit of the American students with their black-tasseled academic caps and their spirited college yells, which they indulged in from time to time in spite of Christiansen's warning to guard their voices, quite as much as the students themselves enjoyed the novelty of visiting an Old World country.

The concert in the capital city was perhaps as great a thrill for the audience as it was for the choir. From the American minister to Norway Schmidt had received word that the royal couple planned to attend the concert and that, in view of their usual punctuality, it would be advisable for the choir to assemble a few minutes early. When the King and Queen arrived the choir was ready, and as the royal pair were seated the singers filed in, quietly took their places, and very beautifully sang the King's Hymn, which Christiansen had specially arranged for the choir. The pleased audience rose and at the close of the hymn there was no doubt that the American singers had won the hearts of the listeners.

From the capital the party traveled north to Fagernes, Hamar, Trondheim, Steinkjer, Levanger, and Verdal, then south through the fjords to Kristiansund. Another long journey by steamer took them back to Bergen for a return engagement eighteen days after their first concert. From Bergen they continued south down the western coast and around the southern bulge of Norway, stopping to sing at Stavanger, Flekkefjord, Mandal, Kristiansand, and Larvik. In Larvik many toasts were raised to the musician whom the citizens were so proud to call their son. Proceeding again to the capital city, the choir sang a second concert there to a crowded house. They visited a few other Norwegian cities in the southeastern part of the country before they sailed for Göteborg and Malmö in Sweden. Crossing the Sound to Denmark, they gave their final concert in Copenhagen.

The newspaper reviews in all the cities were full of

praise for Christiansen's directorship, his admirable technique as evidenced by the choir's sure entrances, effective shadings, and pure tone. Most of the critics commented on the religious character of the program, and seemed particularly interested in the fact that at home the choir sang regularly in the service of the Lutheran church. They agreed that the achievement of this choir was a sad comment on their own culture and on the condition of church music in Norway, for nothing like it existed in the country. And furthermore, they said, it would be impossible to produce such an organization in a country as distracted by political and social issues as Norway. One noted critic and composer wrote after hearing the concert: "There is musical culture reposing in this Norwegian choir from the far West, but they did not acquire that culture from their forefathers. How many in Norway are capable of writing a polyphonic chorus like 'Lover den Herre' [Praise to the Lord] and 'Wake, Awake'—and if I should write them, they would remain here unused."

Perhaps this sheds light on a statement that Christiansen made many years later when someone suggested that he ought to lecture on church music at the University of Oslo. "Yes," he said, "I would like to go there and tell them what America has taught me. Norway gave me much, but America has taught me how to use it." Christiansen was not only preserving the finest in Norway's musical culture and acquainting America with it; he had caught something of the strength and vitality of the New World, too, and was fusing it into his re-creations of Old World chorales and folk melodies.

It was fortunate that the choir made its pilgrimage abroad in 1913, for such a project would have been impossible during the next five or six years of turmoil and reconstruction in Europe. Although America's entrance into the war was delayed for a few years, the uncertain political and economic conditions of the world in general forced retrenchments in civilian living early in the struggle. At St. Olaf College all plans for expansion were severely curtailed in spite of pressing needs, and time that was formerly given to extracurricular activities now went into war work.

For the next five years the tours of the choir were restricted to neighboring states.* They achieved at least two things. Through them the choir was firmly established in the minds of the Norwegian Lutheran people, so that when the time came that financial backing was necessary, these same people, at least those with means, willingly supported an organization which they felt to be theirs. Then, too, the tours prepared the choir technically for the big concert halls on the eastern seaboard. These quiet years gave Christiansen time to experiment, to try one voice combination, then another, in order to get the tonal effect he wanted. He was learning by experience the mechanics of producing an even-toned, well-balanced choir.

Meanwhile Christiansen steadily continued to compose, concentrating his energies increasingly upon that phase of his work. In the fall of 1915 he was granted a year's leave of absence to devote his entire time to composing and writing. Taking his family with him, he went to Minneapolis to spend the year in intensive work.

Upon his return to St. Olaf he was occupied for a time with changes in his department. In 1917 another major consolidation of Lutheran synods took place, establishing the Norwegian Lutheran Church of America, an inclusive and so far stable body. At this time the academy at St. Olaf was dropped, and the college, with a normal enrollment of more than a thousand students, became the largest of the many schools supported by the new organization. Up to this time the School of Music had given no

*No tour was taken in 1919.

special degree; it had awarded a teacher's certificate for completion of the academy course and a diploma to graduates from the college course. Now with some reorganization and adjustment to concentration on the college level, it achieved more mature status and began to grant the Bachelor of Music degree.

By 1919 Christiansen's reputation as an able choral director had been recognized by the University of Minnesota, which offered him a position as director of all choral work at a salary of five thousand dollars a year. But Christiansen had sunk his roots in the congenial soil of St. Olaf and Northfield. He liked the simple, pleasant life with his family safely about him; also he preferred that his children should grow up in the atmosphere of a small town rather than in a city. So he declined the offer.

People have often made the comment that Christiansen could never have produced his choir at any other place than St. Olaf College. They point out that the homogeneous economic, religious, and cultural background of the students makes for a better rapport between director and choir than could be established with a group of more diversified backgrounds. For the kind of work that Christiansen has done it is no doubt true that the psychological conditions have been at their optimum at St. Olaf. And the ready-made and interested audience of Norwegian Lutherans who were willing to support the early tours of the choir undeniably helped it to achieve more than regional recognition. But Christiansen scoffs at the idea that it takes Norwegian Lutherans to make a good choir. He thinks he could have produced an even better one at a larger school, Lutheran or any other, simply because he would have had more material to choose from.

Neither did he remain in Northfield because he felt a holy call to deliver the musical souls of the Norwegian Lutherans from the bondage of bad church music. He would have been just as happy delivering Methodists or Baptists from the same bad church music. No, his reason was simpler than that. He wanted his children to have the fields, hills, and woods, which lay within supper-calling distance of the back porch, for their playground. Though Jake and Olaf were by this time in their last years of college, there were two younger boys, Carl, eight years old, and five-year-old Paul, and after October 8, 1920, a daughter, Elsa Margaret. To give them a happy and healthful childhood was more than compensation for a lower salary to the music director at St. Olaf.

Nineteen nineteen. The war was over. At the little college in southern Minnesota prewar activities were revived. Whispered rumors flew about that the choir might go east on a big tour. "Is it true? I don't know. They say that P. G. is going to New York this summer. Something must be in the air." It was in the air all right, and the new president of the college was doing his utmost to make it a reality.

President Kildahl had left St. Olaf in 1914 to take a professorship at Luther Theological Seminary in St. Paul. His successor, L. A. Vigness, served only during the war years. The new president, Lars W. Boe, had been the secretary of all Lutheran charities in the Northwest during the war, and afterward he continued to take a leading part in the work of the National Lutheran Council, a product of the united efforts of all American Lutherans during the war.

Mohn the pioneer, Kildahl the visionary and idealist—these had been the presidents who had built the school for Norwegian Lutherans in the Middle West. Now there was Boe, the fighting politician. He faced the problem of guiding his college and church through a period in which ecclesiastical interests and Old World loyalties were to be put more and more on the defensive and sometimes into a not altogether fortunate alliance with conservative and even reactionary powers. The massive, square-jawed individual who resolutely took over the leadership of St. Olaf College in 1918 knew what he wanted and usually got it.

He had been the pastor of a small congregation in Iowa in the early years of the century; from 1904 to 1915 he had been the president of Waldorf College, a small Lutheran school in that state. During his years there he had also found time to serve in the Iowa legislature, in the House from 1909 to 1911, in the Senate from 1913 to 1915. A farsighted man, he viewed the problems of St. Olaf College in the larger context of the Lutheran church, not merely the Norwegian Lutheran church, but the Lutheran church of the future, which would embrace all peoples of that faith in America. It was natural that with this viewpoint he could see the potential power of the choir as a cultural tie in the great work of cementing the Lutherans into one body.

In July of 1919 President Boe sent the manager of the choir, Professor P. G. Schmidt, to New York to survey conditions, and, if possible, make plans for an eastern tour. Meanwhile President Boe himself made good use of his connections with the National Lutheran Council, whose headquarters were in New York. On August 2 he wrote to the Reverend Lauritz Larsen, president of the Council, that Schmidt was on his way to New York to make arrangements for a choir tour, and said: "This concert tour will mean much to the choir and also to the college. You know enough about the choir to know that they can sing artistically enough to fairly represent what we Norwegians can do. The trip in one respect is looked upon as a visit to Lutheran strongholds, and will, in a way, mean much to our student body in that they will become acquainted with other Lutherans."

In New York Schmidt made contacts with pastors of the various Lutheran synods, the members of the National Council, members of the Lutheran Men's Club of New York, and the management of the *Musical Courier*. Martin Hanson, a well-established New York impresario in whose colorful background Danish and Spanish-Jewish strains intermingled, was brought into the affair, and at a meeting of representatives from the National Lutheran Council with Hanson and Schmidt, it was decided that Hanson should draw up plans and terms for a month's tour under his general management.

A New York committee of seven members was formed, and when through them and Schmidt guarantors were found who were willing to assume responsibility to the amount of thirty thousand dollars, Hanson began laying the groundwork for an advertising campaign. The final list of thirty-six guarantors included many Easterners, an encouraging fact to the Lutheran leaders of the Middle West, who hoped in this way to establish a community of interest with their coreligionists in other sections of the country. President Boe gave public expression to this attitude in the letter printed in the official program of the choir tour: "The choir comes as a representative of the Lutheran congregations of the West with greetings to the Lutherans of the East. It is hoped that thru its presentation of our common heritage we may become more conscious of our spiritual ancestry and of our common faith."

The big job was under way. At the autumn tryouts Christiansen made selections more carefully than ever before. No voice could be included that might prove potentially dangerous to the ensemble. When the voices had been chosen, strenuous daily rehearsals were begun on a repertoire that included Bach for the first time,

Mendelssohn, Gretchaninoff, Grieg, Christiansen's new composition, "Hosanna," and several of his chorale arrangements.*

There were some on the campus who thought it a foolhardy venture for so young and inexperienced a group to invade the sophisticated circles of the East. Even friends, though they outwardly gave every encouragement to the undertaking, were inwardly apprehensive. Christiansen ignored all comments. The choir students had stood the test of a long and arduous winter of work. He had confidence in them; he was proud to present them to the public.

On April 5, 1920, the choir sang its first concert in Orchestra Hall in Chicago. The critics were enthusiastic. The choir was happy. Hanson, Schmidt, and the guarantors were relieved. The tour had got off to a good start, and they took the Chicagoans' response as a sign for the future. But they realized, too, that when they left Chicago behind, they were coming to a land of alien corn. They were leaving their friends in the Mississippi Valley. Before them were strange cities, industrial centers, shipping centers, world centers with novelties on every street corner, in every shop window, and behind every door, were it art museum, theater, or concert hall. In the small towns of Minnesota, Wisconsin, Iowa, and the Dakotas people thought uncritically that the choir was good because it came from St. Olaf, a college they knew and loved. But in New York it was to be: "St. Olaf? What's that? A small denominational college in the West? St. Olaf Choir? Never heard of it."

It was a little frightening, but the right dose of nervous tension makes a choir sing well. Fort Wayne, Springfield, Columbus, Pittsburgh, Lancaster, Washington, Baltimore,

*See Appendix C for the program.

127

Philadelphia—and then, New York! On Sunday there was a concert in Brooklyn at the Academy of Music; on Monday a concert at Paterson, New Jersey; and on Tuesday evening, Carnegie Hall. Martin Hanson, dapper in tails and pin stripes, watched the box office, saw the lights lower over three thousand listeners, heard the comments of the critics during the intermission, and then rushed backstage with a beaming face. "The critics are wild, the critics are wild!" Christiansen and the choir had made it. New York had listened and liked it, liked it very much.

The critics commented on the freshness, the youth, the vigor of the choir and its singing. In the *Globe and Commercial Advertiser* the reviewer wrote:

It was quite the most refreshing occasion of this long and overcrowded season. Mr. Christiansen has trained the choir to veritable virtuosity and it sang with the resilient, irresistible vitality of youth and the intense conviction of a centuries-old tradition.

Frequently the choir was compared to the Bach Choir of Bethlehem, as in the review in *Musical America*:

Only from the Bach choir of Bethlehem and the Mendelssohn choir of Toronto have New Yorkers in the past fifteen years heard choral singing as surprisingly fine as that provided by the St. Olaf Lutheran Choir. There were moments when it equalled in point of sheer facility the best that either of the older organizations has ever done here and seemed virtually to establish a new local record for flawless finish of unaccompanied song.

James Huneker said in the New York *World*, "This choir sings with the precision of a small orchestra," and the critic for *The New York Times*, Richard Aldrich, called it "one of the few 'virtuoso' choirs that have been here in recent years," commenting particularly on its "remarkable flexibility under the conductor's beat," the unusual plasticity of phrase, subtlety of accent, and rhythmic quality. News of these opinions was heartwarming to those who had been anxiously watching and waiting for reports.

Homeward bound through Albany, Rochester, Buffalo, Cleveland, Toledo, Akron, with return engagements at Fort Wayne and Chicago, the choir met the same delighted applause. As one reviewer confessed, "When these singers walked upon the stage, the thought of many was that 'it is just another bunch of college singers.' But from the moment that Dr. F. Melius Christiansen let fall his baton . . . the audience realized that they were different from the rest." Everywhere their concert was acclaimed one of the most delightful musical surprises of recent years.

Then Northfield, and the long and exciting trip was over. The band and the student body were at the station to meet the returning singers and escort them to the college, where everyone gathered at the chapel to exchange greetings. To the tributes of admiration Christiansen replied briefly that he was ashamed to accept all the praise bestowed upon him; the important thing, he said, was that they were all back safely. He disliked the demonstrations that attended homecomings and receptions. Characteristic of his quiet and humble attitude toward his accomplishment is a statement he made in a letter to President Boe while the choir was on tour a few years later:

Please do not say anything or do anything in our honor when we come home. Only say you are glad we came back without accidents. We shall all be glad to get home and give you a concert on the hill. As great as it is to be greeted by thousands of people at concerts there is nothing quite so great as to sing for our own faculty and students at St. Olaf. We have special interest and love for them.

In 1921 the choir again toured the eastern cities under the management of Hanson and with the assistance of the New York committee of the previous year. After the tour President Boe wrote to the secretary of the committee, Lauritz Larsen, "We appreciate the splendid backing we received from you people, and my only hope is we can finally get the foundation going in such a way as to get the support for choral singing throughout our Lutheran Church." Plans had been made to celebrate the tenth anniversary of the choir during Commencement of that year, and Boe invited the members of the committee in New York to be present for the occasion. Larsen and Martin Hanson came to St. Olaf for the festivities, and a tentative schedule for the next year's tour was discussed.

The last two years had brought professional happiness and success to Christiansen, but once more sorrow broke in upon his family life. Early in August 1921, the car in which Mrs. Christiansen and ten-year-old Carl were riding with friends in Minneapolis collided with a streetcar and burst into flame. Both Carl and his mother were burned badly. Carl lived only a day. Mrs. Christiansen, after a period of grave danger, began slowly to recover. In a letter to Harry E. Eilert, one of the officers of the New York committee, President Boe said of the event, "I do not know as yet what effect it will have on Christiansen. He is still somewhat dazed and it may have more effect on him and his future work than I can tell just at present."

Christiansen could not adjust himself to Carl's death. For many months afterward he was hard and bitter; he grew older quickly in those months. Again the only surcease from his grief was work. From the period that followed Carl's death came one of his finest compositions, "Psalm 50," into which he poured the best that was in him. Dedicated to the "St. Olaf A Cappella Choir," it was first sung in 1923, but though well liked by audiences, it has been used on only four other programs since that time.

In 1922 the choir once again toured the eastern cities.

By this time critics agreed that the St. Olaf Lutheran Choir had come to stand for the best in a cappella singing. Deems Taylor in the New York *World* singled out the several features of the choir that have long since come to be the standard commentaries in reviews: clarity of diction, perfection of attack and release, the discipline of the group, the mystery of the pitch, and Christiansen's complete mastery over the choir. Taylor concluded his review with, "Indeed the only criticism heard during the evening was voiced by a neighbor who thought they were too perfect to be human."

Nor did the significance of the choir's point of origin escape the critics. A Brooklyn reviewer commented:

The choir is composed principally of descendants of the Scandinavian settlers of the northwest. They may be said to represent the other side of the picture of rural Minnesota painted by Sinclair Lewis. The freshness and charm of their youthful voices, the inspiring vigor with which they attacked the revered classics of the hymnology of their church, the unfailing precision and correctness of their command of the musical art, seems to indicate that the novelist was wrong, and that Gopher Prairie and its environs are dispensers and not despisers of culture.

The heavy costs of the two previous tours had not been fully covered by the yields from the concerts, but in 1922 the choir returned with material as well as artistic laurels. In a letter to Eugene Simpson, fellow student with Christiansen in Germany and author of a history of the choir's early years, President Boe wrote: "The Choir certainly had a successful tour this year. Financially they were able to repay all guarantors of the first trip, paying all expenses, and we have been able to set aside $10,000 for a Music Hall." From that time on the tours were profitable financially, and in four or five years enough money was accumulated in the building fund to erect a sizable wing of the new limestone Music Hall which had been in blueprints for several years.

After 1922 the college dropped its connection with Martin Hanson and the New York committee, and Professor Schmidt took over the sole management of the tours. In the following years the choir toured the western states, central states, the South, and the East again, gradually gaining for itself a national reputation as one of the most accomplished choral groups in the country. Indeed, Herman Devries of Chicago in 1924 called it "the greatest of its kind in America, and perhaps in the world. . . . If Mgr. Rella came all the way from Rome to show us the Vatican singers, we can safely send Christiansen and the St. Olaf Choir on a visit to Rome." When the choir sang at the Metropolitan in New York in February 1929 the list of patrons and patronesses for the concert included such well-known names as S. Parkes Cadman, Walter Damrosch, Clarence Dickinson, Otto Kahn, Henry Goddard Leach, and Theodore Tiedemann.

The management of the choir tours became almost a full-time job. Professor P. G. Schmidt was relieved of his teaching duties and became the manager of all musical organizations on the campus. He arranges for appearances of other groups, such as the "second" choir under the direction of Professor Oscar Overby, quartets, or in some years a male chorus, planning the short tours they take. In addition he is the director of the artist and lecture course series which has brought to the campus, among a host of artists and writers, such figures as Kirsten Flagstad, Roland Hayes, Gregor Piatigorsky, Christopher Morley, Sigrid Undset, and Carl Sandburg. A widely traveled and cultured person, master of several languages, Schmidt is admirably fitted for the work and has the qualities that make for an impresario par excellence.

Gracious, dignified, and handsome, he arranges matters with a baggage company or hotel management as gracefully as he acknowledges on behalf of Christiansen and the choir the luncheon tendered them by a wealthy patron of the arts.

The choir student perhaps thinks of "P. G.," as he is affectionately called, as the person who claps his hands for attention and gives orders where to meet and how to get to such and such a place at seven-thirty sharp; who hands out the all-important allowance; and who can be the most entertaining person in the crowd when the long train rides become a bore. He does all that and much more of which the well-cared-for choir member is hardly aware. A fleet of taxis is at the station to meet the train and take the choir immediately to the hotel. At the hotel, rooms have been assigned, mail is out, everything is in order. Before the students leave for their rooms P. G. announces that there will be cars at the hotel at three o'clock to take the students on a sight-seeing tour of the city and that at four-thirty they have all been invited to So-and-So's estate to see his famous gardens and to have tea.

In Philadelphia they visit Independence Hall and the United States Mint. Boston's historic sites are part of their program, perhaps with lunch at the famous Cock Horse Inn on Brattle Street. Wall Street, the Exchange, Old Trinity, and Radio City are on the "must" list for the choir's New York visit. Between concerts the students also attend plays, go to the opera, and spend their entire day's food allowance on lunch at Delmonico's or at the Waldorf-Astoria. Each student is given a fixed allowance for food which more than adequately takes care of his needs. With the extra spending money given them by generous parents, the students collect trinkets

133

and mementos from antique shops, bookstores, and haberdasheries, returning from the trip with an incredible assortment of oddments in their crammed suitcases.

Illness and accidents are unavoidable in a group of sixty people, and it is Professor Schmidt who is responsible for seeing that the students are protected against such possibilities. There are occasional disciplinary matters to handle, endless business details to arrange, luncheons and dinners to attend, and speeches to make. No sooner is the trip over than Schmidt is at work again on the next year's plans. Requests are already waiting for the choir to sing here or there the next year, and before he has finished settling the affairs of one tour, he is deep in correspondence for the next one, planning the advertising, negotiating with hotel managers and railroad companies.

During the tours Professor Schmidt relieves Christiansen of as much worry and excitement as possible, and Christiansen himself watches his health carefully. Writing to President Boe from New York in 1927, Christiansen said:

It is important that I am in good physical and spiritual condition because the singing of the choir is so dependent on how I feel. I am not sentimental when I say that the spiritual condition is very important in this work. We must give genuine expression to those beautiful words and not merely "vain repetitions." May we all be true to our calling. True to our master and true in our work for the master. And may we also be true to Art! The spirit of art is very much like the spirit of Christ. Here, too, truthfulness is essential if it is to reach the hearts of the listeners.

This passage is reminiscent of Christiansen's oft-repeated statement that art is his religion and his religion is art.

Next to Schmidt in service to the choir has been its soloist, Gertrude Boe Overby. As a student at St. Olaf

College she began her career with the choir in 1920. Her marriage to Oscar Overby, a member of the music faculty, enabled Christiansen to continue using her voice. Except for a year of study in New York and an occasional year's absence necessitated by the exigencies of a growing family, she has been the choir's principal soloist throughout these many years. In her singing Christiansen found a rare combination of an ensemble voice and a solo voice. Gertrude Boe Overby will be remembered particularly for her solo contributions in Christiansen's "Beautiful Savior," an arrangement of a traditional melody, which has long been a favorite closing number on the concert program of the choir; his "Lost in the Night," an arrangement of a Finnish folk tune; and his "Lullaby on Christmas Eve," a delicate song, admirably suited to her voice.

Christiansen's relationship with the choir members remained relatively impersonal. His natural dignity and reserve called forth deference rather than familiarity; he was not the kind of teacher to whom the students took their personal difficulties. But he liked them, and encouraged those who worked with him to further the cause of music among the people. When one of the band members was offered a position as head of the music department at a small Lutheran college, Christiansen proceeded to give him advice on the management of such a department. According to the student, this advice was "enthusiastic, explosive, and disconnected." To this same student he later wrote one of his rare letters, congratulating him and expressing his pleasure that a young, energetic person was to be in charge of music education at the institution concerned. Characteristically, he concluded his letter with a general observation: "People do not always understand the profound and learned; they do understand the straightforward and direct. Keep the people interested in what is high—keep your ideal high."

Christiansen's birthday always called for a celebration by the choir, usually at the Christiansens' comfortable but unpretentious home on St. Olaf Avenue. As had been his custom in former years with the band, Christiansen always closed the party with a talk about the responsibilities of being a member of the choir; those who were in it for the glory and prestige it gave them on the campus were not worthy to be members. There must be only one motive for membership: the desire to preserve fine art and the willingness to sacrifice and work toward that end.

One year when the choir met for rehearsal on the morning of April 1, the members decided to sing birthday greetings to their director. His habit upon entering the rehearsal room was to go directly to the piano and strike a chord to indicate the number he wanted them to sing. On this particular morning the choir was prepared to sing "Happy Birthday" when this happened. Christiansen came in, made straight for the piano with that grim, there's-work-to-be-done look on his face, sat down, and played "Happy Birthday" for himself. The deflated singers admitted that they should have known he would be one step ahead of them. He always was.

Only rarely did Christiansen venture outside the realm of music in his talks to the choir, but when he did it was with effect. For years now the choir has sung almost annually in Rochester, which is not far from Northfield, and sometimes the group is entertained after the concert in the home of some Mayo Clinic staff member. On one such occasion at the home of Dr. Donald C. Balfour, director of the Mayo Foundation, Christiansen sat slumped in his chair, seemingly half asleep and entirely indifferent to his surroundings. Only seemingly so. Suddenly he jumped to his feet and called for attention. "I want you to look around you at this home," he told the choir mem-

The St. Olaf Choir, 1938

The Christiansen Choral School, 1940

bers. "It can teach you something about living." He pointed out the evidences everywhere of its owners' many enriching interests: the books lining its walls, its pictures and prints, the flowers from a small adjoining conservatory, the organ with its stacks of well-thumbed music. "These things tell you the doctor and his wife know what things count in life," said Christiansen. "When you have homes of your own, try to make them like this."

On another visit to Rochester Christiansen gave a good demonstration of artistic temperament. This time the choir was singing an extra concert in the chapel of the Sisters of St. Francis at St. Mary's Hospital. Like most audiences, the group of nuns, nurses, and a few ambulatory patients wanted to hear "Beautiful Savior," and Dr. Balfour carried their request to Christiansen during the intermission. No, they couldn't do that song, said the director positively. Urged to reconsider, he kept shaking his head. Something about the setting wasn't just right for "Beautiful Savior."

He and his host were standing in an outside doorway, and Christiansen stood for a moment looking out at the lovely hospital lawn, fresh and spring-green in the May sun. "There!" he exclaimed. "We'll sing it out there."

The word went round the hospital quickly; windows were thrown open and convalescent patients were wheeled or carried to the balconies. When the chapel concert was finished, the choir and its audience moved outside for the encore. Christiansen's impulse had been right. Some of the listeners have heard the choir sing "Beautiful Savior" many times, but never, they say, with such unearthly beauty as that morning under the trees on the hospital lawn.

Christiansen has always been an exceptionally bad correspondent. He wrote letters rarely, and for the most part his mail remained unanswered. He would sometimes let it lie on his desk for several weeks, perhaps thinking that the morrow or the day after would prove more convenient for taking care of correspondence. The days passed and gradually the letters found their way into his wastebasket. A secretary he would have scorned.

His carelessness in regard to mail has undoubtedly been annoying to many who have written to him for information about his work. But on the other hand, the fact that he has cared so little whether or not other people are interested in him is part of his humbleness and simplicity, also a part of the natural strength and self-reliance of a man bent upon his job to the exclusion of almost everything else. That he scarcely ever reads or shows any interest in the reviews of the choir's performances is a fact testified to by his closest associates.

Christiansen did occasionally write to President Boe, and in some of these letters there are expressions of his opinions that give us insight into his mind and feelings. In them, too, we glimpse the affectionate regard and admiration the two men felt for each other. President Boe nearly always addressed Christiansen as "Kong Kristian," the Norwegian for King Kristian. Christiansen stands apart as a kingly figure, and Boe admired the stately, aristocratic bearing of the white-haired Norseman. Two of these letters in which Christiansen writes as a musician and Boe as the college administrator and politician, and in which both show traits of their Norwegian ancestry, are worth quoting.

While the choir was on its winter tour in 1935, some of the officials in the Norwegian Lutheran church proposed that a Bach festival be given in celebration of the two hundred and fiftieth anniversary of the great musician's birth. It was thought that the choirs and choruses from St. Olaf and Luther colleges and the choirs of several of the Lutheran churches in the Twin Cities could participate. Favoring the idea as a chance to further a friendly and cooperative feeling between the two colleges and among the people of the church in general, President Boe immediately wrote to Christiansen about it. His answer is characteristic—blunt and to the point.*

DEAR FRIEND:

Bach Festival! Those people do not know what they do, because they do not know the Bach literature—all Bach male voice writing is only transcriptions done by other composers. A so-called Bach chorale is a folk tune arranged in contrapuntal style for mixed voices. A Bach Motet is an a cappella composition for mixed voices of which we sing one third of a number—A Bach Cantata is written for Orchestra, Chorus, and Organ and should be sung by a larger chorus of mixed voices. The Bach Passion Music is written for Orchestra and Chorus. If you want a Bach Festival it should consist either of Cantatas or the Passion music sung by a large chorus with Orchestra accompaniment. This would require a body of singers like the Apollo Club in Chicago or possibly the Philharmonic of Mpls. Otherwise it may be possible to sing some of the easier Cantatas with Orchestra or only Organ if you give the Church choirs a whole year to work on them. We are not ready to take part in a festival of that kind. It is easy to plan but it would be advisable to get some actual truths to reckon in with the planning. It would take us too long a time to prepare for such a festival and the result of the work would be rather commonplace after all our attempts. We have nothing against the idea itself if it could be done and done respectably, but we should not, out of respect for Bach and the art of music, be allowed to be led into a trap by well meaning ignorance.

With greetings and best wishes,
Yours,
Kong Kristian

In reply Boe briefly refers to the proposed Bach festival, which was immediately dropped, and then expresses his feelings for the work Christiansen is doing.

*The letter was not dated, but was received in the office of the president on February 11, 1935.

Feb. 11, 1935

KJAERE [DEAR] KONG KRISTIAN:

Mange tak for dit brev. [Many thanks for your letter.]
Whenever you speak as a musician I bow my head in rever-
ence and say to myself "saa maa det bli" [so be it]. You are
right in what you say. I am sorry that we did not earlier get
at the proposition of working for a Bach festival. . . .

It is a little difficult for us Norwegians to give expression
to more gentle feelings. We are good at hitting back, but not
much good otherwise. I can only tell you what you know
already, that deep down in my heart there is real appreciation
of what you are doing and what you have done for St. Olaf,
and what you have put into the life of our Norwegian people
and the country itself, an appreciation of that which is best.
I think of how you have gone on year after year. You
objected once when I said that the test comes as to whether a
man can keep on a high level. I may not have been fortunate
in putting it that way, but I do know that it is difficult even
to keep going up hill all the time. That you have been doing.
As your youth has left you I have sensed in the choir a
"modenhet" [ripening] that has made your music even more
beautiful. I am looking for an increasing amount of beauty in
your music and in inspiration, even though the years are
slipping by. Noise and action are fine, but the things that
appeal to the deeper nature of man are worth a lot more. Our
country has lived through its day of action. I am hoping that
they will from now on take on something of the characteristics
of the European countries, a deeper appreciation of all the
finest things that lie in art and religion. Your contribution
has almost been prophetic of that development. So welcome
home to Northfield.

Yours very truly,
L. W. Boe

In the decade from 1920 to 1930 Christiansen established himself firmly in the choral consciousness of
America. With Schmidt and President Boe he felt the
time had come for another trip to Europe. In 1930
the Lutheran church the world over was making plans
to celebrate the four hundredth anniversary of the Augsburg Confession, and it was decided that a tour through

Norway and Germany, the land of the Reformation, during the summer of that year would be appropriate.

Like the 1913 tour this later one took the choir to the principal cities of Norway. The climax of the visit was the choir's participation in the huge anniversary festival held in the *Domkirke* at Trondheim with King Haakon, the Queen, and the Crown Prince present. As upon the choir's previous visit, the press notices called attention to Christiansen's Norwegian birth, his amazing success in America, and the appropriateness of his returning to the land of his birth with a choir that had its roots in the culture of the Old World. There is much human interest in the reviews as well as a generous recognition of the director's technical skill.

In Germany the choir sang in Berlin, Leipzig, Frankfurt, Nürnberg, Wittenberg, Nördlingen, Naumburg, and Eisenach. Since Germany itself has been the home of some of the best a cappella choirs in the world, one could legitimately expect that here, where there were no racial ties to heighten the receptiveness of the audiences, a more critical spirit would exist. The critics commented on the similarities and differences between "deutscher und amerikanischer Chorkultur." "The latter," wrote the critic in the *Leipziger Abendpost,* "expresses itself not so much by emphasis of the inner spirit, as by exhausting all sound effects, this to the extreme, and by a precision, the virtuosity of which approaches the automatic."

In the same vein a Berlin critic, after deploring the fact that the choir had been permitted to sing in a cathedral where the sound was caught in the vault, continued, "It is hard to say whether the singers are to be held responsible for a certain monotony of expression. . . . Divorced from its originally religious purpose, and as far as our feeling is concerned, not wholly endowed with independent musical meaning, the performance still commands respect and one should like to hear the singers again under more favorable conditions."

Another Berlin critic said of the singing, and particularly of the Nicolai-Christiansen "Wachet Auf" (Wake, Awake): "It gives us such an idea of a cappella singing as we do not believe ever to have experienced before in such perfection. The Bach, however, he felt was without "the Bachian accent; almost elegant, but not fresh or overwhelming." A Frankfurt critic declared that the American choir ranked among the best of its kind and that it deserved to be mentioned in the "immediate neighborhood of the leading European musical bodies." And lastly from the *Eisenacher Tagespost:*

> The absolute certainty and purity with which the whole choir intones and hits the key as one voice without any preceding pitch being given is admirable. It would be scarcely comprehensible if it were not that all members have an extraordinarily well-developed absolute pitch discrimination and also without incessant practice in singing together. . . . The choir is like an orchestra or gigantic organ upon which the conductor plays with the virtuosity of a master. . . . beautiful then again the soft, sonorous fullness of the mezzavoce; quite magnificent the pianissimo chords, evanescent in fragile purity.

Upon their return to America in late August, Christiansen received a telegram from President Herbert Hoover: "I cordially congratulate you and the members of St. Olaf Choir upon the splendid reception accorded you and them in Europe and my felicitations upon your happy return to the community and people whom you have so well represented in the field of musical art."

One can scarcely blame Christiansen if at the end of the tour he was gratified that his choir, recruited from the farms and small villages of the Middle West, had stood the test of singing in the cathedrals of Old World cities whose musical preeminence and traditions are as ancient as the cathedrals themselves.

Throughout the thirties the appearances of the choir in the principal cities of America drew audiences of increasing size. Enthusiasm for a cappella singing mounted; directors and singers were eager to learn proper techniques. They flocked to the concerts of the St. Olaf Choir to listen and watch while Christiansen, "a wizard of the baton," as he was called by some reviewers, drew from his students music of impelling beauty. There seemed to be no "off" years; each choir performed as brilliantly as the preceding one. Even Christiansen's advancing years did not blunt the freshness and vitality of the performances. When the choir toured the East in 1941—Christiansen was then in his seventieth year—a Pittsburgh critic wrote, "Dr. Christiansen has lost none of his magic in welding together a chorus of remarkable talents," and Herman Devries in the Chicago *Herald-American* called the St. Olaf Lutheran Choir the "King of Choirs." Almost apologetic for having to repeat the obvious, Richard Davis said in the Milwaukee *Journal:* "There seems no point in reasserting the conviction that the sturdy F. Melius Christiansen, white haired director of the chorus, is the ablest man in his field today. Certainly no man, in any case, has done more to raise the standards of choral music. For generations to come the effect of his devoted service will surely be felt."

A few days later the music critic for the Buffalo *Evening News* wrote of Christiansen, ". . . he is a perfectionist who knows exactly what he wants before he asks his singers to give it to him. Thus, when balance, blending, phrasing, nuance and color are so precisely wedded, as in the unaccompanied singing of the St. Olaf Choir, to the musical line and textual meaning, it can only be because a musician of high abilities, patience and sincerity has grasped the essential message of the score and imparted it to his singers."

CHAPTER 8

How Does He Do It?

YEAR after year, from coast to coast, in the comments made about the St. Olaf Choir, whose personnel changes with each year, the question is asked, "How does he do it?" for each year the same plasticity, unity, and intensity, the same "celestial purity" and almost unhuman perfection has marked this group of singers. The answer lies not in the superior quality of the voices that make up the choirs, since Christiansen chooses largely the average, untrained voice, but in the nature of the director.

Christiansen has been an experimenter; his studio and rehearsal hours have been his laboratory, where he toiled and analyzed with the patience of a scientist over test tubes or a microscope. He experimented with voices, ears, and personalities, fitting, matching, and blending until he found the combination with which he could work. His level of aspiration, which was to attain as near perfection as is humanly possible, meant for him long hours of painstaking study in the physics of sound and intonation, in the mechanics of voice and language. There was no magic, no hidden trick. A choir director from a large midwestern city made annual visits to St. Olaf College for several years to observe choir rehearsals, hoping to discover the secret of Christiansen's success. "I guess he thought the Lord was whispering something in my ear," said Christiansen. "Finally I told him it was just a problem in physics, and he went home and never came back."

Believing that the perfect choir is an organism in which every member loses his identity for the sake of the ensemble, Christiansen carefully tested voices, ears, and personalities to discover their adaptability to this organism. Years of experience taught him what to look for, and it was rare that a voice, once chosen, did not fit satisfactorily into the ensemble. Every September in his studio overlooking the pine trees of Norway Valley, Christiansen conducted a voice clinic. Hundreds of nervous and frightened students waited in line, and one by one he put them through a rigorous examination in his search for the twenty or twenty-five new voices which he needed each year to complete his choir. *What* did he look for, and *how* did he build his choir?

To many directors the voice is the only important consideration in choosing choir members, but to Christiansen the ear has been equally significant. "When we organize choirs, we try out *ears* as well as voices!" he emphasized. "I play a scale for the singer, to see if the ear is fine enough to sing pure distances, and usually if I stop the singer at A he is below the pitch." His own extreme sensitivity to exactness of pitch was increased during his years of violin study, and he has found that those of his students who play the violin, cello, or viola have, in general, a better ear than others.

After checking the ear for accuracy of pitch, Christiansen tested the voice, and the first requisite was that it have blending quality. For this he has certain fundamental criteria. Foremost among them: the voice must be *straight*. The smooth tone that Christiansen tried to develop in all sections was dependent on the straightness of each individual voice; wavering of tone from one pitch to another made pure intonation an impossibility. Thus although the voice met all the other requirements and the singer exhibited the finest musicianship, the voice could not be used in the ensemble if it had a tremolo. In his vivid language Christiansen said, "The voice should be straight as an Indian woman's hair or a telegraph wire." His comments to those who tried out were usually direct and blunt, often picturesque. To one young person who sang with a noticeable tremolo he said, "You sound like a Ford car bumping over a corduroy road."

The infrequency of straight voices among singers was one of the greatest difficulties he encountered in organizing his choir, and from years of experience he came to know how diligent must be the director's search for them. Within the choir itself the warfare against "curly voices" was unceasing; members were warned repeatedly during the year to maintain even tones. On one occasion Christiansen was trying out the basses for a solo, and, finding a bad tremolo among them, he said to its possessor, "We are having an ironing party at our house at two o'clock this afternoon; you are invited to come down and get pressed out."

Even in solo singing a tremolo is undesirable. "A great solo voice has *tone-color,* but not a tremolo," Christiansen often told his singers. Only in a large chorus of several hundred voices did he permit the tremolo, for the thick tones of so large a group give ample space for even a "five-foot tremolo," he once said with a chuckle. For the clean and polished singing necessary in a small ensemble the tremolo cannot be tolerated.

Christiansen next demanded that a voice have uniformity of color throughout its range, smoothness of tone, and flexibility. To test for these requirements he would play a scale which the singer was asked to imitate. He found that breathiness of tone and variation of texture and color are common in the vast majority of voices. Although rhythmic feeling is of prime importance for most musicians, Christiansen felt that in the strictly limited sphere of the ensemble singer it is not so essential.

Of specific voice sections, the one that caused the most trouble was the soprano. Most sopranos have a tremolo, and it is more dangerous in that voice than in any other in ensemble singing because of the rapidity of vibration in high tones. He found, too, that the majority of sopranos sharp on higher tones, seemingly because the ear lacks control over these tones. The criterion note for a soprano is high A, which, if it is thin and is sung without effort, is a good indication that the voice is a soprano. A thick, heavy A reveals an alto. The compass of the voice does not alone decide to which division it belongs; the natural timbre and level of the voice is of prime importance. An alto may be able to sing a high B-flat or C, or a baritone a high A, but this is no proof that these voices belong in the soprano and tenor sections.

For his purposes Christiansen found that the small, thin soprano produces the purest ensemble tone. A large voice too often cannot blend properly. In the middle octave of the soprano voice it is relatively easy to get purity, but in the upper register greater skill and ear sensitivity are required for the singer to attain purity. Christiansen designated voices as "fluty," "reedy," or "mixed," and found that most sopranos change from a reedy, or oboe, tone in the lower register to a fluty tone in the upper. The ideal choir voice, of course, has to be uniform in its tone and color.

Although preferring the small, reedy voice for its adaptability and purity, Christiansen could not build his choir entirely on small voices. He therefore included a few of the more brilliant-toned fluty voices for the purpose of achieving climaxes. The brighter tone of a slightly larger voice could be kept from obtruding if it was placed properly, usually in the center of the section with smaller voices on either side. Whether the voice was large or small, the soprano was required to sing a high E with comparative ease.

For the alto section Christiansen chose a dark tone of

cellolike quality, the criterion note being A below middle C. If the voice was rich and colorful without the dreaded tremolo, it merited consideration as a choir voice. The slower vibrations in the alto voice made the task of blending and matching within the section less difficult than in the soprano. A rich, full E below middle C was demanded of an alto.

Corresponding in many ways to the soprano in the women's voices was the tenor in the men's section. There again the problem of purity became more acute because of the increase in the speed of sound vibrations, and exceeding care was taken to secure smooth, reedy-toned voices. Because the baritone part frequently carried the melody, Christiansen, among other patterns in his tryouts for that voice section, asked the person to sing an interval of a sixth in order to test the lyric quality of the voice. A tenor had to reach a high A or B-flat without using a falsetto, and a bass was required to sing a low D without "scraping the bottom of the kettle," as Christiansen said.

The selection of voices for the choir was made with great care and exactness after numerous tryouts. Many a story has been told about Christiansen's comments to those who tried out and were rejected. Somewhat impolite and rather startling, his spontaneous remarks were not as personally intended as they sounded, and usually they were followed by a genial laugh that took the tartness out of the words. The student who had tried bravely to sing his best might be told, "You had better go—I can't squeeze juice out of a dried-up turnip," or, "Go back to the farm and milk cows, but don't try to sing!"

Those who at first hearing met the general requirements were requested to appear for second tryouts, where the new voices were tested in quartet combinations with the old voices to determine their blend and color; very quickly the candidates learned the importance of "intoning" with their neighbors. As one or another among them was recalled for second, third, and fourth tryouts, excitement ran high on the campus, for to "make the 'first' choir" was perhaps the greatest thrill that could come to any St. Olaf student.

Members who had been in the choir a year or more were referred to as "old" members, but they, too, were required to try out each year. Christiansen used this method as a safeguard against carrying dead timber in his choir; unless a voice was essential to the balance of the ensemble, it could not remain. First-year college students were not numerous in the ranks of those chosen for the choir, but if they were admitted it was usually for their potentialities; if no improvement was seen, they were not allowed to remain. Never was the student permitted to relax. Even after the first three months, which were regarded as an apprenticeship, he had continuously to prove his worth.

When, as in rare instances, Christiansen found that a particular voice did not blend as it should, he cut it out. He was no respecter of persons. On one occasion he felt that a certain voice had developed into menacing proportions during three years in the choir. Without warning he paused during a rehearsal and said to the member, "Will you do me the favor of leaving the choir and not returning again." Harsh words these were to one who had worked devotedly for three years, but when an operation is necessary, the surgeon does not dally; he cuts quickly with a sharp knife. Upon the rest of the choir members the incident made an indelible impression.

Christiansen knew and understood personalities, and although he was often merciless with students, he did it in the belief that young people had to be trained to withstand blows and disappointments. He wanted his students to develop self-confidence and initiative; he had no patience with the spiritless and thin-skinned individual who could not accept the truth when it was dealt to him in hard, square fashion. "Be tough. You have to be tough in this world," he once told a group of teachers and singers who were facing the prospect of having their voices tested by him. "We are not always polite, but we are honest with you and we want you to know the *truth*."

The ideal choir personality, said Christiansen, is one with courage, buoyancy, and aesthetic feeling; one who is plastic and responsive to the varying moods of music. "Yet," he added, "there is another type of personality that fits into a choir well: the sturdy, solid type, which may be less pliable but is nevertheless of real value to the choir. I have had many stiff personalities who sing Bach well. It is difficult to find the happy combination of all these qualities which the ideal ensemble singer should have."

The solo voice presented Christiansen with a particular problem. Because there is usually a strong personality behind it, the solo voice has a tendency to dominate rather than amalgamate with the group, and in good ensemble singing no individual voices should be detected apart from others. "Special training is required for ensemble singing," said Christiansen. "If the solo voice can be trained to the ensemble ideal, it is very valuable for its addition of the color and brilliance necessary to choral singing."

Speaking in terms of the ideal, his only yardstick, Christiansen would have limited his choir to forty voices, but for practical purposes he found he must increase his group to sixty; he had to sacrifice the purity gained from using fewer voices in order to achieve brilliant climaxes. In a student choir with voices at an age level of eighteen to twenty-two, the tone of a forty-voice choir would be pure but slightly monotonous and colorless. Mass choruses, on the other hand, produce thrilling climaxes but can less easily attain artistic singing and purity of tone.

Two or even three weeks were frequently required to find the most suitable voices for the vacancies, but at last the painstaking work was over. The disappointed retired to the daily routine of student life, while the "chosen," slightly dizzy with excitement, notified happy parents that they had been accepted on trial.

For many a student the first rehearsal was an unforgettable hour. The members assembled; the stand and podium were in readiness. A low undercurrent of conversation brushed through the group, but when the door opened a minute or two before the hour and Christiansen entered, talking ceased and an almost soldierlike attention came over the choir. In his characteristic, unhurried manner he walked to the stand and arranged his music. There was nothing of the quick and nervous about him. Calm Nordic ruggedness and the aristocratic bearing of one who instinctively lived the wing-collared tradition of the Old World were his. There was nothing of the ascetic in the face of this musician who had spent his life unremittingly and exclusively in the realm of the artistic.

Some twenty hearts thumped anxiously as new members worriedly wondered what was expected of them, and for the first few minutes they were thrilled into nervous uselessness. Old members were eager for another year, and though they exhibited traces of the superiority of the in-group, which was highly impressive to the new members and secretly envied by them, they were not too sophomoric in their attitude. They knew what it meant to work and sing under the shaping power of Christiansen's expressive personality, and for perhaps most of them it had been without a doubt the most stirring emotional and intellectual experience of their lives. There was also about the old members a sobriety that came with the responsibility for passing on to the new members the intense spirit of devotion to the choir.

And Christiansen himself, what did he feel as he looked over his new group of youthful singers, recognizing here and there a family resemblance to others who had sung under his baton—parents, sisters, or brothers? Most of the students came from modest midwestern homes; they were honest and sincere, untried and unsalted, but vital and potential. Perhaps he felt something of the uncertainty of the experimenter, curious to see whether his experiment would work this time. He struck a D major chord on the piano, and with an energetic beat signaled the choir to sing. The attack was ragged. He cut it short. "Start together, please—again! Louder!" Once more it sounded after a moment's hesitation; then holding the chord, he listened to the balance and texture of the group. Granting its unpolished state and its unevenness, he was able to envisage what it could be; he heard its weaknesses, but also its latent strength. Another year of patient drilling lay ahead.

Very important were the sectional rehearsals that were scheduled immediately upon organization of the choir. A student leader was chosen in each of the four sections by its members. It was understood that the leader was to be one who had had two or preferably three years of experience in the choir, a person whose musicianship was unquestionable, who had a dominant enough personality to command the respect of the students, and who could be relied upon to discipline the group. Christiansen felt that giving responsibility to some students in this way made for an individual development that had a salutary effect on the work of the choir as a whole. In the twice-weekly "part practices" held in addition to the daily rehearsals of the choir, the mechanical work of memorizing the music was done, alongside the constant practice of intonation. Christiansen himself occasionally came to these rehearsals to see that this more individual work was being done well, stressing its importance as a foundation for better and speedier results in the larger rehearsals. "A thing cannot be a means of artistic expression unless it is first polished and has approached perfection mechanically," he told the singers.

In a letter written to President Boe while the choir was on its winter tour in 1927 Christiansen indicated the problems confronting him and his hopes for a better training of choir members:

I should like very much to be able to go through the student body in search of material for the choir. If this choir is going to improve—at least keep up its present standard—we must find better material all the time. We are now working on a rather hit and miss proposition. We should have a person who could train *choir voices*—a person who could find them and give them special training. This kind of training is not the common voice training for solo purposes that voice teachers are giving. The basses should be trained downward in their registers and all voices trained to sing straight notes. And they should have private lessons on the choir songs. There are still problems to be solved and improvements to be made with the choir.

Christiansen's wish for a special teacher of choir voices has never been realized; each member in the choir, however, is required to take voice lessons.

Every year, after the first few rehearsals had acquainted him with the weaknesses in the sections, he found it necessary to add voices here and there throughout the choir. When he was satisfied with the proportion and balance of the group, he arranged the seating for the year, using the plan of the "inner choir" as shown on the accompanying chart. He placed the thin, light, even voices in the center of each section for the purpose of singing delicate passages in which absolute purity was necessary, as for instance in accompaniments to a solo voice, or in pianissimo endings of extreme delicacy. The inner choir was always prepared to continue if the director suddenly cut off the rest of the choir. This technique enabled Christiansen to achieve artistic effects through contrast and through the use of a few voices to spin out the tone to a fine thread. The accompanying chart also shows his placement of dark and light voices. The arrangement varied according to individual voice material from year to year, but in general he followed this plan.

One of the major obstacles in the path toward purity in singing, Christiansen discovered, is the barrier of language. If the ensemble singer is made aware of the problems, however, he can do much to mitigate the impurities that find their way into the tone through the words. Christiansen made no innovations in this respect, but stressed what is widely accepted as the best means for attaining purity: unification of vowels and minimization of consonants. "Sing through the consonants!" he ordered. The most troublesome, *p, r, t, s,* and *sh,* were sung very lightly to avoid mouthiness and an unpalatable chewing of words. For a better unification of the vowels Christiansen instructed his singers to place the sounds back in the throat, breaking the vowel stream as little as possible with intervening consonants. For instance, in the opening phrase of Gretchaninoff's "Our Father," the *l* in the words, "Holy, holy, holy," was given scant attention, while the transition from the *o* to a dark-toned *e* was made with an almost imperceptible mouth movement.

Christiansen learned that in pronunciation the greatest annoyance comes from the diphthong, which if unwatched will ruin a vowel tone. Attenuating the vowel change and maintaining as much as possible a unified vowel sound will alleviate the inartistic effect. The poetic word *twilight* is anything but lovely if sung with the

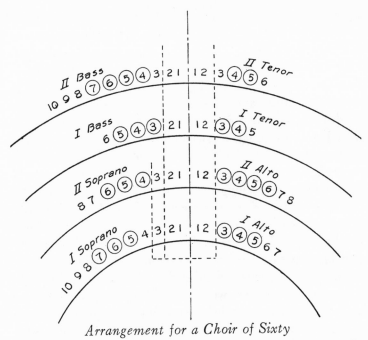

Arrangement for a Choir of Sixty

Key: Uncircled numerals, light thin voices; circled numerals,
heavy dark voices; dotted line, inner choir.

orthodox pronunciation of the word, but sung as a con-
tinuous *ah* broken by a minimum of *w* and *l*, the word
loses its otherwise whining effect. Very familiar in rehearsals was Christiansen's exaggerated demonstration of
the "wanging" sound of diphthongs in an effort to show the
choir members what a baneful thing it is in singing, and
how carefully they had to guard against it.

Although clear diction is obviously one of the first essen-
tials in choral work, and though Christiansen demanded
it of his singers, his major concern was with the production of *pure tone.* Some critics have complained that
Christiansen sacrificed intelligibility for good tone; on the
other hand, a reading of reviews of choir concerts since

1920 reveals that a majority of the critics have commented on the clarity and crispness of the diction.

There was nothing iconoclastic in the rules Christiansen used; they were the common rules of pronunciation in singing, but to achieve the best effects they had to be studied carefully and experimented with again and again. Highly important for the choir conductor, too, he believed, is a thorough knowledge of the physics of sound.

Breathing is another basic consideration in a cappella work. In his book on choir singing Christiansen wrote: "To develop large lung capacity and control of breath is the principal work of the singer." Control of the breath gives the tone body and color, whereas incorrect breathing produces a leaky voice with an unpleasantly fuzzy tone. Needless to say, Christiansen demanded rigid adherence to the breathing marks he designated, permitting no liberties on this score. He worked for long passages sung in a single breath. In sustained background singing, however, the choir was trained to steal breath, alternate singers breathing when their neighbors were singing, thus avoiding a break in the tone. This was used especially in the humming accompaniments for solo numbers.

Since its debut as a concert choir, one of the novel distinctions of the St. Olaf Choir has been its method of getting the pitch. No technique for securing it was visible during the concerts. Consequently, many myths were propagated far and wide concerning the much discussed feat of apparently fetching the pitch out of the air.

Thinking that Christiansen used a tuning fork or a pitch pipe, as did most choral directors, audiences watched him carefully between numbers as he stepped down from the podium and engaged in a casual word or two with one or another of the members in the front row. In reality he was asking his regular question: "What is the next number?" This was his method of preparing the students for the change of mood in the following number. Or he might be taking the occasion to tell the altos or the sopranos to "Wake up!" if he felt their singing had been sluggish. But there was no giving of the pitch. Many listeners came to the conclusion that the singers were trained to find the pitch for the subsequent number from the final chord of the preceding selection through relative key progression.

When the choir first appeared in eastern concert halls in 1920 and 1922, the critics were baffled by the phenomenon, and nearly every review commented on this feature. Some critics were known even to listen to a concert from the wings in their sleuthing attempts to discover the secret. After the concert at the Metropolitan in 1922, Deems Taylor wrote in the New York *World,* "No one knows yet how they got the pitch. They would finish a number exactly on the pitch (their intonation never faltered throughout) and begin the next one in a widely unrelated tonality, without any sign of hesitation or of audible prompting."

As a matter of cold fact the furor about the pitch came about quite unwittingly. Christiansen adopted his particular technique because of its efficiency and unobtrusiveness, not for a moment regarding it as a trick. He never tried or cared to bring before the public the mechanical organization of the choir. His sole purpose always was to raise the level of choral music, and to do this he needed a choir in which mechanical details were handled faultlessly. Through the scores of young music directors he has trained his technique has spread, and it is no longer quite the mysterious rite it once was. Critics have almost ceased commenting on it, for in musical circles, especially since the swift and widespread growth of a cappella choirs, it is common knowledge now that Christiansen used the "planted" pitch pipe.

Scattered throughout the choir were small single-tone

pitch pipes, one for each pitch needed during the program. If a full chord introduced the number, a member in the section singing the root note gave the pitch. If the number began in one voice part, naturally that section held the pipe. During the applause the pipe was blown so softly that it was audible only to those standing next to the holder, after which the pitch spread grapevine method through the choir. The entire procedure occupied but a few seconds; by the time the applause had died away and the rustling programs were quieted the choir was prepared for the opening chord of the new number. Although Christiansen himself and occasional choir members had what is popularly termed "absolute pitch," he did not think it feasible to rely on this form of pitch-giving for concert work. It put too much responsibility on one individual.

Christiansen's style of directing, unlike that of so many conductors, cannot be said to have stemmed from the influence of a great teacher. His mode of expression was his own. His philosophy of directing, however, was derived largely from one source, a slim German volume, *Der moderne Dirigent* (The Modern Director), by a relatively obscure German musician, Arthur Laser, who himself had been much influenced by Hans von Bülow. In this volume, declared Christiansen, he found a formulation of his own theories on conducting. Knowing Christiansen's oft-expressed belief that it is the duty of every human being to develop his individuality to its fullest, one senses the familiar when reading Laser. The passages that Christiansen underscored as he studied the book reveal the ideas that apparently were most significant to him: The director is first of all an artist who must infuse into the work of the original artist (the composer) his own individuality, for artistry and individuality are inseparable. His interpretation must express his own conception

of the spirit of the composition even if this means breaking with tradition, for the artist who clings to the letter
is only half an artist. Between the director and the group
he directs there must be a *geistiges Band* (spiritual tie) if
the group is to understand the former's interpretation and
style. The visible manner of directing should in no way
attract attention by any exaggerated gesticulation, which
makes it impossible for the director to preserve the com-
posure he must have if he is to command the sympathy
and respect of his group and of the audience. Each motion
of the director must have a purpose and must follow directly from a thought.

Christiansen's manner of conducting seems to have
been guided by these ideas, for there was nothing ex-
travagant, nothing superfluous in it. It was vigorous and
forceful, but without mannerism and without frenzy;
there was no bending, no podium cavorting, but crisp,
economic motions of the arm. He agreed with the majority of conductors in a sparing use of the left hand.
Although the outstanding characteristic of his directing
was dynamic energy, he was equally skillful in smooth-
flowing legato and lyric passages.

One of his particular techniques was that of the "delayed attack," in which, after the initial upbeat, there was
a pause before the choir attacked the chord. It is difficult
to explain how the singers were able to time their entrance
so accurately to a single point, but the very purpose of
this type of attack is to unify the group. Psychologically
the delayed attack depends on the singers' feeling for the
right moment. The length of the delay varied greatly.
Sometimes the choir was so eager to get into the number
it literally jumped the beat, while at other times if the
group was nervous or fatigued the response was slow. A
second or two might elapse before the group sang, and
even then Christiansen would have to pull the first chord

out of the choir almost painfully, as the strain and the tenseness of his face indicated. It was quite evident that the choir would not attack until the singers felt complete unity. Christiansen contended that to be artistic a choir must be trained in this technique. Constant drilling on this point eventually brought a precise yet unexplosive attack.

Less difficult, of course, but equally important for artistic singing, were the releases, which also had to be absolutely unified. "They must be like the end of a sawed-off log! Clean!" he hammered at the students day after day.

Christiansen's remarkable results in choral training were achieved through a clear understanding of the physical laws that govern the human voice, the ear, and the breathing apparatus and an intelligent application of them. Infinite patience and capacity for detail, a highly sensitized ear that did not permit the minutest fault to escape unnoticed, and a personality that bound his singers to him in complete devotion were the native qualities that united to place him among the chosen in this field of music.

Christiansen's choir rehearsals were sixty minutes of energetic work, vivid language, discipline, and attention. He worked his singers as strenuously mentally as vocally, and said to them again and again, "Please concentrate! It is essential for good singing. Why do choirs flat? Because they lack the ability to concentrate!"

He did not employ technical phraseology to convey to his students what he wanted. When the sopranos slid up or down the scale singing Bach, he frowned at them and scolded, "Don't make kettle handles when you sing. Sing notes! Listen to the piano," and he played the phrase. "Now, you sing like that." In his composition, "Sunbeam Out of Heaven," he wanted the words "Pretty little sunbeam" sung "like a kitten running down the stairs on light paws."

Once when the sopranos were singing with too heavy and dark a tone, he asked them to sing it more "pink," meaning light yet with color and warmth; and another time he wanted a high, floating tone to be "pure blue." After some particularly clumsy phrasing, he told the choir, "You sing as if you were throwing water out of a pail and splashing it against a wall, instead of letting it drop from a silver spoon like little pearls." When the tenors had been singing with a thin, colorless tone, he barked at them, "Your notes are too *bony*; put some *meat* on them!" He accented words in his stubby sentences in a dynamic fashion, as if to italicize his ideas in the minds of the students. Wanting a chord in Gretchaninoff sung with a full and driving force, he told them to "chew into a building" with it. And one day when he felt that the singing of a certain chord in Grieg lacked majesty, he said, "I want this to be like the dome of a great cathedral." Depth, resonance, and loftiness grew into the chord as the choir sang it.

Unavoidably the singers sometimes became so absorbed in the mechanics of singing that the spirit lagged behind. When he sensed this mechanical quality creeping into the choir, Christiansen took time to talk to the students about the ideal toward which they were striving, and the necessity of the spirit as well as the law in singing. Perfection of technique was not enough. "You sing notes as if you are pulling sausages out of a tight hole; as if it is hard work. The value of singing is that which is *more* than the actual singing; you can't sing unless you have the love of singing in your hearts."

His expressive face mirrored the varying emotions the music kindled in him, changing constantly while he directed. His entire face listened, alive to every part, yet in perfect control of the whole. A sharp twist would cross his face when a note faltered or was impure, but as he held it until it gradually blended, his face would relax into a smile. Once, lingering over the beauty of a fifth perfectly in tune at last, he said after releasing it, "I would like to die in moments like that."

Many comments have been made about the perfect discipline and control that Christiansen exerted over his choir. One music critic remarked that Christiansen's technique of directing was too individual to be characterized as belonging to any particular school—German, French, or Italian; if anything, it belonged to the school of hypnotism. Said somewhat lightly, the remark yet contained much truth. Christiansen had an almost hypnotic effect on his choir. His eyes compelled constant and unwavering attention, and he used them during concerts to speak the language which at rehearsals his students heard. The singers responded instantly to the darting flash that warned them of a dangerous chord, or that perhaps commanded them to "Sing together!" When his eyes twinkled and a Peer Gynt roguishness came over him, he infected the singers with the same madcap spirit and the music capered gaily and waggishly for a few measures. In a phrase of fragile loveliness his eyes begged them to sing it gently and delicately, fearful lest the heaviness of their voices should crush the flowerlike beauty. The singers would forget for a moment the world of things and people, so completely were they under the spell of his personality. Inherently and unconsciously he had the ability to dramatize his strong and deep emotions, and by this means he was able to show his singers the quintessence of his inmost feelings, as he had to do if a *geistiges Band* were to exist between him and them and enable him to bring from them the deepest and best that was in them.

From start to finish the concert was a mutual give-and-take. A frown at the tenors subdued an obstreperous third that clamored for attention like a noisy child; a protrusion of the lower jaw and a challenging look at the basses brought a crumbling thunder as of the very elements themselves; a sly, mischievous smile toward the alto section made them creep after the sopranos in a cat-and-mouse play of melody, and a triumphant grin at the sopranos hurried them on as they nimbled up the scale eluding the tagging altos. Little wonder that his students enjoyed singing for him. In both rehearsals and concerts he gave them insight into the hidden beauties of the music, not so often through words as from the moods that shadowed his face.

A concert was very taxing mentally, emotionally, and physically, and when it was over Christiansen preferred the rest and quiet of his hotel room to the admiring palaver of the social gatherings that were so often planned in his honor. Likewise the public's penchant for autographs was to him a dull nuisance from which he tried to escape, but occasionally, particularly for children, he genially signed programs. More often he smiled his way through the enthusiastic crowd, climbed into a waiting car, and as he settled back, relieved that another concert had been well received, he reached into his pocket and took out a peppermint drop. He always kept a supply of this favorite pick-up in one of his pockets.

In later years it became easier for him to respond graciously to those who sought him during intermissions to thank him or to compliment him on his work. Doubtless he appreciated their kindly motives, but usually he had little to say to them, not out of haughtiness, but because Nordic inarticulateness and a tinge of shyness prevented him.

He was not interested in the sophisticated superficialities, the ballyhoo, and the grand manner that accompanied concert work. He endured as much as was necessary and ignored as much as possible. He believed that even without a play for its favor the public will come to hear good music if it is artistically performed. Newspaper reviews were of little consequence to him. While the students spent the first hour on the train going through the morning editions for reviews of the concert sung the night before, Christiansen would find a crossword puzzle in the paper and settle himself contentedly to solve it. This was a hobby that brought him pleasure and relaxation and one in which he indulged almost daily.

The average concertgoer accepts an evening of music with little thought of the long hours that have gone into planning it. During the summer months Christiansen analyzed music, new and old, and reflected on the possible make-up of his choir for the coming year. Perhaps they could do Mendelssohn's "Savior of Sinners" with the tenor who had revealed a voice of solo caliber; possibly his own new number, written the early part of the summer, would work out nicely in the last group, or as an optional number after the second group. Thus his thoughts would knit and unravel next year's program until it fitted his mood, and, more important than anything else, until it was in his own mind representative of the best in sacred music literature. The program remained tentative, of course, until he had appraised the capabilities of the new ensemble. He was sometimes forced to discard a number because its mood did not suit the temperament of the choir for that particular year, or, more frequently, because there was no solo voice that lived itself into the music.

Christiansen frequently spent a part of his summer vacation visiting the large music libraries in the East for the purpose of studying the work being done by other choral composers. He considered program-making one of the most important and difficult tasks confronting the a cappella director. "This has been my bugbear, my greatest worry and work. If I helped lay the foundation for a cappella singing in this country, program-making has been the hardest and most important work I have done," Christiansen said one day. It involved trips to Boston, New York, and Europe for the sole purpose of visiting publishing houses in an effort to find good a cappella music. In July 1923 he wrote to President Boe from his summer home at Sister Bay, Wisconsin: "I was in Boston about 3 weeks and went through the great City Library music department for choir music. Found very little usable material. I found mostly antiques. Interesting as it was, it is not modern enough to be practical. I picked up material here and there and had it sent here for study and careful inspection."

Christiansen spent the summer of 1926 in Europe, visiting England, Germany, and his home in Norway. In Manchester, England, he spent several days as the guest of his old Leipzig school friend, Samuel Langford, successor to Ernest Newman in the post of music critic for the *Manchester Guardian.* Langford was of the opinion at the time that choral singing in England was on a sharp decline. Christiansen, however, was much impressed by the English school of composers, particularly Arnold Bax, Edward Elgar, Gustav Holst, Vaughn Williams, Geoffrey and Martin Shaw, Ralph Dunstan, and Richard Terry. He also became very enthusiastic about the Elizabethan polyphonic writers and upon his return to America said the public would soon hear the St. Olaf Choir singing Gibbons, Byrd, and Morley. But his enthusiasm waned, for the English works did not appear on the programs.

Christiansen found that virtually nothing was being done in choral composition among the modern Scandinavians, but in Germany he discovered a rich school. Most interesting to him was the work of Georg Schumann, Arnold Mendelssohn (a kinsman of the great Felix), Max Reger, Friedrich Koch, and Kurt Thomas.

If Christiansen believed that the program must be representative of the best in choral music, what in his judgment was the best? His first choice was the folk song. With its melodious simplicity and subjectivity, it appealed to his emotional temperament. Growing and developing in the culture of a people generation after generation, the folk melody expressed their universal feelings; and because Christiansen's passion was for truth, with the belief that it lies in common human experience, or, as he often said, in "universals," he found in the folk melody the finest artistic expression of that human experience. With his own roots groping deep into Norwegian culture, it was natural that many of his compositions were arrangements of old Scandinavian folk songs, and some of these were sung yearly by the choir. "If the public is to respect our profession, we must educate them to know the *best,* and the folk song is the best because it has lived through the wear and tear of many centuries," he said on one occasion. Closely second, of course, were the sacred compositions of the great classic masters. "Good taste is that taste which has been washed in the folk song and the classics."

Speaking to a group of choral directors about the construction of a program, Christiansen advised, "The program must present a unified whole. A choral program should be a *choral program* and nothing else. Don't throw in horn or violin solos. Instrumental relief is not needed, for when the program becomes a musical kaleidoscope, it is cheapened."

Within the generic unity of the program, however, there must be contrast. In his own programs he obtained variety by choosing compositions from the different schools of sacred music, each with its varying forms of musical expression: the objective intellectualism of the sixteenth- and seventeenth-century German classicists, the romanticism of the nineteenth-century Germans, the minor-noted introspection of the Russian writers, the poignant lyricism of the folk song, and occasionally the arresting harmonizations of contemporary composers. Dividing his program into three groups, he would begin with the heavier classical numbers, leaving for the next two groups the more romantic and descriptive composers, the modern Russians, and the melodious folk song.*

Aside from a preponderant use of his own original compositions and his arrangements of Scandinavian folk melodies, he leaned most heavily on the nineteenth- and twentieth-century German and Russian composers, then on the sixteenth-, seventeenth-, and eighteenth-century Germans. He used only a minor sprinkling from the well-known sixteenth-century Italian school; Palestrina, di Lasso, Victoria, and Ingegneri each appeared only once over a period of more than thirty years of choir concerts; from the seventeenth-century Neapolitan school Durante's "Misericordias Domini" has appeared on five programs. There has been no recognition of the old English school— Byrd, Tallis, Gibbons, Tomkins—and of the modern English composers only Elgar and Gibbs have been used. Critics have occasionally expressed a desire for more works of the sixteenth- and seventeenth-century composers, but, although he willingly conceded the great musical art of that age, Christiansen shied from the classical mode, feeling more at ease with nineteenth-century romanticism.

In the field of choral music Christiansen has made a signal contribution, perhaps not as a composer, not as a theorist, but certainly as a practitioner. Because of his passion for perfection of detail and his patient but inspired devotion to choral art, he has been one of the finest directors ever to appear on the stage of choral America.

*See Appendix C for the programs.

167

CHAPTER 9

The Nation Sings

GRADUALLY as Christiansen's name and the reputation of his choir spread beyond the Norwegian Lutheran churches to educational institutions and music circles on the national scene, concrete recognition was accorded the St. Olaf director's growing influence. In 1922 Muhlenberg College, a German Lutheran institution in Allentown, Pennsylvania, granted him an honorary Doctor of Music degree. On June 12, 1928, Capital University in Columbus, Ohio, in dedicating its new music hall, granted degrees to Christiansen, to Nikolai Sokoloff, conductor of the Cleveland Orchestra, and to James Cooke, head of the Presser Foundation and editor of the music magazine *Etude*. A week later Christiansen received his third honorary Doctor of Music, this time at Oberlin College. And in 1937 the University of Minnesota conferred one of its rare honorary degrees upon the director who had brought distinction to his state in the field of music.

Christiansen felt that these degrees were tributes, as well as benefits, to the choir and its work rather than personal triumphs. In a letter to President Boe about the Ohio trip in 1928 he made this terse comment: "It cost 150 dollars to St. Olaf and for the sake of the Choir work I think the money well spent."

Further evidence of Christiansen's standing in national circles was the frequent mention of him and his work in the choral music discussions at the meetings of national music groups. Charles Boyd devoted a paragraph to Christiansen in his paper, "Choir Development Since 1876, and the Preeminent Choirmasters," given before the

Music Teachers National Association in 1928. At a meeting of the same association in 1934, Henry Veld, director of the Augustana College Choir at Rock Island, Illinois, opened his discussion on choral conducting with this statement: "Beginning with the pioneer work of Dr. F. Melius Christiansen of St. Olaf's College some twenty-five years ago, the art of unaccompanied singing has made great progress in America, largely through his influence."

In 1935 the well-known choral enthusiast, Mrs. William Arms Fisher, told the same body that America in the five-year period from 1930 to 1935 had become choral-minded. As stimulating influences she mentioned the visiting choral groups of the Old World, the Sistine Chapel Choir, the Symphonic Russian Choir, the Prague Teachers' Chorus, and the various boys' choirs. She continued, "The public appetite was further whetted in the meantime by the annual tours of noted American groups. The St. Olaf Choir was among the first to develop a high state of perfection. Its tours brought a rapidly increasing host of concert patrons into the consciousness of unaccompanied singing."

The frightened Norwegian boy who had come to America with his violin case under his arm had earned the right to be ranked with Buck, Davison, Dickinson, Lutkin, Wolle, and Williamson, the great names in America's choral history. In 1940 a music critic said of Christiansen, "He is one of the great choral directors, if not the greatest, in the country today." Peter Lutkin, who was pioneering in a cappella singing at Northwestern University at the same time that Christiansen was laying the foundations for the choir at St. Olaf College, at one time spoke of Christiansen as the "prince of choir masters," and gave him most of the credit for having started the a cappella movement in this country.

Lutkin had organized an a cappella choir among his

students in 1906 for the purpose of demonstrating the music of Palestrina in a lecture to an Evanston women's club. He was so fascinated with the study of Palestrina and other polyphonic masters that the choir became a permanent group under his direction. Lutkin, however, made no attempt to go beyond Evanston audiences with his choir; the fact that Northwestern University, quite unlike St. Olaf College, was backed by wealth and was already a recognized institution made it unnecessary to use the choir for advertising purposes.

In the winter of 1927 Lutkin invited Christiansen to give a series of lectures in a new course in church music which he was initiating at the university. Christiansen accepted and spent a week on the Northwestern campus lecturing on various phases of choir conducting.

Christiansen's influence on choral techniques has spread first over the Middle West and finally over the entire country through several channels. Many of his own students have gone into the high schools and colleges of the Upper Mississippi Valley as well as other parts of the country to teach music and direct glee clubs and choirs. They have carried Christiansen's artistic ideals with them, and whether they work in small towns of a few hundred people or in larger cities, their choruses and choirs reveal an unmistakable Christiansen touch.

In California the choral work of Benjamin Edwards and William Erlandson has brought recognition to the a cappella choirs at junior colleges in Los Angeles and San Jose. In Parkland, Washington, Gunnar Malmin has used the Christiansen technique with his choir at Pacific Lutheran College. Choirs in the Nebraska colleges of Hastings, Hebron, Dana, and Midland have been directed by St. Olaf-trained musicians. Although not a St. Olaf graduate, John Rosborough, director of the Cathedral Choir at Lincoln, Nebraska, visited St. Olaf several times, spending many hours attending rehearsals and consulting with Christiansen.

Outstanding choral work has been done by former St. Olaf students in the high schools and colleges of Erie, Pennsylvania, Rochester and Buffalo, New York, and Ashland, Wisconsin. Not only as a director, but also as a composer of choral music, Morton Luvaas has brought distinction to Allegheny College in Meadville, Pennsylvania. And when the Upsala College A Cappella Choir of East Orange, New Jersey, took its spring tour in 1940, a reviewer in the Worcester *Gazette* wrote of the director, Gladys Grindeland, a former member of the St. Olaf Choir, "Miss Grindeland's training with Dr. F. Melius Christiansen, famed director of the St. Olaf Choir of Northfield, Minnesota, was reflected in the splendid performance given by the choir in many difficult numbers they presented. Unusual tonal blending was noted throughout the program."

Christiansen's own sons, Olaf and Paul, have likewise devoted themselves to the furtherance of the a cappella movement. In 1929 Olaf Christiansen started the a cappella choir at Oberlin College, where he continued to direct all choral activities until 1942. Paul Christiansen, after studying at St. Olaf and Oberlin colleges and at the Eastman School of Music, became the head of the music department at Concordia College, Moorhead, Minnesota, where he directs an a cappella choir that in many respects follows the pattern and tradition of the St. Olaf Choir.

The choral work of one St. Olaf-trained student has received particular recognition during World War II. Hjalmar F. Hanson, a chaplain in the United States Navy, was for two years the director of the one-thousand voice choir at the Great Lakes Naval Training Station. By radio and by screen—forty-five picked voices from the choir sang in Paramount's picture *The Navy Way*—the music of this choir has been heard by millions of people. When Hanson left for sea duty in 1944 his place with the choir was taken by Lieutenant Commander Sigvart Steen, another former St. Olaf Choir member. But the work of most of Christiansen's students has been less glamorous. Quietly during the last two decades hundreds of them have gone into the schools and communities of the nation. Through them Christiansen's principles of a cappella singing have increased the number of high-grade church, school, and community choirs in which the nation is singing.

Within the Norwegian Lutheran church the meetings of the Choral Union became a stimulus for the betterment of choral singing. In 1911 the loosely organized choruses and festivals that had sprung from the Norwegian Lutheran Singers' Union of Christiansen's Augsburg days had been formally organized into the United Norwegian Lutheran Church Choral Union with Christiansen as director and Paul M. Glasoe, St. Olaf College faculty member, as president. When with the merger of the three large synods in 1917 the group became the National Choral Union of the Norwegian Lutheran Church of America, the director and president remained the same.

The organization of the Choral Union theoretically followed the organization of the Norwegian Lutheran church in its circuit, district, and national plan, but lack of funds prevented the district choral unions from becoming active groups. Many circuits within the church, however, could point with pride to a robust choral union of a hundred or more members. Very often a former St. Olaf Choir member has been the director of a circuit or perhaps a district choral union. One such leader is the Reverend Alvin Snesrud, formerly of Los Angeles, who was indefatigable in carrying forward Christiansen's ideals through the Choral Union of Southern California.

As director of the National Choral Union, Christiansen

has been an incalculable force in raising the standard of music within that church body. Since 1917 the National Choral Union has met biennially with the Young People's Luther League, conventions having been held in Red Wing (Minnesota), Seattle, Duluth, Fargo, Sioux Falls, Chicago, Minneapolis, Los Angeles, and Billings. For all except two of the festivals Christiansen has been the director. Attendance has increased over the years to such an extent that now Chicago is the only midwestern city that has facilities for the large chorus of two to three thousand singers who come from all parts of the country. One of the most successful of these festivals was held in Los Angeles in the summer of 1939. Without a doubt such a concert as this one given in the Hollywood Bowl with Christiansen directing three thousand singers before an audience of several thousand has an energizing effect on a great many lovers of the choral art.

The tours of the St. Olaf Choir have been, of course, the most important single means through which Christiansen's influence has made itself felt. Very rarely is a concert given at which there is not a block of seats reserved for some high school chorus or church choir. A specific case in point is the unusual city of Flint, Michigan, where music as a community enterprise has been developed further than in any other American urban center. This city, whose own high school a cappella choir was invited to sing at the Second International Conference of Music Educators in Lausanne, Switzerland, in 1932, has had as a part of its annual musical program a series of concerts by professional groups. Zanzig, in writing about this phase of Flint's musical life, said, "The inclusion among these, at various times, of the St. Olaf Choir, the Westminster Choir, and the Russian Symphonic Choir is said to have had a large influence in the development of choral singing in the community."

Christiansen has been a great admirer of William Norton, Flint's music director, who for many years has supervised all the music not only in the city's schools but in the whole community. Two of Christiansen's sons, Jake and Olaf, have taught in the school system at Flint, and Christiansen himself has been in contact with Norton for many years. It has been Norton's custom to send Christiansen the annual report of the Community Music Association, and when Christiansen said, "Norton has done one of the outstanding works in this country for music," he knew whereof he spoke. Norton once asked Christiansen to come to Flint to settle a long-standing dispute about which of three church choirs was the best. What Solomon-like judgment Christiansen gave is of little interest, but the fact that he was appealed to in this fashion is indicative of his status in his field.

A noticeable change has taken place in the high schools during the last decade or more: The choir has largely replaced the old glee clubs and the mixed chorus, particularly the latter. The girls' and boys' glee clubs are still in the picture, but in most schools attention is now centered on choir singing. Speaking of Christiansen's part in this change, Peter Tkach, one of the leading music teachers in the Minneapolis school system, said, "One of the finest things Christiansen has done was to shove the glee club out of the picture. He has been one of the most influential men in this whole generation to raise high schools from the cheaper and lighter form of the glee club to the higher level of the choir."

In 1936 Christiansen noticed in the paper one day that the a cappella choir of West High School in Minneapolis was to give its annual spring concert that evening; among the numbers listed on the program was his own "Psalm 50." He was immediately interested, for he thought the number too difficult to be sung by high school choirs, and naturally he was curious to see what these youngsters would do with it. He drove to Minneapolis for the concert and was highly pleased with the performance. He saw also that Peter Tkach, the young director, was a real artist. After the concert he talked to him and to the students, thanking them for their excellent performance. This began a friendship of value both to Christiansen and to Tkach, and every year thereafter Christiansen attended the concert of the West High School Choir.

According to Tkach, the majority of Christiansen's own works are not suitable for the high school choir; he has written consciously for the St. Olaf Choir, with the result that the range is too wide for the high-school-age voice. Of late years Christiansen has taken more interest in choral work in the high schools and has made some rather unsuccessful attempts to compose for that age voice. In his conscious striving toward simplicity he drops below the musical maturity-level of the youthful performers, as Tkach once said, and thus fails to hold their interest.

There is no doubt that Christiansen's influence on choral singing throughout the country has been increasing steadily. Records of the sale of his music through the Augsburg Publishing House reveal a noticeable increase beginning with the year 1930. Lutheran church choirs outside the Norwegian Lutheran church, as well as other Protestant church choirs, began to use his compositions. Although most of his music was sold to church and college choirs, the sales to high school choruses also expanded appreciably as high school music contests became more popular.

Geographically the middle and western states have shown the most interest in Christiansen's music; except for Texas, which has a large Lutheran community, the southern states have been only mildly interested; the sales in eastern states have been increasing yearly. Leading states in the use of Christiansen numbers are Minnesota, North Dakota, South Dakota, Illinois, Nebraska, Wisconsin, Michigan, Iowa, Montana, Kansas, and Ohio.

The year 1935 marks the beginning of an important new phase in Christiansen's career, for in the summer of that year the Christiansen Choral School was started. The idea very likely was born at the Christiansens' summer home in Sister Bay, Wisconsin, the preceding year. Christiansen, his son Olaf, and Olaf's brother-in-law, Neil Kjos, a music publisher in Chicago, had long talks together on various phases of their work; very often the discussions pointed to the need for a short summer course for choral directors, a course that would combine brevity and intensity with vacation-like surroundings. With his business ability and his wide contacts on the commercial side of the musical world, Neil Kjos was the ideal person to manage such a venture.

The first two weeks' session was held at Winona Lake, Indiana, and more than two hundred directors were enrolled. Because they could not accommodate all those who applied for admission, the Christiansens decided that thereafter they would conduct two sessions. The undertaking had succeeded beyond their hopes. The musicians who had come to the school were impressed by the work; they were stimulated by the friendliness and enthusiasm of the staff; and they were grateful for the chance to meet and discuss problems with their co-workers in the choral field. Olaf remembers well how his father, who usually reacted to any success with matter-of-factness, was visibly moved on the last day of the session by the expressions of gratitude from the many directors as they bade him good-by.

The next year, in 1936, a June–July session was held in Ephraim, Wisconsin, and an August session again at

Winona Lake. Many who had come the first year returned and have continued to do so year after year. After trying out a number of locations scattered over the country for the 1937–39 sessions, in 1940 Kjos secured Ferry Hall, a girls' school in Lake Forest, a suburb of Chicago, for the first session, and Penn Hall, a similar school in Chambersburg, Pennsylvania, for the second. These accommodations proved so ideal—dormitory, dining hall, practice studios, auditoriums, tennis courts, and golf links —that they were used again in 1941 and 1942. No session was held in 1943 because of wartime uncertainties, but the work was to be resumed at Ferry Hall in 1944.

In the nine years of its existence some twenty-five hundred directors have attended the Christiansen Choral School, 55 per cent of them high school choral directors, 25 per cent church choir directors, and 20 per cent college choral directors. From nearly every state in the Union they have come, with the greatest number from Pennsylvania, Ohio, Illinois, Minnesota, Wisconsin, Iowa, and Indiana. Nearly all ecclesiastical bodies have been represented, for the school is of course nondenominational in character.

The course is excellently planned to suit the needs of the three groups of directors who attend. Beginning at eight o'clock and ending at twelve, there are four hour-classes in conducting, choir rehearsal, high school voice and ensemble, and church choir. After lunch a high school symposium gives that group an opportunity to discuss such problems as they have encountered in their work. From two-thirty to three-thirty Christiansen conducts a class in the analysis and interpretation of selected choir music, using a small choir to demonstrate his points. The rest of the afternoon is given over to various forms of recreation—tennis, golf, swimming, badminton—or, very often, to extra rehearsals by small groups here and there in various practice rooms. In the evening there is a thirty-minute voice-building class, after which the group enjoys an hour of madrigal singing or breaks up into small madrigal ensembles.

Until 1939 the classes in high school work were taught by Carol Pitts, director of music in Central High School, Omaha, Nebraska. In the summer of 1940 Peter Tkach of the Minneapolis public school system took over this phase of the course. With a special class of thirty high school boys and girls which he recruits from the neighborhood, Tkach demonstrates how a junior or senior high school choir can be developed through teaching correct posture, breathing, enunciation without vowel disturbance, consonant formation, tone quality, intensity, and volume.

Olaf Christiansen teaches the classes in choir conducting and church choir, which deal with the many phases of organization and rehearsal procedure, the function of music in the church service, and the aims and ideals of church music.

The benevolent senior member of the staff, called by many simply "the Doctor," is the shining figure who draws the men and women directors from all parts of the country. Like his students at St. Olaf, even these more seasoned musicians fear him, but—there is neither sentimentality nor exaggeration in this—they love him too. His sincerity, his deep love for his art, and his honest, earthy speech bring him the respect and utmost admiration of all who come to work with him. One person said in speaking about Christiansen, "You go home from the Choral School and direct in a different way. You can't help it after being near him."

Christiansen makes his class in choir rehearsal as much like the rehearsals of his own St. Olaf Choir as possible. He begins by trying out all the voices, explaining to the group why this particular voice is a good ensemble voice, why another is not. His methods here are just as precise as when he chooses members for his own choir, and as he takes the class through the procedure of eliminating voices, matching them by means of quartets, balancing the parts, and finally selecting about thirty-five voices for a choir, he impresses on the group the importance of these initial steps in the formation of an a cappella choir.

Using this small choir for the duration of the course, he teaches the assembled group how to secure correct intonation, precision of attack and release, chordal balance—in short, all the methods he himself uses to attain a superior a cappella choir. At the end of the two weeks' drill the selected choir gives a concert with all the form and ceremony of a choir on tour singing before a large house. And to tell the truth, there are just as many shaking knees and dry mouths in this improvised choir as there are in Christiansen's St. Olaf Choir just before the first number of the opening concert of the season.

Expressions of gratitude from the students have been numerous. Undoubtedly they would all agree with the young director who wrote to Neil Kjos after one of the sessions: "We are by now gently settling back to earth after another glorious experience at C.C.S. Have seen a good many of the crowd and heard from many; they all report the same thing. . . . As for me each year I get something from that school that I can't explain. Most of all you get an enthusiasm and a zeal which will carry you over many otherwise dull periods."

Until the advent of the Choral School, Christiansen had not been so interested in teaching his methods to others; but through his contact with these young directors he saw the value that was to be gained from imparting what he had learned through years of labor and thought to others who would carry on the work. That the Choral School is well serving this purpose can be seen in a letter from one of the directors to Kjos: "We agree that the last session was an even greater inspiration and help in our profession than the first one we attended, and we thought that the first one couldn't be surpassed. . . . We are all keyed up for the one to come—will be there with 'empty buckets' and will come away with them filled to overflowing." Christiansen realized as he grew older that perhaps his greatest service to the art he loved was to fill the "empty buckets" of the many who came to him seeking knowledge and inspiration.

CHAPTER 10

The Choral Composer

INCREASINGLY through the years Christiansen's attention turned toward composition. It is difficult to see where, with his multiplying activities, he could find time for the concentrated endeavor such creative work demands, but the most clear-cut memory of his father that Olaf Christiansen has carried from childhood is of the man's terrific capacity for work, his self-discipline for the sake of his art.

Despite the new and demanding duties he assumed when he moved to St. Olaf College, Christiansen did not immediately give up his early ambition to become a concert violinist. When not on the campus for classes or rehearsals, he worked at home, practicing or composing. The boys remember vividly how their father would walk around the house with his violin under his chin memorizing concertos. Later when composition began to absorb his attention, they remember how he would write a few bars of a melody, play it on the piano, get up and putter about, lie down to smoke his pipe, then jump up suddenly and hurry to the piano with a new idea or a variation of the old. One evening, after sitting in the music room a long time in the dark, he came out into the room where the children were playing and said, "Composing is seeking into the unknown."

In the middle of the night his family would sometimes hear him prowling around in the dark in search of one of the many "motive books" he had lying about. The habit of jotting snatches of melody into a music notebook had been with him since boyhood, and very often a new composition would be built on a theme that he had hastily scribbled into his motive book several years before. In the course of the years a hundred or more such books had accumulated, and they were scattered among the stacks of music that littered his piano and desk in the music room, or, for that matter, almost anywhere around the house. One morning at breakfast he showed Olaf a melody written on a leaf in one of these books and said, "This is what you sang in your sleep last night." Sometimes the family was awakened in the morning by the sound of the piano. Christiansen had risen early to work. Whenever they heard him playing the waltz from *Carmen* they knew he was moody and low in spirits.

The leave of absence granted him in 1915–16 gave him the longest period he ever had during his active years to devote wholly to composition. During that year he wrote and published two small books. The first, *School of Choir Singing,* contains material for a one-year course of instruction in music theory, the elements of tone production, pronunciation, breath control, blending of voices, and the choice and interpretation of music, plus a section of vocal exercises. The second, *Practical Modulation,* is a book of organ exercises designed to aid the organ instructor in his teaching. The year also brought a short so-called cantata, *Store ting har Herren gjort* (Wondrous Things the Lord Hath Done),* for chorus and baritone solo with organ or piano accompaniment; a long cantata, *Reformation Cantata,* with orchestral accompaniment; "Song-Service" No. 7 with four chorales; and the last three booklets in the *Lette lyrisk-religiøse sange* (Easy lyric-religious songs), containing fourteen songs. In addition he collaborated with Carl A. Mellby in editing *The Collects of the Lutheran Church.*

*The text was written by J. N. Kildahl. It was published in English in the *St. Olaf Choir Series,* Vol. III, 1920.

Store ting har Herren gjort was written for the occasion of the union of the three Lutheran synods in 1917 and is a song of thanks and praise to the Lord that the synodical fences which had kept the Norwegian Lutherans in separate pastures have at long last been broken down. The *Reformation Cantata,* unfolding the story of the Reformed Church from its beginning in ancient prophecy, was used widely by Lutheran church choirs and was sung frequently at choral union festivals.

In 1917 Christiansen wrote an oratorio, *The Prodigal Son,* which he also scored for orchestra. This, however, was not so popular as the cantata of the year before, and, according to Christiansen, has had but a single performance. In speaking of this work he expressed his views about oratorios in general, saying, somewhat dogmatically perhaps, that they are a past form of music and that people are not interested in listening to them in this day and age. Whether or not this is so, it is certain that Christiansen himself has not cared for oratorio.

The year 1919 marked the beginning of the *St. Olaf Choir Series,* edited by Christiansen and published by the Augsburg Publishing House, the company that has brought out most of his works. Volumes I and II, issued in a single binding, contain fifty selected anthems of Bach, Mendelssohn, Handel, Mozart, and other composers of religious music. The succeeding volumes contain only Christiansen compositions, arranged or original. The entire series numbers twelve volumes and includes two hundred and sixteen choir numbers. In it Christiansen republished in English many of the earlier compositions that had appeared in Norwegian in the *Sanggudstjenester* (Song Services). One need not go beyond the *St. Olaf Choir Series* to get a fairly complete picture of Christiansen as a composer of choral music. His choral compositions outside of this series are relatively few, and it is through this series that he is known today.

A glance through the programs of the various high school a cappella groups that have sung at the meetings of the National Music Teachers Association shows that the music of Christiansen and of Noble Cain appears more frequently than that of any other American composers of a cappella music. Although Christiansen composed largely for the college choir, quite a few of his choral works have been popular with high school a cappella organizations. A survey of one hundred and sixty Wisconsin high schools showed that the songs most frequently used for a cappella choirs were Glinka's "Cherubim Song," De Pearsall's "When Allan-a-Dale Went a-Hunting," Sibelius' "Dear Land of Home," then Christiansen's "Beautiful Savior," "Praise to the Lord," and "Today There Is Ringing." Also receiving frequent listing were his well-known "Lost in the Night" and "Wake, Awake." The ten best sellers among Christiansen's compositions in order of number of sales are: "Beautiful Savior," "Today There Is Ringing," "Vigil," "Lamb of God," "Lost in the Night," "Source of Calm Repose," "O Sacred Head," "Lord of Spirits," "Praise to the Lord," and "The Fairest of Roses."

It has been noted that in Christiansen's first prolific burst of serious choral composition his creativity sought expression in strict contrapuntal arrangements of sixteenth-century chorale melodies (his "developed chorales"), many of which are his most popular works. During the middle twenties, however, a change of style began to manifest itself. Instead of such rugged pieces as "Wake, Awake" and "Praise to the Lord" Christiansen began to select chorales of a more lyric type for his arrangements, as for instance "The Morning Star," "From Heaven Above," and "Deck Thyself, My Soul with Gladness." At the same time a romantic touch seems to have found its way into the arrangements themselves. Gravitation toward a more melodic line is also seen in his increasing use of Scandinavian folk melodies for his themes. The plaintive, emotional coloring and texture of the folk songs appealed to him as beauty in its truest sense.

Glancing through the *St. Olaf Choir Series*, one sees that the majority of his chorale arrangements were published in Volumes IV, V, and VI from 1919 to 1925. The five-year period following this yields no chorales, but five or six Norwegian folk melodies and about the same number of compositions with original melodies. Also one notices that having passed through the "chorale period" his music becomes programmatic in character. As early as 1919, in "As Sinks Beneath the Ocean," there is an attempt at a tone poem, but the tendency does not become outspoken until the later twenties. The appearance in 1931 of "Celestial Spring," a motet in four movements, may perhaps be regarded as a milepost. It is unquestionably program music, descriptive, written for its tonal effects and to show the virtuosity of an admirably trained choir. At this point Christiansen began to write for his public. Also, many of the compositions were written for his choir alone and for its great tours, for they are definitely beyond the range of the average choral group.

The compositions succeeding the "Celestial Spring" suite show a side of Christiansen that had not appeared before in his music. The dignity and seriousness of his earlier work have given way to a lighter mood; a sense of humor has invaded the music. The mellowness and romantic poignancy of older age, particularly noticeable in the suite written in 1935, "From Grief to Glory," with its four parts called "Decadence," "Love in Grief," "Spring Returns," and "Life," manifests itself increasingly in the compositions of the thirties. It is unhappily the case that the Christiansen of this later period rather frequently drops to the level of the banal, the saccharine, and some-times even to the cute in such works as "Sunbeam Out of Heaven" and "Beauty in Humility."

In his advancing years Christiansen composed even more prolifically than he did as a younger man, but he worked differently. Whereas formerly he had composed slowly, thinking long about a piece of work, letting it ripen, as it were, in his mind and meticulously reworking it, as he grew older his composing became more erratic. He had creative spurts in which he literally tossed off several compositions in two or three weeks' time. As a matter of fact, in a period of less than three weeks during the winter of 1942 he composed and sent to the publishers a book of about a dozen organ pieces. However, these were designed for use by the average church organist in small communities and were necessarily rather simple in structure.

The change in Christiansen's compositions has been paralleled by his changing conception of the possibilities of choir singing and by a different approach to the inter-pretation of choral music. He gradually began to think of the choir not as a group of voices, but as a symphony orchestra. During rehearsals, for instance, he tried to produce with soprano voices the effect of a flute, or through the high humming of a few voices the fine tone of a violin. Frequently he told the altos that he wanted a passage sung with cellolike quality. One of his numbers, "When Curtained Darkness," concludes with a brief solo passage for the alto voice, and from this singer he asked for the tone effect of a horn sounding in the distance. He tried many voices in the phrase and was not satisfied until he found one that had the quality of a muted horn.

In striving for symphonic effects he did not so much attempt a direct imitation of individual instruments, al-though he often used the language of instruments to convey his meaning to the choir; he sought rather to produce the general style and quality of an orchestra with its clarity and equability of tone. This was a more imaginative and poetic conception of the human voice than he had hitherto held, and it went well with the simultaneous tendency toward tone poems in his compositions.

Christiansen's level of aspiration was always higher than the achievement of his last best choir. He heard the perfect choir when he composed and when he directed, and for this choir he strove year after year. He felt always the challenge of the inch above. Naturally the choir had its ups and downs; some years the voice material on the campus was poor, other years exceptionally good. He produced a good choir every time, but some years it was richer in tone quality and better soloists were available. Still, there was a subtle change in the singing of the choir in the twenty years from 1920 to 1940, a change that came about partly because of the mellowing of Christiansen's personality and partly because of the metamorphosis in his work as a composer.

As the years advanced there was an increasing refinement of tone, a heightened precision and care in the singing of the choir, with the result that there was more artistry but a trifle less spirit. Even the choir's rendition of Bach, Mendelssohn, and the Italian masters was influenced by their diet of "orchestrated" vocal music. They began to sing Bach's "Be Not Afraid" or "Sing Ye" with too little real vitality, with too little understanding of it as music. This was pointed out even as early as 1922 in a review written by H. E. Krehbiel for the New York *Tribune*. The judgment of this reviewer is representative of the criticism Christiansen and the choir have received from time to time throughout the years.

The choir . . . is a marvel in the quality of its tone, its precision, its purity of intonation, its command of nuances, its responsiveness to the wishes of its conductor. We wish we could bestow as much admiration on his taste and judgment in selection and interpretation as we gladly do on his skill as a trainer and his sense of tonal beauty. But we cannot like some of his harmonizations of the stout old Lutheran chorales which he substituted for those of the old masters who introduced them into the Protestant service, nor the undignified catchpenny effects to which he is willing to resort.

Such singers as his, whose tonal utterance has the beauty and equability of a perfect organ, with a hundred times the potential expressiveness of the instrument, ought to make a revelation of the music of the church from Orlando di Lasso down to today. They were tremendously uplifting in three psalm anthems by Georg Schumann and the motet by Gustav Schreck and in the sustained portions of Bach's motet for double chorus, "The Spirit Also Helpeth Us"; but all the allegros were robbed of dignity and breadth and made finicky by an obvious desire for crisp decisiveness, and the splendid music suffered in consequence. But when the musical ear was so successfully wooed everywhere else by the equable flow of the beautiful voices and truly seraphic serenity, it seems churlish even to wish that anything had been different than it was. We shall enjoy no such choral treat till the choir comes to us again.

Connected also with the change from the chorale to program music was Christiansen's declining interest in the text. Until about 1925, to use that date as a convenient peg, the religious significance of the text was of prime importance to him. He was writing church music, so he used for his texts poetry with a definitely religious inspiration. Perhaps "Psalm 50" is the peak of this period. There more than in any other composition he achieved a complete union of text and music. The bulk of his music after "Celestial Spring," however, cannot strictly be called church music. If a religious theme appears at all in the texts, it is in the form of a diluted pantheism. And the increasingly secularized texts were, on the whole, greatly inferior to those of his earlier compositions. They are usually poor poetry, if they should even be called poetry, both in their aesthetic qualities and in their thought. A colleague in the music department has furnished Christiansen with many of the lyrics for his later compositions, and it is obvious that the writer is choosing words merely for their vowel content, not for their meaning. Christiansen himself seemed finally to care little whether the text made sense or nonsense; the words to him served merely as convenient frames upon which to hang a clothing of music.

This means, of course, that the importance of the songs came to rest in the music and scarcely at all in the words —certainly with an unfortunate effect on the spirit of the singing. The choir student of the twenties sang the program with force and conviction; the chorales, the Bach, Mendelssohn, and Gretchaninoff were an expression of his own spirit. The choir student of 1940 sang:

> O rippling rill in lonely hollow
> Your limpid lay I fain would follow
> In quest of gates ajar.
> From dismal dell, where'er you sally,
> You eddy on in tuneful rally
> To scented fields afar.

> Impelling pulse in ceaseless motion
> Your raptures lead to roar of ocean,
> To die, be born anew;
> For rills will rise from deepest fountain
> In God be lifted to the mountain,
> Redeemed in sparkling dew.

Certainly part of a singer's power over an audience and his appeal to it lies in his ability to enter into the meaning of the words and convey to the audience the emotions they arouse in him. With a text as meaningless as the one quoted the singers can only turn their attention solely to the music. Before long they are singing merely notes; the performance is as mechanically perfect as if a button had been pressed to release a stream of perfectly planned and executed chords, but of value beyond beauty of sound there is none.

Thus the singing of the St. Olaf Choir became too well oiled, too monotonously good to stir the listener deeply, however much he marveled at the discipline and training of the group, at the depth and resonance that Christiansen had developed in their voices. One is led to wonder: Did Christiansen in his progress toward the Ideal Choir sacrifice the true spirit of music for technical perfection? Did he forget that choral music by definition is a combination of words *and* music?

CHAPTER II

Passing of the Pioneers

THE summers that Christiansen did not spend on tour with the choir or traveling for other professional reasons were spent at the family's summer home at Sister Bay, Wisconsin, located on the peninsula that juts out into Lake Michigan. Ever since about 1900 the Christiansens have gone there for their summers, and if Christiansen could have had his heart's desire, he probably would have chosen to live there all his life. He had spent his childhood looking out to sea; he still dearly loved the water and longed to be near it. He told a story about himself once which, though related laughingly, revealed the nostalgia he felt for the sea. One day when he felt particularly homesick, he stopped his car on the bank of Northfield's gentle-flowing Cannon River. Curving his hand to form a telescope, he squinted through the small opening at the river. All he could see was water, even when he moved his head slowly from side to side. Having satisfied himself that he was looking at a wide expanse of sea, he drove home.

As the children grew up, married, and had children of their own, they, too, built homes on the forty-three-acre plot at Sister Bay, which had originally been the property of Mrs. Christiansen's paternal grandfather. Soon there was a little Christiansen colony on the Bay: a daughter Elsa and her husband; three sons—Jake, director of athletics at Concordia College in Moorhead, Minnesota; Paul, director of music at the same school; Olaf, his father's heir apparent at St. Olaf College; their wives and about a dozen grandchildren.

In this atmosphere of children's shouts and laughter, bright sunshine, and unhurried days Christiansen has been his happiest. He would spend most of his time out-of-doors, improving the grounds and tinkering on the dock. Set apart from the cottage is a rustic studio where he could shut himself away to practice or compose if he wished, but Christiansen did little of this during the summer months. Undoubtedly he thought and planned for the coming year's work as he spaded, chopped trees, and carried stones to the pier, but he went to Sister Bay mainly to rest and store up energy for the year ahead.

At the milestone of three score years and ten everything about Christiansen still indicated his Norwegian origin: his speech, with the broad accents and inflection of the tongue he had spoken exclusively until his maturity; his square jaw, rough-hewn face, and proudly carried head with its shock of crisp white hair; his robust, solid appearance. He still retained much of his force, conviction, and dynamic energy. There remained in him something of the austere severity of a Prussian general who demands absolute obedience and attention when work is to be done and to whom incompetence is unendurable. His curt command would still throw students into chilled fright; indications of temper still smoldered beneath the surface when a phrase was sloppily executed. But the frequency of his sudden angered explosions had diminished with the passing years; the fiery flash of the eye and the sarcastic shout had given way to a merry twinkle and a good-natured quip, followed by a chuckling bob of his shoulders.

Widening age differences between Christiansen and his students brought a *rapprochement* that was not there in former years. As the master's once insatiable drive for work ebbed, he found more time for chatting with students, advising them in their professions, counseling them with the wisdom harvested from a full life. He has always been interested in them and their problems; more, he has always loved the strength of their youth, their keen appetite for life. At the end of one rehearsal in which the choir had given its very best in the sheer joy of working for him, he laid down his baton, looked at the group, and in a quiet, humble way said, "I love every one of you."

At some time or other during his years of service at St. Olaf Christiansen has taught almost all the courses in the music department, but as he advanced in years, his hours of teaching were reduced and adjusted to his other work. Perhaps the most popular course has been his class in choir conducting, which every student majoring in music was required to take. Even nonmusic students took the course if they could get Christiansen's permission. When Christiansen was forced to cut down his teaching load, his courses in double counterpoint, canon and fugue, and advanced composition were continued in the form of private lessons to selected students of exceptional ability.

One cannot deny that the public school music course has been neglected at St. Olaf, that it has suffered from the emphasis given to choral work. But, on the other hand, the School of Music has achieved a reputation fair enough to make the demand for St. Olaf-trained music teachers in Minnesota and neighboring states exceed, in most years, the number of graduates. If the all-round musical training of the students has perhaps not met the highest standard, at least in the choral field the graduates have had exceptional training under Christiansen, and this has made for their success as music teachers.

His very real achievements, as well as the national acclaim he has won, have made Christiansen one of Minnesota's favorite sons, much beloved and revered throughout the state. Since 1926 his choir and the Minneapolis Symphony, the two most renowned musical organizations in the state, indeed in the region, have given a joint concert each year in the huge Northrop Memorial Auditorium on the campus of the University of Minnesota, and this annual musical event draws audiences of five thousand and more from all over the state. At the concert in 1935 Christiansen himself directed the orchestra in a few numbers, including, fittingly enough, selections from Grieg's *Peer Gynt Suite.* He could hardly have failed to be reminded of those days years before when he was an unknown violinist in this then equally obscure orchestra.

At the 1942 concert the Minneapolis Symphony played one of Paul Christiansen's compositions, a symphonic movement entitled "The Vials of Wrath." This youngest son in the Christiansen family has already shown evidence of gifts as a composer that may in time exceed, in breadth at least, those of his father.

At the next year's concert some of the choir numbers were directed by Paul's older brother Olaf. After the concert at Buffalo during the choir's tour in January 1941, Christiansen had written to President Boe: "I wish you would make arrangements with Olaf to become my assistant for next year. I feel that should be done for the security of the Choir and my other work. . . . I don't want the Choir to die with me—not even sag. The sagging process is apt to begin next year—the way I feel on this trip."

The audiences were in no way aware of the director's diminishing energies, as the reviews show, but Christiansen knew, as great creators of enduring institutions must always know, the importance of handing responsibility on to a successor while he could still be present to assist in the transfer of public confidence and favor. After a year's delay President Boe acceded to Christiansen's request, and Olaf was called from Oberlin College to become his father's assistant in 1942–43. After he had shared the responsibility for two seasons, in directing before the public as well as in training the choir, it was announced in the spring of 1944 that F. Melius Christiansen was permanently surrendering the director's baton to his son. Olaf, with a splendid record of achievement at Oberlin and an excellent director in his own right, is fully equal to the task, and the change should bring no dimming of the choir's glory.

One may suspect that retirement will not be easy for Christiansen. He has always been so fully occupied with his work that he has developed few other interests to fill his hours. Concentration on his profession has prevented him even from being "a good neighbor," as he said. Seldom, if ever, has he identified himself with a nonmusical campus cause, and as far as the town is concerned he has been entirely lacking in Rotarian spirit. Few social engagements disturbed his days. Neither he nor Mrs. Christiansen participated as actively in faculty social life or student affairs as the average professor and his wife in a college town. Mrs. Christiansen, not a member of the Lutheran church, was not drawn into the Ladies' Aid Society or the church suppers and bazaars that kept the majority of the faculty wives engaged.

In spite of his relative isolation, however, Christiansen had a few contacts with friends and colleagues. He and the venerable Minneapolis music educator, Thaddeus Philander Giddings, were friends of long standing, admiring each other greatly. Christiansen was never a believer in Giddings' *do-re-mi* method of teaching music, and over it they had a great deal of good-natured argument and banter, in which no offense was meant and none taken. In the beginning of Christiansen's career as a concert choral conductor Giddings often had to urge him to use more of his own compositions on his choir programs.

Occasionally, too, the Carlyle Scotts of Minneapolis,

whom Christiansen had first met in Leipzig, would visit the Christiansens in Northfield. They enjoyed exchanging stories of the early days when Christiansen was a struggling violinist and Carlyle Scott a young pianist at the University of Minnesota, teaching in a building which was so cold in winter that before his students arrived for lessons he warmed the piano keys by placing his muffler first on the radiator, then laying it full length on the keyboard.

Among Christiansen's friends on the St. Olaf faculty was his neighbor on the "Avenue," Paul M. Glasoe, who in addition to being head of the chemistry department, took an active interest in Christiansen's work in the National Choral Union, of which Glasoe was president. A student of Lutheran hymnody, Professor Glasoe for many years conducted a Sunday evening "Chorale Hour" over WCAL, the St. Olaf College radio station.

Paul G. Schmidt, Christiansen's professional confrere since the days of the first band tours, has also been one of his closest personal friends. Perhaps no person on the campus has known and understood Christiansen so well as he. Certainly Christiansen has shared with Schmidt more than with anyone else his hopes and fears, his ideals, his disappointments, and his successes. Christiansen's welfare, both personal and professional, has been in a sense Schmidt's life work. Each has been a loyal friend to the other.

The small group with whom Christiansen was on more intimate terms also included President Boe, Carl Mellby, Ole E. Rölvaag, who was head of the Norwegian department, and gruff-looking but good-natured Erik Hetle, who had started teaching in the physics department the same year that Christiansen joined the staff. Hetle's droll tongue and Norwegian stories were particularly appreciated by this little circle of inveterate pipe-smokers. Christiansen thoroughly enjoyed swapping good stories with his friends. Stories even found their way into his letters, as in one written to President Boe shortly before school opened in the fall of 1936. After discussing a departmental problem that had arisen, Christiansen continued:

Here is hoping that there will be a few good singers among the many students coming to St. Olaf this year. The country looks to St. O. for the ideal Choir of the U. S. Prof. Schmidt talked about a trip to the west coast. I hope, in case we are going, that he will be given the freest opportunity to make it a success—for, what is the use of going if it is to be a failure. "Nobody knows what trouble I is in" when we have to sing to empty houses on account of poor management. No matter how great an artist is giving a Concert, it has to be managed in the right way in order to have a crowd and—peculiar as it may seem—the artist sings as well as the size of the audience, provided of course that he is an artist. When I use the word "provided" it reminds me of a story: There was a meeting held by a negro congregation in the South. They had Bible study and the subject was: "And there shall be weeping and gnashing of teeth." One of the members asked the question, What about those old people that have no teeth? The parson who did not want to be stumped answered: "Teeth will be provided!"

. . . I wish the curtains in my studio might be drycleaned and mended.

Love and greetings from all,

Your friend,

F. M. Christiansen

Although Carl Mellby taught history and sociology, his extensive knowledge of music was recognized and put to use in frequent reviews for the local newspapers. Sometimes when Mellby dropped in for an evening's chat, Christiansen would show his friend the composition he was working on; together they would sit at the piano, Christiansen playing phrases as they discussed the composition. Mellby with his more objective training as a

197

historian often argued against Christiansen's romantic tendencies.

Like Christiansen, Rölvaag was immersed in his work and indifferent to social life except for occasional evenings with his close friends. Coming to America from Norway at the age of twenty, Rölvaag had suffered the agony of immigrant years as had Christiansen and so many others. Attendance at a Lutheran academy in South Dakota and four years of college at St. Olaf molded the mind of the young newcomer, who had already begun to express himself in writing. After a year's study at the University of Christiania, he returned to St. Olaf to begin teaching Norwegian language and literature the same fall that Christiansen went to Leipzig after the band tour.

Rölvaag, ideologist as well as artist, tried through his writings to awaken in the people of the Central Northwest an understanding of their European heritage. He believed in the cultural potentialities of the region because of its distinct ethnic composition, its history, and its religious mood, and through his novels he sought to express the aspirations he sensed in the souls of his people. Almost simultaneously during the middle and late twenties, these two Norwegian Americans, Rölvaag and Christiansen, were drawing national attention to themselves and to St. Olaf, Rölvaag with his powerful pioneer stories, *Giants in the Earth* and its sequels, and Christiansen with his chorale-singing choir. It has been said, with a measure of truth, that St. Olaf College was rescued from mediocrity by these two geniuses. By the end of the decade Rölvaag was nationally recognized as one of the finest writers in America.

In 1925 the Norwegian Americans celebrated the centennial anniversary of the coming of the first Norwegian settlers to America. The Middle West, where the bulk of the Norwegian population was centered, was alive with activity. Histories were written; a great festival was planned; President Coolidge was invited and came to Minneapolis; bands played "Ja vi elsker" and "The Star-Spangled Banner." Rölvaag delivered an address on "Our Racial Heritage," which again stressed the ideas that were so dominant in his thinking. Christiansen had been asked to write a cantata for the occasion, but the request was made so late that he could not finish the work in time for the celebration proper. The *Centennial Cantata*, as he called it, was not performed until a year later, when it was sung in Minneapolis by the Choral Union of the Norwegian Lutheran church, accompanied by the Minneapolis Symphony.

The terms of service of Christiansen and Rölvaag brought many changes to the college on the hill that provided the setting for their labors. The founders and early supporters of St. Olaf perhaps never dreamed of the beauty that Manitou Heights would some day possess. The approach to the college up St. Olaf Avenue today would be unrecognizable to the buggy travelers of that dirt road more than a half century ago. The avenue is paved; overhead, elm branches interlace to form an arch of green. Trim houses, well-clipped lawns, peony and tulip beds have taken the place of the grainfields and pasture land that adjoined the old street. A lilac hedge extending for almost a block at the foot of the hill blooms a Commencement farewell to every senior class.

To "Old Main" the years have added building after building, most of them of gray limestone in the style of a French medieval castle. An exception among them is the small, brown-stained wooden art studio with its slanting roof, its carved pillars and borders, ornamented with Viking ships and old Norse figures. Through the trees on the northwest edge of the campus one sees the neat buildings of one of the three farms that supply the college with meat and dairy products. Below the hill to the northeast lies the fourteen-acre athletic field, equipped for football, baseball, and track. The southern edge of the campus dips sharply to form what is called Norway Valley. Towering pines make the needle-covered paths a cool, sequestered spot. A natural stage and amphitheater in the valley provide a delightful setting for the outdoor Shakespearean play presented traditionally each spring by the dramatics department.

In many of these physical changes may be seen an expression of a fundamental inner change: the lessening Norwegianism and growing Americanism of the student body. No longer do many of the students come from Norwegian-speaking homes. Most of them, even those of Norwegian ancestry, do not know the language; they study it with as little previous preparation as they do French or German. And the number of students of non-Norwegian stock has been increasing steadily.

When Christiansen went to St. Olaf College at the beginning of the century, the ideological pattern that set the college apart was clear-cut. Although the melting pot had already spilled over into the Middle West and was creating a new type of American to run the wheels of industry, to sit on city councils, and to teach children the principles of "one nation indivisible," St. Olaf still tried to preserve its identity as a distinctly Norwegian-American institution. It succeeded for a while because the ardor of the pioneers was still alive in this generation of its leaders, of whom President Boe, Rölvaag, and Christiansen were typical. They represented a generation whose hearts belonged partly to the old, partly to the new. Close enough to their European heritage to retain its thought and habit patterns, they yet found themselves, only half-willing, clothing their ways and ideas in the outer garments of the American scheme in which they lived.

This generation had to be, and at St. Olaf it had its triumph and reward in the novels that were written within the college walls, the choirs that were sent forth from its portals. Through Rölvaag and Christiansen the sectarian pioneers' college on the hill made an outstanding contribution. But the day arrives when the dwelling of the pioneer is adjoined by one and then another until it becomes a house on a street in a town. He no longer lives his former individualistic life, but becomes a member of a community. So it has been with St. Olaf College. Many who fought to keep it a Norwegian-American stronghold have departed; Rölvaag died in 1931, Lars W. Boe in December 1942. The days of those giants in the earth are gone. What was the living present of yesterday cannot be more than the proud and colorful background of tomorrow.

One of the great generation, F. Melius Christiansen, himself a felicitous symbol of the transition, is still venerably among us. He went to St. Olaf College as a Norwegian American to work as one of them. But as his work matured, it carried him beyond the limitations of the group, linked him to the chain of American life, taught him American concepts and American goals. He no longer considers himself the exponent of a Norwegian-American art; instead he serves an art that transcends ethnic and sectarian demarcations, and he has come to think of his work as a contribution to American music. Christiansen's span is drawing to a close, but his songs and his teachings will live on in the schools and in the concert halls of America.

Sources

DURING the four years of my membership in the St. Olaf Choir I kept a journal of my experiences and in it recorded incidents concerning Christiansen, conversations with him, and the general life of the choir. When the actual work on this biography was begun in 1940, I spent several months in Northfield. During these months and in subsequent visits, Dr. Christiansen generously devoted many hours to me, giving information concerning his family and his own life history. From his immediate family I have received valuable information about the life of the Christiansen household.

Christiansen's friends, likewise, have generously contributed information about his life. Foremost among these are: Paul G. Schmidt, Carl A. Mellby, and the late Lars W. Boe, all of St. Olaf College; Professor H. N. Hendricksen, Carl G. O. Hansen, Mrs. Carlyle Scott, Peter Tkach, O. I. Hertsgaard, Adolph Olsen, and Dr. C. M. Roan, all of Minneapolis; and Neil Kjos of Chicago. I am also indebted to Kenneth Bjørk, professor of history at St. Olaf and a member of the board of editors for the Norwegian-American Historical Association, who read the manuscript with a sharp and critical eye.

Documents and letters relative to Christiansen's childhood and youth in Norway are almost entirely lacking. Except for a school report received at the end of the eighth grade (quoted in Chapter 1) and an official permit to leave Norway (quoted in Chapter 2), both of which are in Christiansen's possession, no records from that period of his life are extant. Consequently, my only source of information was Christiansen's verbal account. Fictionalization, slight in Chapter 1, is negligible in the remainder of the work.

For the general historical background in the Norway chapters I used Knut Gjerset's *History of the Norwegian People* (New York: Macmillan, 1915, 2 vols.), the only history of the Norwegian people written in English. Volume 2, *The Modern Period,* was particularly useful. The most complete and scholarly English-written investigation of Norwegian nationalism during the age of romanticism is Oscar Falnes' *National Romanticism in Norway* (New York: Columbia University Press, 1933). I found his excellent account of the *landsmaal-riksmaal* struggle most valuable in understanding Christiansen's cultural background. A popularized presentation of the Scandinavian countries, their people, customs, industry, and arts, is to be found in Henry Goddard Leach's *Scandinavia of the Scandinavians* (New York: Scribner, 1915).

For material dealing with immigration see Caroline Ware's general article, "Immigration," in the *Encyclopedia of Social Sciences* (1932, vol. 4, pp. 589–95); for European immigration to America, George Stephenson's *A History of American Immigration, 1820–1924* (Boston: Ginn, 1926); for a generalized account of the economic, political, and cultural contributions that immigrant peoples have made to American life, Carl Wittke's *We Who Built America: The Saga of the Immigrant* (New York: Prentice-Hall, 1939). The best analysis and most recent history of Norwegian migration to America is to be found in Theodore Blegen's *Norwegian Migration to America, 1825–1860* (Northfield, Minnesota: Norwegian-American Historical Association, 1931) and his later volume, *Norwegian Migration to America: The American Transition* (1940, published by the same association).

Narrower in scope but valuable for its year-by-year tracing of Norwegian immigration to America with a careful account of names and settlements is George Flom's *A History of Norwegian Immigration to the United States: From the Earliest Beginnings Down to the Year 1848* (Iowa City, Iowa: Privately printed, 1909). Carlton Qualey's *Norwegian Settlement in the United States* (Northfield, Minnesota: Norwegian-American Historical Association, 1938) picks up the story after the immigrant reaches America and follows the westward expansion of Norwegian settlements from the New York settlement into the midwestern states.

The following is a list of publications containing exclusively or prevailingly primary sources pertaining to Norwegian immigration and immigrant life: *Ole Rynning's True Account of America* (translated and edited by Theodore Blegen. Minneapolis: Norwegian-American Historical Association, 1926). The publication of this account in Norway in 1838 was the beginning of the highly important "America letters." It answered thirteen practical questions concerning America and the problems of emigration in a sane and straightforward manner. *Bishop Neumann's Word of Admonition to the Peasants* (1837. Translated and edited by Gunnar Malmin in *Studies and Records,* Norwegian-American Historical Association, 1926, vol. 1, pp. 95–109). Bishop Neumann tried to persuade Norwegians to remain in their own land by pointing out the negative side of emigration, and his pamphlet effectively counteracted the tide of emigration for two or three years. Ole Munch Raeder's *America in the Forties* (translated and edited by Gunnar Malmin. Minneapolis: University of Minnesota Press, 1929). This series of letters written by an eminent Norwegian scholar traveling in America in 1847–48 presents a vivid picture of American life at that time, especially the conditions existing among the Norwegian pioneers. *Studies and Records,* a publication of the Norwegian-American Historical Association, volumes 1 (1926), 2 (1927), 3 (1928), 4 (1929), 5 (1930), 6 (1931), 7 (1932), 8 (1934), 9 (1936), 10 (1938), 11 (1940), 12 (1941), and 13 (1943). These volumes contain articles, diaries, letters, and the like written by the immigrants or about them. They form a record of many of the phases of Norwegian-American life from the earliest pioneer days down to the present time.

Laurence M. Larson in *The Log Book of a Young Immigrant* (Northfield, Minnesota: Norwegian-American Historical Association, 1939) gives a chatty chronicle of the physical, intellectual, and spiritual migration of a Norwegian boy coming to America. The same author in *The Changing West* (Northfield, Minnesota: Norwegian-American Historical Association, 1937) has written eight essays on phases of the changing culture and history of the West, particularly in regard to the tendencies underlying Norwegian-American fiction, scholastic achievement, adjustment of the immigrant, the role of the lay preacher in pioneer life, and the relationship of the immigrant to the "Yankee School." In *Norwegian Emigrant Songs and Ballads* (Minneapolis: University of Minnesota Press, 1936) Theodore Blegen and Martin Ruud have translated and edited a large collection of songs that depict a phase of emigrant life never before uncovered. By this medium the emigrant often revealed the motives for his departure from Norway, his emotions, and the difficulties involved in his adjustment to conditions in the new land.

For the description of Oakland and San Francisco I consulted the *Pictorial History of California* (compiled and edited by Owen C. Coy. University of California Extension Division, no date given); Helen Hunt Jackson's *Bits of Travel at Home* (Boston: Roberts, 1878), in which the author includes descriptions of both cities, though at a time somewhat preceding Christiansen's arrival there; and J. H. Bates's *Notes on a Town in Mexico and California* (New York: Burr Printing House, 1887), which also contains brief descriptions of both cities.

J. Magnus Rohne's *Norwegian American Lutheranism up to 1872* (New York: Macmillan, 1926) presents a straight historical account of the growth of the Lutheran church among the Norwegian Americans, its ultimate divisions and synodical relationships. For a broader treatment, revealing the sociological background of the growth of the Lutheran church in America, see Chapters IV and V of Blegen's *Norwegian Migration to America: The American Transition*. For additional material on the subject see Olaf M. Norlie's *History of the Norwegian People in America* (Minneapolis: Augsburg Publishing House, 1925). The author was appointed to write a general history of the Norwegian people in this country for the Norwegian centennial celebration, but his preoccupation with ecclesiastical matters makes his book mainly valuable as a source of information in that sphere of Norwegian-American life.

For the history of Augsburg College I used Berhard J. Kleven's *The Story of Augsburg* (Builder's Series, No. 1, no date) and Andreas Helland's *Augsburg Seminar Gjennem Femti Aar, 1869–1919* (Minneapolis: Folkebladet Publishing Company's Trykkeri, 1920), both in the Augsburg College Library in Minneapolis. For Christiansen's student life I had, in addition to his own account, information secured from Professor H. N. Hendricksen, student at Augsburg Seminary during Christiansen's freshman year in the college and at present registrar at Augsburg, and from Dr. C. M. Roan of Minneapolis, who knew Christiansen at that time and who kindly turned over to me a letter written him by the Reverend B. L. Sundal, a member of the Augsburg Quartet, containing incidents about Christiansen.

In the office of the Friend Publishing Company in Minneapolis, I was given access to the files of the magazine *Ungdommens Ven,* in which some of Christiansen's early music appeared. From N. N. Rønning personally and through his book *Fifty Years in America* (Minneapolis: Friend Publishing Company, 1938), which contains biographical sketches of many of the figures prominent in Augsburg circles, I gained additional material on the Augsburg period.

To supplement the information given me by individuals, I traced Christiansen's musical activities in Minneapolis by using old programs in his possession and the files of the Minneapolis *Tidende* in the library of the Minnesota State Historical Society in St. Paul. To Adolph Olsen of Minneapolis I am indebted for the account of Christiansen as a violin teacher. The description of the Kjerulf Club and its activities I secured from G. A. Gjertsen of Minneapolis, who was a member of the organization. Carl G. O. Hansen, also a member of the Kjerulf Club and a very active participant in, and writer about, Norwegian-American musical life in Minneapolis, furnished me with valuable background material. In addition to Christiansen's narrative of the Leipzig years I have used details from accounts given me by Mrs. Carlyle Scott of Minneapolis, who was also a student of Hans Sitt at the time Christiansen studied at the Royal Conservatory in Leipzig, and by Dr. Carl A. Mellby of St. Olaf College.

For the general history of Minneapolis music during the second half of the nineteenth century and early years of the twentieth, I used the newspaper files of the Minneapolis *Tribune,* finding a wealth of material in a series of articles by Louise Chapman of the music department of the Minneapolis Public Library. This series, "The First Fifty Years of Music in Minneapolis," appeared in the Minneapolis Sunday *Tribune* for five successive weeks from January 20 to February 24, 1935. From Mrs. Carlyle Scott and from Carlo Fischer, a teacher at Northwestern Conservatory during Christiansen's connection with the institution and cellist in the Danz Symphony and later in the Minneapolis Symphony, I received additional material for this period.

Good histories of St. Olaf College are Carl A. Mellby's *St. Olaf College through Fifty Years, 1874–1924* (Northfield, Minnesota, 1925) and I. F. Grose's *Fifty Memorable Years at St. Olaf* (Northfield, Minnesota: Northfield News, 1925). Both books are in the St. Olaf library. I also used the *St. Olaf College Bulletin,* 1899–1941, on file in the office of the registrar. For the history of St. John's Church I used *St. John's Norwegian Lutheran Church: A Record of the First Fifty Years, 1869–1919* (prepared by a committee. Northfield, Minnesota: Mohn Printing Co., 1920). The files of the *Manitou Messenger,* the St. Olaf College paper, and the *Viking,* the college yearbook, were most valuable for securing a picture of student life and activity during the early years of Christiansen's work at St. Olaf. I have drawn most heavily from volumes 17–29 of the *Manitou Messenger,* covering the years 1903–15.

To O. I. Hertsgaard of Minneapolis, who was a member of the St. Olaf Band when Christiansen went to the college, I am indebted for several of the incidents I have used. Little attention has been given in this work to the musical life at St. Olaf College before 1903, that is, preceding Christiansen's appointment. A detailed account of this period is to be found in Eugene Simpson's *A History of St. Olaf Choir* (Minneapolis: Augsburg Publishing House, 1921). This book, now out of print, gives the history of the St. Olaf Choir from its beginning up through the first eastern tour in 1920. Chapter VIII of Simpson's monograph contains a short sketch of Christiansen's early life. It puts special stress on the first Leipzig period and includes also a short biography of Gustav Schreck. As mentioned in the text, Simpson was a fellow student of Christiansen at Leipzig.

Ole E. Rölvaag has found able biographers in Theodore Jorgenson and Nora Solum of the St. Olaf College faculty: *Ole Edvart Rölvaag: A Biography* (New York: Harper, 1939).

For material on the Choral Union of the Norwegian Lutheran church I am indebted to Dr. Paul M. Glasoe of St. Olaf College, president of the Union. The account of the Lutheran Hymnary Committee was furnished me by Christiansen and by Dr. Mellby. For a history of the music festival movement in America see William Arms Fisher's *Music Festivals in the United States: An Historical Sketch* (Boston: American Choral and Festival Alliance, 1934).

Dr. Lars W. Boe, the late president of St. Olaf College, kindly gave me permission to read and use material from the files of his correspondence with Christiansen, Schmidt, and other individuals concerned with the work of the choir. The files of correspondence, programs, and reviews kept by Professor P. G. Schmidt were also made available to me. The quotations from the *Globe and Commercial Advertiser, Musical America,* and *The New York Times* were taken from Simpson's *A History of St. Olaf Choir,* p. 166. The quotations from all other reviews of the choir concerts were taken from the file of newspaper clippings in the possession of Professor P. G. Schmidt.

Although the major portion of the material in Chapter 8 came directly from Christiansen, either in rehearsals or in discussion with him, I consulted the following works in the preparation of it: Noble Cain, *Choral Music and Its Practice: With Particular Reference to A Cappella Music* (New York: M. Witmark, 1932); William Arms Fisher's introduction to F. M. Christiansen and N. Cain, editors, *A Cappella Chorus Book: For Mixed Voices* (New York: Oliver Ditson, 1932); Henry Coward, *Choral Technique and Interpretation* (London: Novello, 1914); Frederick Wodell, *Choir and Choir Conducting* (12th ed. Philadelphia: Presser, 1930); F. M. Christiansen, *School of Choir Singing* (Minneapolis: Augsburg Publishing House, 1916); and a series of articles by Christiansen collected in *Choir Director's Guide* (Minneapolis: Augsburg Publishing House, 1935). In Arthur Laser's *Der moderne Dirigent* (Leipzig: Breitkopf and Härtel, 1904) the author discusses the role of the director as an interpreting and performing artist. In the first section Laser deals with the philosophical approach to directing, and in the second section he discusses the practical approach.

In preparing Chapter 9 I used the following articles and books: Charles Boyd, "Choir Development Since 1876, and the Preeminent Choirmasters," *Music Teach. Nat. Assoc. Proc.,* 1928, pages 67–80; Henry Veld, "Choral Conducting," *Music Teach. Nat. Assoc. Proc.,* 1934, pages 46–56; Mrs. William Arms Fisher, "America Becomes Choral Conscious," *Music Teach. Nat. Assoc. Proc.,* 1935, pages 223–34; Augustus D. Zanzig, *Music in American Life* (New York: Oxford University Press, 1932); John T. Howard, *Our American Music* (New York: Crowell, 1931). I also had the privilege of reading an unpublished master's thesis by Burnette Thompson, submitted at the Eastman School of Music, Rochester, New York, in 1937. Miss Thompson deals very competently with "The Significance of the St. Olaf Lutheran Choir in American Choral Music." Her viewpoint, however, is strictly that of musical education. The work contains surveys of the frequency with which Christiansen's compositions have been used by high school choruses. No use has been made of them in the present work. The data concerning choral work in the Wisconsin high schools are taken from another unpublished master's thesis, "The Status of Choral Organizations in 160 Wisconsin High Schools," by Hubert L. Edquist, submitted to the College of Education at the University of Minnesota in 1938. Miss Thompson's monograph also contains interesting statistics covering the first three years of the Christiansen Choral School. The figures in the present work were obtained directly from Neil Kjos, manager of the choral school. From Peter Tkach of Minneapolis I received additional material concerning choral practices in high schools, and in particular concerning Christiansen's influence in that sphere. I also had occasion, thanks to the invitation of Dr. Christiansen, to observe the work of the choral school during the summer session of 1940 held at Lake Forest, Illinois.

Biographical sketches of Christiansen are to be found in the following: *Who's Who in America*, 1924–25, 1926–27, 1930–31, 1932–33, 1934–35, 1936–37, 1941–42, 1942–43; *Who is Who in Music, 1941 Edition* (New York: Lee Stern Press, 1941), p. 66; *International Cyclopedia of Music and Musicians* (edited by Oscar Thompson. New York: Dodd, Mead, 1939), p. 335; *Macmillan Encyclopedia of Music and Musicians in One Volume* (compiled and edited by Albert E. Wier. New York: Macmillan, 1938), p. 335; *Baker's Biographical Dictionary of Musicians* (edited by Theodore Baker. 4th ed. New York: G. Schirmer, Inc., 1940), p. 208; *A Dictionary of Modern Music and Musicians* (London: J. M. Dent & Sons, 1924), p. 93.

List of Published Compositions

CHORAL WORKS

CANTATAS

Store Ting har Herren gjort (organ accompaniment, Augsburg, 1916)*
Reformation Cantata (orchestra accompaniment, Augsburg, 1917)
Centennial Cantata (orchestra accompaniment, Augsburg, 1925)

ORATORIOS
Prodigal Son (orchestra and organ accompaniment, Augsburg, 1918)

SMALLER WORKS FOR MIXED CHORUS
12 Korsange (Free Church Publishing Company, 1894)

Sangserie-Idun (1896–99)

Sangbogen, a hymnal edited by Theodore Reimestad and M. Falk Gjertsen (Minneapolis: Syvende Oplag, 1907), contains the following Christiansen original melodies and arrangements: Kun et skridt (arr. F.M.C.). En stund i dødens dale (arr. F.M.C.). Herlige livsens ord (arr. F.M.C.). Vennens røst (arr. F.M.C.). O Jesus Krist, vor frelser (arr. F.M.C.). Frelsens klippe (arr. F.M.C.). Guds naadekald (arr. F.M.C.). En kjaerlig, trofast ven (arr. F.M.C.). Se og lev! (arr. F.M.C.). Ei af denne verden (arr. F.M.C.). Jeg synge vil om Jesus (arr. F.M.C.). I Kristus har jeg livet (arr. F.M.C.). Naar af tunge tvivl (arr. F.M.C.). Til den unge ven (arr. F.M.C.). Oplad! opladt! (Irish folk melody—arr. F.M.C.). Barnesang (folk song—arr. F.M.C.). Kristelig frihed i Guds aand (Reimestad–F.M.C.). Syng, menighed (Reimestad–F.M.C.). En liden stund (Reimestad–F.M.C.). Op, I kristne, ruster eder (Reimestad–F.M.C.). Jeg kysser dine haender (Reimestad–F.M.C.). Kristus er opstanden (Reimestad–F.M.C.). Skilsmissen tung (Reimestad–F.M.C.). Atter paaske-morgen (Reimestad–F.M.C.). Jesus for os døde (Reimestad–F.M.C.). Som foraarssolen (Reimestad–F.M.C.). Jeg har baaret (Reimestad–F.M.C.). Luther (Reimestad–F.M.C.). Nytaarssang (Wennerberg–F.M.C.). Sang til juletraeet (Grieg–F.M.C.). Som sol gaar ned i havet (Grieg–Reimestad–F.M.C.). Frelst! frelst! (Berggreen–F.M.C.). Som markens blomst (Handel–F.M.C.). Guds menighed (Stephen Foster–F.M.C.). Høstsang (O. Paulson–F.M.C.). Farvel, farvel (Wennerberg–F.M.C.).

Fem Koraler (Augsburg, 1906): Vor Gud han er saa fast en borg (Luther–F.M.C.). Zions vaegter haever røsten (Nicolai–F.M.C.). Sørg, o kjaere Fader,

---

*The Augsburg Publishing House, Minneapolis, Minnesota, is referred to throughout as Augsburg.

APPENDIXES

du (Lindeman–F.M.C.). Nu rinder solen op (Zinck's Koralbog–F.M.C.). Af
Høiheden oprunden er (Nicolai–F.M.C.).

Vuggesang om Julekvaelden (arr. for violin and piano. Oslo: Haakon Zaphe,
1907).

Sangerfesthefte No. 1 (Augsburg, 1905): Fuga: It Was Meet that We Should
Make Merry. Behold What Manner of Love. Peasant Wedding March
(Søderman). Mellem glaedens liljer (Vogtländer). Hav tak, Gud og Fader
(Swedish folk melody–F.M.C.). Den store hvide flok (Grieg's arr. for men's
chorus—arr. by F.M.C. for mixed chorus with alto solo). Herre, raek mig.
Bøn (from Handel's "Theodora"). Ungdomssang (Prince Gustav–F.M.C.).
Det ringer (Kjerulf–F.M.C.).

Nationalsange for det skandinavisk-amerikanske folk (Augsburg, 1913): America. Star-Spangled Banner. Norsk faedrelandssang. Du gamla, du fria. Det er
et land.

Sange for blandet Kor (Augsburg, 1914): Hvad er det godt at landet.
Paaskemorgen slukker sorgen. Deilig er jorden (Crusaders' Hymn–F.M.C.).
O hoved høit forhaanet (Hassler–F.M.C.). Lover den Herre (Søhren–
F.M.C.). O Gladsome Light. I Know That My Redeemer Liveth (arr.
F.M.C.). Lamb of God (Søderman). He Is Blessed (Søderman). Hosanna
(Søderman). The Heavens Are Telling. Vor Gud han er saa fast en borg
(Luther–F.M.C.).

Sanggudstjeneste No. 1 (Augsburg, 1907): Kirken den er et gammelt hus
(Lindeman–F.M.C.). I arme synd're. O Jesus se (J. Shop–F.M.C.). I Jesus
søger jeg min fred. O Guds lam uskyldig (German chorale, 1540—arr.
F.M.C.). Sørg, o kjaere Fader du (Lindeman–F.M.C.). Velt alle dine veie
(Mendelssohn–F.M.C.). Jesus, Jesus, Jesus sigter (Lindeman–F.M.C.).
Hjem jeg laenges (Lindeman–F.M.C.). Zions vaegter (Nicolai–F.M.C.).
Den store hvide flok (Grieg–F.M.C.).

Sanggudstjeneste No. 2 (Augsburg, 1908): Et suk igjennem verden gaar.
Bryt frem (Lindeman–F.M.C.). Nu har jeg findet (Neumark–F.M.C.).
O hoved høit forhaanet (Hassler–F.M.C.). Staa fast, min sjael (Zinck's
Koralbog–F.M.C.). Taenk, naar engang (folk melody—arr. F.M.C.). O
taenk, naar engang samles skal (Hermann–F.M.C.).

Sanggudstjeneste No. 3 (Augsburg, 1910): Synger for Herren. Fra grennen ta
din harpe ned. Jeg staar for Gud. Hjerte, lad dig ei indbilde. Jeg saa ham
som barn. Deilig er jorden (Crusaders' Hymn–F.M.C.). Lover den Herre
(Søhren–F.M.C.).

Song-Service No. 4 (Augsburg, 1913): Lord, to Thee I Make Confession.
The Lord Is Full of Compassion. O Bread of Life (Isaac–F.M.C.). Alone
with Thee (Conradi–F.M.C.). The Cross.

Song-Service No. 5 (Augsburg, 1913): Retirement. Lord of Spirits I Surrender
(Reissiger–F.M.C.). Built on a Rock (Lindeman–F.M.C.). The Millennium.
Wake, Awake (Nicolai–F.M.C.).

Sanggudstjeneste No. 6 (Augsburg, 1914): O Jesus se (J. Shop–F.M.C.).
Et undres jeg paa. Hjem jeg laenges (Kjerulf). Fred til bod (Hartmann–
F.M.C.). Op dog, Sion.

MUSIC MASTER OF THE MIDDLE WEST

Song-Service No. 7 (Augsburg, 1916): In Heaven Above (Lindeman–F.M.C.). My Spirit Longeth for Thee. Go and Let My Grave Be Made (Swedish folk melody—arr. F.M.C.). Give Praise.

Lette lyrisk-religiøse Sange No. 1 (Augsburg, 1910): Paaskemorgen. Fred hviler over land og by. Vaaren. Kom Helligaand. Suk. Der skinner en sol. Nu sol i øst oprinder mild. Ungbirken.

Lette lyrisk-religiøse Sange No. 2 (Augsburg, 1910): Bøn. Kun dagligdags. Sukket. Ungdomssang. Du deilige jul. Lysets engel. Naar ene jeg paa veien gaar. Begravelse. Alt staar i Guds faderhaand.

Lette lyrisk-religiøse Sange No. 3 (Augsburg, 1911): Jeg fik en trøst. Det er vaar. Syng kun op! Aa hjelp meg du. Morens sang. Syng med os. Fra himmelen. Laer mig, o skov!

Lette lyrisk-religiøse Sange No. 4 (Augsburg, 1911): Du sidste sommerskjaer. Der ringes paa jord. Laer mig, nattens stjerne. Der er en vei. I skyggen. Et liv i Gud. Den rette dyders mor. Lyksalig det folk.

Lette lyrisk-religiøse Sange No. 5 (Augsburg, 1914): Julen gaar ind. Velkommen igjen. Guds engle i flok. Julen har englelyd. Nu juletraer hjerterne fryder.

Lette lyrisk-religiøse Sange No. 6 (Augsburg, 1916): Som foraarssolen. Løft din bølge. Som den gyldne sol. Som kongebrud.

Lette lyrisk-religiøse Sange No. 7 (Augsburg, 1916): Der gaar et stille tog. Fremad, frem til dristig faerd! Og var det lidet. Jeg ved en blomst.

Lette lyrisk-religiøse Sange No. 8 (Augsburg, 1916): Kom regn fra det høie. Guds søn steg ned at tjene. Veiret. De fagre blomster. Skjøn er morgenstunden. I al sin glans.

The Lutheran Hymnary (Augsburg, 1913) contains the following Christiansen arrangements of chorales: Wie schön leuchtet (Nicolai–F.M.C.). Aus meines Herzens Grunde (German chorale, 1598–F.M.C.). Gaa nu hen og grav min Grav (Swedish melody–F.M.C:). Herr Jesu Christ, dich zu uns wend (Cantionale Sacrum, Gotha, 1651–F.M.C.). Herzlich thut mich verlangen (Neumark–F.M.C.). Wer nur den lieben Gott lässt walten (Neumark–F.M.C.). Kommt her zu mir, spricht Gottes Sohn (German chorale, 1530–F.M.C.). Lobt Gott, ihr Christen (Hermann–F.M.C.). Lobe den Herren, den mächtigen König (Søhren–F.M.C.). Nagelt til et Kors paa Jorden (Zinck's Koralbog, 1801–F.M.C.). Nun ruhen alle Wälder (Isaac–F.M.C.). Nu lader os da grave ned (Hermann–F.M.C.). Nu rinder solen op (Zinck's Koralbog–F.M.C.). O Traurigkeit, O Herzeleid (German chorale, 1628–F.M.C.). O Jesus, for din Pine (Kingo's Gradual, 1699–F.M.C.). O Lam Gottes, unschuldig (German chorale, 1540–F.M.C.). Op alle, som paa Jorden bor (Hermann, 1560–F.M.C.). Paa Gud alene (Zinck's Koralbog, 1801–F.M.C.). Straf mich nicht (Rosenmüller, 1655–F.M.C.).

Sangerhilsen No. 1 (Oslo: A. M. Hanche Forlag, 1920): Vaar i mit hjerte. Guds fred. Fryd dig. Ved kveld. Hvad jeg vil. Lovsynger Herrens navn.

Sangerhilsen No. 2 (Oslo: A. M. Hanche Forlag, n. d.): Zions vaegter haever røsten (Nicolai–F.M.C.).

212

APPENDIXES

Sangerhilsen No. 3 (Oslo: A. M. Hanche Forlag, n. d.): Kirken den er et gammelt hus (Lindeman–F.M.C.). I Himmelen, i Himmelen (Lindeman–F.M.C.).

Sangerhilsen No. 4 (Oslo: A. M. Hanche Forlag, n. d.): Morgenglans av evigheit (Freylinghausen, 1704–F.M.C.). Nu rinder solen op (Zinck's Koralbog, 1801–F.M.C.).

ST. OLAF CHOIR SERIES*

Volume I (1919): 1. Arise, Shine (G. F. Cobb). 2. Asleep in Jesus (Ole Bull). 3. But the Lord Is Mindful of His Own (Mendelssohn). 4. Come to Me (Anon.). 5. Evening Hymn (Witt). 6. Hymn (F. Schubert). 7. If With All Your Hearts (Mendelssohn). 8. Morning (Mendelssohn). 9. Now Is Christ Risen (J. M. Bach). 10. Now the Day Is Over (Oscar Borg). 11. Now the Shades of Night Are Gone (Le Clerc). 12. O Son of God (Curschmann). 13. Praise Ye the Lord (C. Palmer). 14. Sanctus (Luigi Cherubini). 15. Sanctus (Gounod). 16. Sing! Unto the Lord (Mozart). 17. The Guiding Star (Kjerulf). 18. The Light of Bethlehem (F. Abt). 19. The Love of God (Mozart). 20. The Sabbath Call (Kreutzer). 21. The Way Is Long and Dreary (Spitta). 22. The Word of God (Grieg). 23. Thou Wilt Keep Him (George Leach). 24. Upward (H. Wetterling—ladies' voices). 25. What Holy Calm (Beethoven).

Volume II (1919): 26. A Song of Praise (Beethoven). 27. A Cheerful Heart (C. Isenmann). 28. And the Glory of the Lord (Handel). 29. Behold a Host (Grieg). 30. Behold I Bring You Good Tidings (John Goss). 31. Blessed Is He Who Cometh (Gounod). 32. Break Forth into Joy (J. Barnby). 33. Funeral Hymn (F. A. Reissiger). 34. Hail to the Brightness (F. A. Reissiger). 35. Heavenly Dwelling (F. Schubert). 36. How Beautiful (J. Stainer). 37. Jubilate, Amen (Kjerulf). 38. Landsighting (Grieg). 39. Near Is the Lord (J. Rheinberger). 40. O Rest in the Lord (Mendelssohn). 41. Parting and Meeting (Mendelssohn). 42. Pilgrims' Chorus (Wagner). 43. Pleasant Are Thy Courts (W. Lagerkrantz—ladies' voices). 44. Praise Ye the Lord (M. Vulpius). 45. Prayer (F. H. Himmel). 46. Song of the Pilgrim (J. S. Bach). 47. The Promised Land (A. Søderman). 48. Those Eternal Bowers (Joh. Svendsen). 49. Thine, O Lord (James Kent). 50. 'Tis the Evening's Holy Hour (Beethoven).

Volume III (1920): 51. Beautiful Savior (Crusaders' Hymn–F.M.C.). 52. Before Thee, God. 53. Christmas Hymn (chorale—arr. F.M.C.). 54. Come Thou Last Summer Ray. 55. Dayspring of Eternity (arr. F.M.C.). 56. Grace Wonderful. 57. Hosanna. 58. Prayer. 59. Take Down Thy Harp. 60. The Flower of Love. 61. The Mother's Song. 62. The Rainbow Bridge of Prayer. 63. Today There Is Ringing. 64. The Vision of Christ (Norwegian folk song —arr. F.M.C.). 65. Wondrous Things the Lord Hath Done.

Volume IV (1920): 66. Angel Bright. 67. Ascension. 68. As Sinks Beneath the Ocean. 69. A Life in God. 70. Cast Down, Yet Hoping in God. 71. Father Most Holy (Crüger–F.M.C.). 72. Funeral Hymn. 73. O Happy Day (folk song—arr. F.M.C.). 74. Onward. 75. O Sacred Head (Hassler–F.M.C.).

*Compiled and edited by F. M. Christiansen, Augsburg.

MUSIC MASTER OF THE MIDDLE WEST

76. Praise to the Lord (Søhren–F.M.C.). 77. Sighing Soul, Hear. 78. The Bride of the King. 79. The Christian Virtues' Mother. 80. The Enchanting Word.

Volume V (1922): 81. How Fair the Church of Christ Shall Stand (Schumann's Gesangbuch, 1539–F.M.C.). 82. Psalm 50. 83. God Our Father. 84. Hear Me. 85. Night, and a Lonely Star. 86. Come, Thou Savior of Our Race (Erfurt Enchiridion, 1524–F.M.C.). 87. All My Heart. 88. O Darkest Woe (J. Shop–F.M.C.). 89. The Morning Star (Nicolai–F.M.C.). 90. In dulci jubilo. 91. This Is the Sight That Gladdens (Crüger–F.M.C.). 92. O Wondrous Type (pre-Reformation chorale–F.M.C.). 93. Welcome. 94. Christmas Hath Angels' Voice. 95. The Christmas Tree.

Volume VI (1926): 96. Good Tidings to Zion. 97. Put Up the Sword! 98. O Absalom, My Son! 99. Brethren (J. Chr. Bach–F.M.C.). 100. A Snow Mountain. 101. From Heaven Above (Schumann's Gesangbuch–F.M.C.). 102. Wake, Awake (Nicolai–F.M.C.). 103. O Bread of Life (Isaac–F.M.C). 104. Built on a Rock (Lindeman–F.M.C.). 105. Deck Thyself, My Soul, with Gladness (Crüger–F.M.C.). 106. In Heaven Above (Norwegian folk song–F.M.C.). 107. Light of Light (chorale—arr. F.M.C.). 108. Give Praise (chorale—arr. F.M.C.). 109. A Christmas Carol.

Volume VII (1932): 110. Clap Your Hands. 111. Thou Art, O God. 112. Blest Are the Pure in Heart. 113. Source of Calm Repose (Norwegian folk song—arr. F.M.C.). 114. Here, As We Come. 115. Be True. 116. So Soberly and Softly (Norwegian folk song–F.M.C.). 117. Consider the Lilies. 118. Thou Grace Divine. 119. Lost in the Night (Finnish folk song–F.M.C.). 120. Rise My Soul. 121. What Joy to Reach the Harbor (Norwegian folk song–F.M.C.). 122. The Fairest of Roses (melody from 1542—arr. F.M.C.). 123. Lord of Spirits (Reissiger–F.M.C.). 124. When God Paints the Sunset (Norwegian folk song–F.M.C.). 125. Celestial Spring (a motet-cycle in four movements): No. I, The Spirit's Yearning. 126. Celestial Spring: No. II, Exaltation. 127. Celestial Spring: No. III, Regeneration. 128. Celestial Spring: No. IV, Glorification.

Volume VIII (1933): 129. Thy Kingdom Come. 130. Vigil. 131. Hallelujah to the Lord. 132. Here Leave Your Sorrow. 133. Lamb of God (German chorale —arr. F.M.C.). 134. The Old Home. 135. Good-Will and Peace. 136. Lullaby on Christmas Eve. 137. Bridal Song. 138. Aspiration. 139. Joy. 140. Sunbeam Out of Heaven. 141. Vistas of Song. 142. Blessed Jesus. 143. This Night. 144. Behold a Host (Grieg–F.M.C.). 145. Temples Eternal. 146. Christmas Starlight. 147. Angels Made an Arbor. 148. Evening Hymn. 149. Beautiful Yuletide. 150. Kingdom of God.

Volume IX (1935): 151. (a) Lamb of God, (b) He Is Blessed (Søderman). 152. Hosanna in the Highest (arr. F.M.C.). 153. Marah. 154. The Voice Within. 155. Rock and Refuge (Norwegian folk song—arr. F.M.C.). 156. Longing for Home (Norwegian folk song—arr. F.M.C.). 157. A Carpenter Cut the Manger Wood. 158. The Yuletide. 159. O Heart Attuned to Sadness (Norwegian folk song—arr. F.M.C.). 160. Golden Harps Are Sounding (arr. F.M.C.). 161. I Know That My Redeemer Liveth (arr. F.M.C.). 162. I Know a Home Eternal (arr. F.M.C.). 163. Sabbath Morn (arr. F.M.C.).

APPENDIXES

164. Father, O Hear Me (arr. F.M.C.). 165. The Heavens Resound (arr. F.M.C.). 166. In Heavenly Love (Mendelssohn–F.M.C.).

Volume X (1936): 167. There Is a Song on Zion's Mountains. 168. Sing, and Let Your Song Be New. 169. Day Is Dying. 170. Sing Praise to God 171. Song of Praise (J. S. Bach–F.M.C.). 172. Come Soothing Death (J. S. Bach–F.M.C.). 173. Easter Bells. 174. From Grief to Glory: Verse I, Decadence. 175. From Grief to Glory: Verse II, Love in Grief. 176. From Grief to Glory: Verse III, Spring Returns. 177. From Grief to Glory: Verse IV, Life. 178. My God How Wonderful (from the Scotch Psalter, 1615—arr. F.M.C.). 179. Mother's Day Song (Norse folk song—arr. F.M.C.). 180. King of Glory. 181. Lo, How a Rose (Praetorius—arr. F.M.C.).

Volume XI (1938–41): 182. The New Song (Norwegian folk song—arr F.M.C.). 183. A Son of God (Gastorius—arr. F.M.C.). 184. What Is Life 185. Beauty in Humility. 186. Immortal Love. 187. A Cradle Hymn. 188. Thine Be the Glory. 189. Christ in the Temple. 190. Deep Within. 191. When Curtained Darkness. 192. Born Anew. 193. The Sun Has Gone Down. 194. The Spires. 195. There Many Shall Come. 196. Wonders Are Wrought. 197. At Dayspring. 198. I Praise Thee (J. B. König–F.M.C.). 199. Have Mercy and Spare (chorale from Kingo's Gradual, 1699—arr. F.M.C.). 200. Heaven and Earth.

Volume XII (1942–44): 201. Let All Mortal Flesh Keep Silence (French folk song–F.M.C.). 202. Unto Us. 203. My Peace I Give unto Thee. 204. O Darkest Woe, No. 2 (German chorale–F.M.C.). 205. What Thanks I Owe Thee. 206. O Day Full of Grace (Weyse–F.M.C.). 207. As Sinks Beneath the Ocean, No. 2. 208. A Poet Lived in Galilee (Swedish folk tune–F.M.C.). 209. Thy Kingdom Come, O Lord. 210. Thy Word. 211. Through the Solemn Midnight Ringing. 212. My Psalm. 213. Two Wedding Songs, S.S.A. 214. Bless the Lord, O My Soul. 215. It Came upon the Midnight Clear. 216. The Angel's Hand.

ADDITIONAL SONGS FOR MIXED VOICES

I'll Go Home Again (Chicago: Neil Kjos, 1940)

As Pearly Raindrops Play (Chicago: Neil Kjos, 1941)

Autumn's Art (Chicago: Neil Kjos, 1942)

Song of Mary (Chicago: Neil Kjos, 1942)

LADIES' VOICES

Fifty Famous Hymns (Augsburg, 1914)

MEN'S VOICES

Kor- og Kvartetsang for Mansstemmer (Augsburg, 1902): Ungdomssang. Steinbrytervise. Aftensang. Ungbirken. Moderens sang.

Ud! Ud! (Oslo: Norsk Musikforlag, n. d.)

Aa eg veit meg eit land (Oslo: Norsk Musikforlag, n. d.)

Som sol gaar ned i havet (Oslo: Norsk Musikforlag, n. d.)

MUSIC MASTER OF THE MIDDLE WEST

VIOLIN

Kjølstavisa (New York: Carl Fischer, 1903)

Romance (New York: Carl Fischer, 1903)

PIANO

Bonny Castle Waltzes (Chicago: National Music Co., 1892)

ORGAN

St. Olaf Organ Series (Augsburg, n. d.): Canon in the Octave. Consolation. Festival Overture. Folk-tone. Funeral March No. 1. Funeral March No. 2. Hope. Hymn and Prayer. Legende. March. March Triumphale. Melody in G. Offertory in F, No. 1. Offertory in F, No. 2. Pastoral. Prayer. Prelude and Fuga. Song. Sunday Morning. The Shepherd Flute. Vision.

Organ Music for Church and Home (edited by F.M.C., Augsburg, 1942): Jesu, Joy of Man's Desiring (J. S. Bach). Sorrow (F.M.C.). Built on the Rock (Lindeman–C. Teilman). Melody (Christian Sinding). A Psalmtune (E. Grieg). The Last Voyage (E. Alnaes). Margretes Cradlesong (E. Grieg). Jesus Is My All (Folksong). Andantino (Folksong). Prelude (J. Haarklou). Thema (Beethoven). Adagio (Mendelssohn). Saeter Jentens Søndag (O. Bull). Air from Suite No. 5 (Handel). Andante (Mozart). Chorus from "Judas Maccabaeus" (Handel). Lied ohne Worte (Mendelssohn). Evening Prayer (J. Svendsen). Largo (Handel). Bridal March from "Lohengrin" (Wagner). Dead March from "Saul" ·(Handel). Ave Maris Stella (E. Grieg). Prelude (Rink). Wedding March (Mendelssohn). Jubilate (S. Lie). Chorale (I. Holter). Ritornello (O. Olsen). Jubilate, Amen (H. Kjerulf). Andante Funèbre (J. Svendsen). Melody (J. Halvorsen). Prelude (Chr. Cappelen). A Hymn (E. Alnaes). Aases Death (E. Grieg). Prelude (Chopin). Fuga (J. S. Bach). Supplication (F.M.C.). Albumblatt (E. Neupert). Lullaby on Christmas Eve (F.M.C.).

BAND

First Norwegian Rhapsody (Witmark, 1932)

Second Norwegian Rhapsody (Witmark, 1938)

MISCELLANEOUS

The Collects of the Lutheran Church (with C. A. Mellby. Augsburg, 1916)

Song Festival Collection (Augsburg, 1917)

Chorales and Choruses (Augsburg, 1920)

Hymns and Choruses (Augsburg, 1923)

School of Choir Singing (Augsburg, 1917)

Practical Modulation (Augsburg, 1917)

A Cappella Chorus Book: For Mixed Voices (edited by F. M. Christiansen and N. Cain. Introduction by W. A. Fisher. New York: Oliver Ditson, 1932)

Young Men's Choral Assembly for Schools (New York: G. Schirmer, n. d.)

Tours

OF THE ST. OLAF LUTHERAN CHOIR
1920–44

Year	Area	Months	Year	Area	Months
1920	East	April	1931	South	January–February
1921	East	April	1932	East and	January–February
1922	East	January–February		South	
1923	Midwest	April	1933	Midwest	April
1924	West	December–January	1934	East	January–February
	Central	April	1935	East	January–February
1925	West	January	1936	Central	April
1926	East and	April	1937	West	April
	South		1938	East	January–February
1927	East	January	1939	Central	April
	West	June–July	1940	West	January–February
1928	Central	January–February	1941	East	January–February
	and South		1942	South	January–February
1929	East	January–February	1943	Midwest	April
1930	East	January–February	1944*	Midwest	April
	Europe	June–August			

*Christiansen retired as the active director of the choir during this year. He did not accompany the group on its annual tour.

Programs

OF THE ST. OLAF LUTHERAN CHOIR
1912–44

1912

Der ringes paa jord ....Christiansen
Deilig er jorden (Crusaders' Hymn) ....Folk melody—Christiansen
Song Cycle ....A. Søderman
    a. Lamb of God   b. He Is Blessed   c. Hosanna
I Know That My Redeemer Liveth ....Handel–Christiansen
Jeg saa ham som barn ....Norwegian folk song–Christiansen
O Jesus, se ....Shop–Christiansen
O hoved høit forhaanet ....Hassler–Christiansen
Som sol gaar ned i havet ....Christiansen
Det ringer fra alle taarne ....Kjerulf–Christiansen
Lover den Herre ....Søhren–Christiansen

1913
(NORWAY)

Der ringes paa jord ....Christiansen
Moderens Sang ....Christiansen
Hvad est du dog skjøn ....Grieg
Lover den Herre ....Søhren–Christiansen

Come Ye Disconsolate ....Samuel Webbe
Still, Still with Thee ....Franz Abt
Lead Kindly Light ....Franz Abt
Ladies' Quartet

Alone with Thee ....J. G. Conradi
Deilig er jorden (Crusaders' Hymn) ....Folk melody–Christiansen
Fra "Hør os Herre"—Sang-cyklus ....A. Søderman
Som sol gaar ned ....Christiansen
Wake, Awake ....Nicolai–Christiansen

1914

Der ringes paa jord ....Christiansen
O Jesu, se min Skam og Ve ....Arr. by Christiansen
Lover den Herre ....Søhren–Christiansen

Holy Spirit Dove Divine ....Gottschalk
Den store hvide flok ....Grieg–Christiansen
Still, Still with Thee ....Franz Abt
Ladies' Quartet

218

APPENDIXES

Built on a Rock ....Lindeman–Christiansen
Kun dagligdags ....Christiansen
Herre, hvor laenge? ....Handel–Christiansen
Deilig er jorden (Crusaders' Hymn) ....Folk melody–Christiansen
Retirement ....Christiansen
Domine Exaudi ....Grieg
O Bread of Life ....Isaac–Christiansen
Wake, Awake ....Nicolai–Christiansen

1917
In Heavenly Love Abiding ....Mendelssohn
My God, My God (Psalm 22) ....Mendelssohn
How Blest Are They ....Tschaikowsky

Violin Solo:
Second Movement from D-minor Concerto ....Wieniawski
Souvenir ....Drdla
Miss Alma Rasmussen

O hoved høit forhaanet ....Hassler–Christiansen
O Bread of Life ....Isaac–Christiansen
In Heaven Above ....Lindeman–Christiansen
Lover den Herre ....Søhren–Christiansen
Violin Solo:
Air for the G String ....Bach
Romance ....Svendsen
Deilig er jorden (Crusaders' Hymn) ....Folk melody–Christiansen
Som sol gaar ned ....Christiansen
Taenk naar engang ....Folk melody–Christiansen
Wake, Awake ....Nicolai–Christiansen

1918
In Heavenly Love Abiding ....Mendelssohn
Cherubim Song ....Glinka
In Heaven Above ....Lindeman–Christiansen
Christmas Song ....Rimsky-Korsakoff
O Praise Ye ....Arensky
The Nightingale ....Tschaikowsky
Song Cycle ....Søderman
    a. Lamb of God   b. He Is Blessed   c. Hosanna
Moderens Sang ....Christiansen
Som sol gaar ned ....Christiansen
Wake, Awake ....Nicolai–Christiansen

1920
(FIRST EASTERN TOUR)
Blessing, Glory, and Wisdom ....Bach
Praise to the Lord ....Søhren–Christiansen
Built on a Rock ....Lindeman–Christiansen

MUSIC MASTER OF THE MIDDLE WEST

A Mighty Fortress Is Our God ....Luther–Christiansen
The Word of God ....Grieg
Savior of Sinners ....Mendelssohn
O God, Hear My Prayer ....Gretchaninoff
Father, Most Holy ....Crüger
Hosanna ....Christiansen
Beautiful Savior (Crusaders' Hymn) ....Folk melody–Christiansen
Wake, Awake ....Nicolai–Christiansen

1921

The Spirit Also Helpeth Us ....Bach
Truth Eternal ....Gustav Schreck
Song Cycle ....Søderman
O Praise Ye God ....Tschaikowsky
Bless the Lord ....Tschesnokoff
Agnus Dei ....Kalinnikof
O How Shall I Receive Thee (Motet for Advent) ......Gustav Schreck
The Morning Star ....Nicolai–Christiansen
Built on a Rock ....'.Lindeman–Christiansen
All My Heart ....Ebeling–Christiansen
A Christmas Song ....Christiansen
In dulci jubilo ....14th century melody–Christiansen

1922

The Spirit Also Helpeth Us ....Bach
O Sacred Head Now Wounded ....Hassler–Christiansen
How Fair the Church of Christ Shall Stand ....Chorale from
                          Schumann's Gesangbuch–arr. by Christiansen
It Is a Good Thing (Psalm 92) ....Georg Schumann
Yea Through Death's Gloomy Vale (Psalm 23) ....Georg Schumann
Lord, How Long? (Psalm 13) ....Georg Schumann
O How Shall I Receive Thee (Motet for Advent) ....Gustav Schreck
Praise the Lord, O My Soul ....Gretchaninoff
A Christmas Song ....Christiansen
In dulci jubilo ....14th century melody–Christiansen
Praise to the Lord ....Søhren–Christiansen

1923

Be Not Afraid ....Bach
O Darkest Woe ....Shop–Christiansen
This Is the Sight that Gladdens ....Crüger–Christiansen
Magnificat ....Stanley Avery
The Morning Star ....Nicolai–Christiansen
Earth, in Singing ....Schumann
In dulci jubilo ....14th century melody–Christiansen
O How Shall I Receive Thee (Motet for Advent) ......Gustav Schreck
Nunc dimittis ....Gretchaninoff
How Fair the Church of Christ Shall Stand ....Chorale from
                          Schumann's Gesangbuch–arr. by Christiansen
Psalm 50 ....Christiansen

APPENDIXES

1924

Come, Jesu, Come ....Bach
O Wondrous Type ....Latin chorale–Christiansen
A Crown of Grace ....Brahms
Make Me, O Lord God, Pure in Heart ....Brahms
Our Father ....Gretchaninoff
Come, Thou Savior of Our Race ....Latin chorale–Christiansen
O Sacred Head Now Wounded ....Hassler–Christiansen
Hosanna ....Gustav Schreck
Who Can Comprehend Thee? ....Peter Lutkin
Glory Be to God ....Rachmaninoff
The Three Kings ....Catalonian Nativity Song–arr. by Romeau
Wake, Awake ....Nicolai–Christiansen

1925

Sing Ye ....Bach
O Bread of Life ....Isaac–Christiansen
Hosanna ....Christiansen
Beautiful Savior (Crusaders' Hymn) ....Folk melody–Christiansen
Savior of Sinners ....Felix Mendelssohn
How Fair the Church of Christ Shall Stand ....Chorale from
                            Schumann's Gesangbuch–arr. by Christiansen
Welcome ....Christiansen
O How Shall I Receive Thee (Motet for Advent) ....Gustav Schreck
Our Father ....Gretchaninoff
A Snow Mountain ....Christiansen
In dulci jubilo ....14th century melody–Christiansen
Wake, Awake ....Nicolai–Christiansen

1926

Sing Ye ....Bach
Misericordias domini ....Durante
Benedictus qui venit ....Liszt
Put Up the Sword ....Christiansen
Yea Through Death's Gloomy Vale ....Georg Schumann
Come, Guest Divine ....Georg Schumann
From Heaven Above ....Chorale from Schumann's
                                   Gesangbuch–arr. by Christiansen
Whence, Then, Cometh Wisdom? ....Gustav Schreck
O Sacred Head Now Wounded ....Hassler–Christiansen
Deck Thyself, My Soul, With Gladness ....Crüger–Christiansen
In Heaven Above ....Lindeman–Christiansen
Praise to the Lord.............................Søhren–Christiansen

1927

The Spirit Also Helpeth Us ....Bach
Cherubim Song ....Glinka
Deck Thyself, My Soul, with Gladness ....Crüger–Christiansen
Benedictus qui venit ....Liszt

221

Now Sinks the Sun ....Horatio W. Parker
Two Sacred Folk Songs ....Grieg
    Hvad est du dog skjøn   Gudsson har gjort mig frie
O Gladsome Light ....Gretchaninoff
Two German Christmas Songs ....Arr. by Kranz
    Heiligste Nacht   Geistliches Wiegenlied
O How Shall I Receive Thee (Motet for Advent)........Gustav Schreck

1928

Jesu, Priceless Treasure (from the motet) ....Bach
How Fair the Church of Christ Shall Stand ....Chorale from
                Schumann's Gesangbuch–arr. by Christiansen
Go, Song of Mine ....Edward Elgar
Hosanna ....Christiansen
May Our Mouths Be Filled with Thy Praise ....Rachmaninoff
Salvation Is Created ....Tschesnokoff
From Heaven Above ....Chorale from
                Schumann's Gesangbuch–arr. by Christiansen
The Morning Star ....Nicolai–Christiansen
So Soberly ....Norwegian folk melody–Christiansen
Marienlied ....Arr. by Fisher
Wake, Awake ....Nicolai–Christiansen

1929

Sing Ye ....Bach
Misericordias domini ....Durante
The Morning Star ....Nicolai–Christiansen
Go, Song of Mine ....Edward Elgar
Be Thyself My Surety Now ....Max Reger
Mary's Cradle Song on the Twelfth Day ....Georg Schumann
Ihr Kinder Zions freut euch ....Arnold Mendelssohn
Glory Be to God ....Rachmaninoff
So Soberly ....Norwegian folk melody–Christiansen
Clap Your Hands ....:....Christiansen
Beautiful Savior (Crusaders' Hymn) ....Folk melody–Christiansen

1930
(EUROPEAN TOUR)

Sing Ye ....Bach
Cherubim Song ....Glinka
Benedictus qui venit ....Liszt
Nu funden er den Saele Stund ....Christiansen
O hoved høit forhaanet ....Hassler–Christiansen
Savior of Sinners ....Felix Mendelssohn
Deilig er jorden (Crusaders' Hymn) ....Folk melody–Christiansen
O How Shall I Receive Thee (Motet for Advent).......Gustav Schreck
Himmelen, i Himmelen ....Lindeman–Christiansen
Lost in the Night ....Finnish folk song–Christiansen
Wake, Awake ....Nicolai–Christiansen

APPENDIXES

1931

Be Not Afraid ....Bach
All Creatures of Our God and King ....Armstrong Gibbs
Come Holy Spirit ....Georg Schumann
O Praise Ye God ....Tschaikowsky
Agnus Dei ....Kalinnikoff
Regeneration ....Christiansen
A Snow Mountain ....Christiansen
Psalm 50 ....Christiansen
Motet zum Weihnachtsfest ....Arnold Mendelssohn
Salvation Is Created ....Tschesnokoff
Hosanna ....Christiansen
Marienlied ....Arr. by F. A. Fisher
Beautiful Savior (Crusaders' Hymn) ....Folk melody–Christiansen

1932

Agnus Dei ....Kalinnikoff
This Is the Sight That Gladdens ....Crüger–Christiansen
Be Not Afraid ....Bach
Be Jubilant My Spirit ....Heinrich Schmid
When God Paints the Sunset.................Folk melody–Christiansen
Celestial Spring ....Christiansen
      I. The Spirit's Yearning   II. Exaltation
     III. Regeneration   IV. Glorification
Das Geläut zu Speir ....Ludwig Senfl
O Praise Ye God ....Tschaikowsky
Two German Christmas Songs ....Arr. by Kranz
     Heiligste Nacht   Geistliches Wiegenlied
Praise to the Lord ....Søhren–Christiansen

1933

Our Father ....Gretchaninoff
Three Sacred Songs ....Georg Schumann
     Yea, Through the Vale   Behold, How Good
       How Long Wilt Thou Forget
Hvad est du dog skjøn ....Grieg
Celestial Spring ....Christiansen
Magnificat ....Stanley Avery
Creator of Beauty ....Christiansen
All My Heart This Night Rejoices ....Christiansen
O How Shall I Receive Thee (Motet for Advent)........Gustav Schreck

1934

O God Our Great Jehovah ....Richard Kountz
Here Leave Your Sorrow ....Danish folk melody–Christiansen
Misericordias domini ....Durante
Sing Ye ....Bach
Our Days Are As a Shadow ....Bach

It Is a Good Thing to Give Thanks ....Schvedof
Hosanna ....Christiansen
Regeneration ....Christiansen
Savior of Sinners ....Felix Mendelssohn
Beyond the Haze ....Paul Christiansen
So Soberly ....Folk song–Christiansen
Lullaby on Christmas Eve ....Christiansen
Beautiful Savior (Crusaders' Hymn) ....Folk melody–Christiansen

1935

Ascendit Deus ....Jacobus Gallus
Angels Made an Arbor ....Christiansen
Hvad est du dog skjøn ....Grieg
Sing Ye ....Bach
Yea, through the Vale of Death ....Georg Schumann
Behold, How Good ....Georg Schumann
Psalm 50 ....Christiansen
Kingdom of God ....16th century chorale–Christiansen
Heiligste Nacht ....Arr. by Kranz
O Heart Attuned to Sadness ....Swedish folk song–Christiansen
Vistas of Song ....Christiansen

1936

Be Not Afraid ....Bach
Come, Soothing Death ....Bach
Song of Praise ....Bach
Wake, Awake ....Nicolai–Christiansen
Kingdom of God ....16th century chorale–Christiansen
From Grief to Glory ....Christiansen
    I. Decadence   II. Love in Grief   III. Spring Returns   IV. Life
Rock and Refuge ....Swedish folk melody–arr. by Christiansen
Vistas of Song ....Christiansen
From Heaven Above ....Chorale from
    Schumann's Gesangbuch–arr. by Christiansen
O How Shall I Receive Thee (Motet for Advent) ....Gustav Schreck

1937

Finale from "Apostrophe to the Heavenly Host" ....Healy Willan
The Spirit Also Helpeth Us ....Bach
Nunc dimittis ....Gretchaninoff
Autumn Woods ....Paul Christiansen
When God Paints the Sunset............Norse folk melody–Christiansen
Exaltation (Part II, Celestial Spring) ....Christiansen
Regeneration (Part III, Celestial Spring) ....Christiansen
Easter Bells ....Christiansen
In excelsis gloria ....Breton melody–arr. by Morton Luvaas
Thanksgiving Motet ....Arnold Mendelssohn
Lost in the Night ....Finnish folk melody–Christiansen
Beautiful Savior (Crusaders' Hymn) ....Folk melody–Christiansen

1938

Sing Ye ....Bach
Hvad est du dog skjøn ....Grieg
Misericordias domini ....Durante
Finale from "Apostrophe to the Heavenly Host" ....Healy Willan
Cherubim Song ....Glinka
We Have No Other Guide ....Schvedof
The Twenty-Third Psalm ....Gustav Schreck
Autumn Woods ....Paul Christiansen
Lo, How a Rose E'er Blooming ....Rhenish folk melody–Christiansen
Beauty in Humility ....Christiansen
Lost in the Night ....Finnish folk melody–Christiansen
Praise to the Lord ....Søhren–Christiansen

1939

Be Not Afraid ....Bach
Tenebrae Factae Sunt ....Palestrina
Psalm 50 ....Christiansen
O Thou Gladsome Light ....Gretchaninoff
Unto the Lord ....Paul Christiansen
Magnificat ....Paul Christiansen
Benedictus ....E. Paladilhe
O Be Joyful, All Ye Lands ....Gretchaninoff
Clap Your Hands ....Christiansen
Aspiration ....Norse folk melody–Christiansen
Wake, Awake ....Nicolai–Christiansen

1940

O Praise Ye God ....Tschaikowsky
Tenebrae Factae Sunt ....Marc Antonio Ingegneri
Restoration ....Benjamin Edwards
O How Shall I Receive Thee (Motet for Advent) ....Gustav Schreck
Benedictus qui venit ....Liszt
As a Flower ....Paul Christiansen
Sing to God ....Paul Christiansen
From Grief to Glory ....Christiansen
From Heaven Above ....Chorale from
 Schumann's Gesangbuch–arr. by Christiansen
Beauty in Humility ....Christiansen
Lost in the Night ....Finnish folk melody–Christiansen
Wake, Awake ....Nicolai–Christiansen

1941

O Savior, Throw the Heavens Wide ....Brahms
O Sacred Head ....Hassler–Christiansen
We Have No Other Guide ....Schvedof
The Lord Reigneth ....Paul Christiansen
Savior of Sinners ....Felix Mendelssohn

Thanksgiving Motet ....Arnold Mendelssohn
Come, Guest Divine ....Georg Schumann
Faith Victorious ....Gretchaninoff
When Curtained Darkness ....Christiansen
Beauty in Humility ....Christiansen
Sing unto Him ....Morton Luvaas
Lullaby on Christmas Eve ....Christiansen
Doxology ....Bourgeois

1942

Born Today (Hodie Christus Natus Est) ....J. P. Sweelinck
O Magnum Mysterium ....Tomas Luis de Victoria
The Spirit Also Helpeth Us ....Bach
Finale from "Apostrophe to the Heavenly Host" ....Healy Willan
Our Father ....Gretchaninoff
O Darkest Woe ....J. Shop–Christiansen
Psalm 50 ....Christiansen
Born Anew ....Christiansen
Lost in the Night ....Finnish folk song–Christiansen
Marienlied ....Arr. by Fisher
Heaven and Earth ....Christiansen

1943

Adoramus te, Christe ....Giuseppe Corsi
O Nata Lux ....Thomas Tallis
Prayer to Jesus ....George Oldroyd
Jesu, Priceless Treasure ....Bach
Our Father ....Gretchaninoff
Nunc dimittis ....Gretchaninoff
Praise the Lord, O My Soul ....Gretchaninoff
O How Shall I Receive Thee (Motet for Advent)........Gustav Schreck
Built on the Rock ....Lindeman–Christiansen
O Darkest Woe ....J. Shop–Christiansen
From Heaven Above ....Chorale from
                Schumann's Gesangbuch–arr. by Christiansen
Beautiful Savior (Crusaders' Hymn) ....Folk melody–Christiansen

1944

Surrexit Pastor Bonus ....Orlando di Lasso
Christus Factus Est ....Felice Anerio
Bénédiction Avant le Repas ....Claude Le Jeune
Come, Soothing Death ....J. S. Bach
Wake, Awake ....Nicolai–Christiansen
The Trumpets of Zion ....Olaf C. Christiansen
Only Begotten Son ....Gretchaninoff
Prayer to Jesus ....George Oldroyd
Apostrophe to the Heavenly Host ....Healy Willan
Dayspring of Eternity ....Freylinghausen–Christiansen

APPENDIXES

Index